G
Families Don't Just Happen

To Maxine.
May God continue to
bless and guide you and your
family.
Catherine Harris Scott

Also by
Catherine Musco Garcia-Prats and Joseph A. Garcia-Prats, M.D.

Good Marriages Don't Just Happen:
Keeping Our Relationship Alive While Raising Our Ten Sons

Also by
Joseph A. Garcia-Prats, M.D. and
Sharon Simmons Hornfischer, R.N., B.S.N.

What To Do When Your Baby Is Premature:
A Parent's Handbook for Coping with High-Risk Pregnancy and Caring
for the Preterm Infant

A deep gratitude to our literary agent
Jim Hornfischer for his guidance and support
of our endeavors.

Good Families Don't Just Happen

*What we learned from raising our
10 sons and how it can work for you*

Catherine Musco Garcia-Prats & Joseph A. Garcia-Prats, M.D.
with Claire Cassidy

BOSCO
Publishing

Published by
Bosco Publishing
5502 Lymbar Drive, Houston, TX 77096-5022

ISBN: 0-9763294-0-9

Printed in the United States of America

First published by Adams Media Corporation (ISBN: 1-55850-804-X)

Library of Congress Control Number: 2005920342

For information on quantity discounts for bulk purchases contact
Bosco Publishing.
Web site: www.boscopubliching.com
Telephone: 713-721-1582
Fax: 713-721-9147

To our sons,
Tony, David, Chris, Joe Pat,
Matthew, Mark, Tommy, Danny,
Jamie, and Timmy,
with love and appreciation for the joy
they have brought to our lives.

Table of Contents

Introduction
by Fr. Brian Zinnamon, S.J.
ix

Prologue
In Our Spare Time
xiii

Chapter One
In the Beginning: Strong Relationships Build Strong Families
1

Chapter Two
Becoming a Family: Enriched by the Uniqueness of Each Individual
17

Chapter Three
Positive Parenting Produces Positive Results
37

Chapter Four
*To Be the Garcia-Prats Not the Garcia-Brats: Raising Disciplined,
Responsible, Caring Children*
55

Chapter Five
Recognizing and Fulfilling Our Parental Responsibilities
79

Chapter Six
*Teaching By Example: Living What You Want
Your Children to Learn*
101

Chapter Seven
Instilling the Love of Learning
119

Chapter Eight
Faith and Family
145

Chapter Nine
*Developing Support Systems:
Getting By with a Lot of Help from Our Friends*
165

Chapter Ten
Coping with Time, Fatigue, and Life's Stresses
185

Chapter Eleven
Traditions, Memories, and "Fun"-damentals
207

Chapter Twelve
*The Boys Talk–"Our Two Cents"
by Tony and David Garcia-Prats*
217

Epilogue
Mission Accomplished–and the Beat Goes On
231

Suggested Reading from the Garcia-Prats' Home Library
237

Play Dough Recipe
239

Introduction

Fr. Brian Zinnamon, S.J.
President
Strake Jesuit College Preparatory
Houston, Texas

I was standing in the middle of the Strake Jesuit school cafeteria, which was my assigned post during an open house. The school was hosting more than twelve hundred eighth graders and their families who were deciding if Jesuit was the high school for them. Open house is a night we at Jesuit attempt to be on our best behavior and survive. It is a challenge to make a huge crowd feel welcome in such a short period of time. I was the last stop on the tour and by this time many people were overwhelmed by the size of our campus and the amount of information they were expected to absorb.

In the midst of all this chaos, I met a prospective mother and her son and I suddenly realized there was something very familiar about her. I recognized her from my distant past, but as a Jesuit priest I have lived and studied in many different places. Thank goodness she remembered where we had met first. We both attended Loyola University in New Orleans some twenty years earlier. After we reminisced for a few moments, Cathy said that I would be very glad to have her son, Tony, attend our school next year. Knowing a mother's pride, I reassured her that he seemed like a very fine young man and one we would enjoy having among our students. "You don't understand what I mean, Father.

Tony has nine younger brothers." This is the kind of family every president of an all-boys school dreams about on nights like these. I gave her a hug and told her we were going to be very good friends for a long time.

Besides a steady enrollment prospect for the school, we have received so many benefits from knowing this family. Both Joe and Cathy have been very involved with our parents organization. They are great volunteers and participants in school projects. At least one of them attends most of their sons' activities supporting not only their boys but cheering on others as well. Two of the boys have now graduated in the top quarter of their class. Tony, the oldest, was salutatorian. We have three more of the boys in school with us at this writing and all are doing very well. It is amazing to many people how well adjusted these young men are. They are on time for school each morning with their homework completed and their assignments done. They are prepared for class each day. It is a mystery to some parents who have far fewer children how this can be. Other mothers race up to school with forgotten lunches or a forgotten book. One exasperated mother exploded one morning, "I cannot believe my son forgot his Spanish book at home for the third day in a row. Why does this not happen in the Garcia-Prats family?"

Well, sometimes it does, but not twice. Cathy and Joe do not rescue their sons on minor things and, therefore, the boys learn responsibility and consequences at a very young age. If one forgets his lunch, he will either beg food from his friends or go hungry. If one goes hungry on Monday, he probably won't forget his lunch on Tuesday. The lesson is learned. If one forgets his homework on his desk at home, and the teacher keeps him after school to complete the assignments and he has to take the bus home because his ride left, he does not forget his assignment the next day.

Teaching children to take responsibility for their actions or suffer the consequences is a major principle in helping young people mature and develop self-esteem. Children who can do for themselves are children who feel good about themselves. Too often parents overprotect children and keep them from growing up. Cathy and Joe do not give in to "peace at any price." In the Garcia-Prats family everybody has to pitch in and help.

This truly amazing couple value responsibility while at the same time teach their children they are loved and how they are to love others.

The secret of this successful family is there is enough love to go around for everybody and some left over for lots of good friends as well. Cathy and Joe have made choices about their priorities and values in life. They live in a modest home. Their lifestyle is simple. They have given up the trappings of a consumeristic society. Cathy and Joe love each other and take great delight in raising their children. They provide a very healthy and happy environment in which children grow and mature. God is at the center of their lives. As you read through the chapters of this book, you will be witnessing a family in process, living very ordinary lives that become extraordinary because of their deep faith and the love they share. They respect the individual needs of their sons and see them as unique and beautiful gifts from God.

The Roman Catholic Church loves families and children. As a Catholic priest it gives me great joy to be a part of this family's life. The Church is a community of people who ideally support and love one another. This family's values center upon building a stronger community by their example and making their mark by helping others. Many wonder how they find the time. Busy people find the time to do important things and the things that they value. I suspect the Garcia-Prats family has gotten used to being stared at when they appear somewhere together. I also know they think of themselves as quite ordinary folks who love one another. Actually, the success of this family lies in their faith in God, their value in the human person, and their consistency in how they love another.

Prologue

In Our Spare Time

I f you bungle raising your children, I don't think whatever else you do well matters very much.

–Jacqueline Kennedy Onassis

As the family goes, so goes the nation and so goes the whole world in which we live.

–Pope John Paul II

When people learn we have ten children, all boys, the responses are interesting, to say the least. One woman, who met us at a party, teased Cathy, "So, you're the lady with the ten boys. I heard your husband was a doctor—I figured he was a brain surgeon and had given you a lobotomy!" Some people actually think we are crazy. Most people look at us in disbelief. And, there are those who believe, like us, that we are truly blessed to have ten sons.

When we got married twenty-three years ago, we planned to have a big family, which to us then meant four or five children. Having ten children sort of evolved. It was not, we assure you, a continued effort to try to have a daughter—the most frequently asked question. Nor did we have ten children for religious reasons, the second frequently asked question. We are Catholic, but our Church does not teach us to have any specific number of children. It does teach us to be responsible parents, responsible parenting defined as meeting the emotional, physical, educational, and spiritual needs of a child.

Each of our sons adds a special touch to our family. We knew every time we decided to have another child that we could physically and emotionally handle the needs of the new baby as well as those of his older brothers. We often tease the boys that it is their fault we have so many kids, and, in many ways, this is true. Tony was a great kid, and then David was a great kid, and so on and so on.

As parents of this expanding family, we were always pleased we weren't the only ones excited each time we were expecting another child. The boys, too, were thrilled and shared in our joy. We fondly remember the evening we told the boys (seven at the time) at dinner that we had some exciting news to share with them. "Can we guess? Can we guess?" they asked. So they began guessing: "We won the lottery?" "We're going to Disney World?" "We won the ten million dollar sweepstakes?" David then asked excitedly, "Is it *better* than winning the ten million dollar sweepstakes?" We nodded. David jumped up and yelled, "We're going to have another baby!" The kitchen exploded with cheers. We thought we'd suffocate from the hugs and kisses.

A few years later when we announced our pregnancy with Jamie (our ninth), the younger brothers looked at Tony, who was taking biology at the time, and asked, "What are the odds, Tony, it'll be a boy? Can you figure it out?" They were beginning to wonder if their luck (defined as having all boys) was running out. "It doesn't look good, guys," Tony pondered. "Only 1 in 512 families that have nine children have all the same sex." But they were determined to keep the faith, and did so again when we were expecting our tenth (the odds having doubled to 1 in 1024). Moments like these eased the nausea and discomforts of pregnancy, knowing the boys treasure each other as much as we treasure them.

Watching our older sons grow into fine young men has been rewarding and a source of great joy, reassuring us that we are being responsible parents and encouraging us in our efforts with our younger sons. When others comment how well behaved and caring our sons are, we feel extremely proud. We are also pleased at how they get along at home and how easy it is to go places with them—no matter how many are with us—because they are well behaved and help each other.

Over the years, friends, teachers, and neighbors who observed our sons urged us to write a book. Our pat answer was always, "Sure, in our spare time!" We considered the idea and actually thought we would title the book "In Our Spare Time." As you can imagine, the amount of spare time has not increased; but other events occurred in our lives that spurred our efforts to write.

One year after the birth of our tenth son, Timmy, an article featuring our family appeared in *The Houston Post.* The reporter, Claire Cassidy, went beyond the novelty of a family with ten sons. She focused on the fact that after interviewing teachers and others who knew us, what impressed them most about our family was not that the boys excelled in academics and sports, but that they were courteous, responsible, and compassionate. The article mentioned how our family worked together and somehow kept an air of calm in the midst of potential chaos. The story related how we dealt with day-to-day activities, stayed organized, and through it all enjoyed our sons immensely. The article highlighted parenting tips we had provided the reporter. She told readers, "This is a positive story about good kids and a good family."

Until the feature was published, we were unaware of its exact context and focus. To have all our years of parenting so fondly praised overwhelmed us with pride. We were also overwhelmed at the response to the article: innumerable phone calls, letters, and cards. People's comments ranged from "remarkable," "refreshing," "positive," "super," "inspiring," "rewarding," and "To think you accomplished this in the '90s" to "One of the best human interest stories I've read. You haven't heard the last from it." Pediatricians told us they copied the article and shared it with patients. One even wrote, "I wish I could make it required reading for all parents." We received invitations to speak to various groups. A magazine and cable television station sent reporters to do stories about our family.

The article struck a chord with readers. People wanted to know what we had done—What was our formula for raising good kids and for having a good family? Their questions forced us to sit back and analyze what we were doing that made a difference. We realized that, as a whole, people want to be good parents and have a good family, and they are eager to learn how.

The headline in the newspaper article proclaimed, "A Perfect 10." But we are not about perfection. How can we expect perfection from our children, our family, when we, their parents, are not perfect? What we *are* about is having a good family with children who are responsible, loving, caring, well educated, and respectful of God and His world. We want our children to know that their self-worth and success is measured in nonmonetary terms: by who they are, what they do, and how they live their lives.

One evening at dinner, after we had decided to write our book, we asked the boys for suggestions for a title. The suggestions were many, varied, and humorous, such as "Raising Ten Boys and a Dog," "What's a Parent to Do?" "The Art of Parenting," and even "To Hell and Back." Then David suggested, "Good Families Don't Just Happen." We realized this was a true statement. It takes more than having children to have a good family; in order to have a good family one must start with good parenting. For so long our society has asked, "What's wrong with children today?" We've been struck by the understanding that the problem does not begin with our children but with their parents. Although parents love their children, they often lose sight of what is really important and what they need to do to raise good children. We *know* parenting is challenging and demanding, but we also know that when done well and with love, the rewards are immeasurable.

How do we learn to parent when so much of parenting seems to be on-the-job training? For us, our ability to parent, like our family, evolved. We did have an advantage because both of us were dedicated to children professionally before we began our family. Joe did his training in pediatrics and specialized in neonatology, the care of the critically ill newborn. He is the director of a newborn nursery at one of Houston's largest teaching hospitals. Cathy's background is elementary education; she taught first grade before having the boys.

Whereas this "expertise" has been helpful, it has not been enough. As young parents in the 1970s, we decided what we wanted for our children, and then set out to accomplish our goals. Did we do it alone? Of course not. We observed other parents, read books, asked questions, attended seminars, and prayed a lot—and continue to do these things today. We lovingly acknowledge there have been many positive influences in our lives that have guided us in our choices over the years: our parents, our siblings, friends, teachers, and our Jesuit education.

We also acknowledge that the foundation of our family is our strong marriage. The love and commitment we have for each other provides the boys with an unspoken sense of security. We treat each other with mutual respect, even relishing each other's differences. The fact that we have different talents and interests only strengthens our marriage and our family. Imagine the gaps we would have to fill if we were good at the same things.

We also understand the need for a strong belief in God that guides us through rough times and gives us a sense of purpose and serenity. In Ecclesiastes 4:7-12, this role of God in one's marriage is expressed as a three-ply cord. A prayer from our church's marriage preparation program reads, "We believe it is your Spirit that lighted our way to one another so that we could become a 'two' that is better than 'one.' Individually and mutually, Lord, we commit ourselves to you. We ask you to be an inseparable part of our togetherness—a 'three-ply cord' of husband, wife, and God—that is not easily broken."

At the 1996 Strake Jesuit College Preparatory Mother-Son Luncheon, the guest speaker, Mr. Jim "Mattress Mac" McIngvale, owner and president of Gallery Furniture, in Houston, repeatedly reminded the boys, "Successful people do what unsuccessful people are unwilling to do." To paraphrase Mr. McIngvale, **"Successful parents do what unsuccessful parents are unwilling to do."**

For the past two decades, we have worked hard, laughed, cried, and grown together as a couple and a family. We share with you now our experiences and insights, knowing and accepting, of course, that we don't have all the answers. The concepts presented in this book are the heart of a philosophy that has worked well for us. We live our philosophy, making choices every day in the best interest of our family. We believe you can integrate and adapt these ideas to your family, regardless of size, culture, or composition.

Enjoy reading this book, but most of all, respect, love, and appreciate your children. As we said earlier, parenting is challenging and demanding, but when done well and with love, there is no greater reward for ourselves and for society.

Catherine Musco Garcia-Prats and
Joseph Garcia-Prats
Houston, Texas

Chapter 1

In the Beginning: Strong Relationships Build Strong Families

L *ove is patient; love is kind. Love is not jealous, it does not put on airs, it is not snobbish. Love is never rude, it is not self-seeking, it is not prone to anger; neither does it brood over injuries. Love does not rejoice in what is wrong but rejoices with the truth. There is no limit to love's forbearance, to its trust, its hope, its power to endure. . . . There are in the end three things that last: faith, hope and love, and the greatest of these is love.*

—1 Corinthians 13:4-7, 13

In the beginning, there were just the two of us, although that's hard to imagine now. Joe was the young, eager, pediatric intern and Cathy was the new college grad, the ink still wet on her diploma. Cathy graduated from Loyola University on Monday, we had rehearsal dinner on Tuesday, and we were married in New Orleans on Wednesday. What a whirlwind week. Often, we joke that we started off on fast forward and we're still looking for the pause button.

When we took our marriage vows twenty-three years ago, we committed our lives to each other. The words, "For better or for worse, for richer or for poorer, in sickness and in health, till death do us part," were spoken sincerely and with conviction. **That commitment, or covenant—a permanent and unconditional relationship—meant we would work with each other, solve our problems and make changes when necessary to strengthen our marriage and make each other better individuals.** We were not unlike most recently wedded couples who also held the same ideals and felt the same confidence about their own marriages. We told ourselves, like the Mission Control commander brainstorming methods to rescue Apollo 13, "Failure is not an option."

Since then, we have come so far. We maintain the same ideals today that we did then, but we better understand *how* to make those ideals a reality. **Good marriages don't just happen.** We need love, respect, trust, compromise, and good communication skills along with shared goals and values, forgiveness, laughter, and acceptance of each other and of change. Building a loving, lasting, joy-filled relationship entails constant effort and a strong commitment by both spouses. Although we knew twenty-three years ago that we loved and respected each other, and that we shared similar goals, values, and commitments, it's what we *didn't* know that created our stumbling blocks.

Making the Necessary Adjustments, Choices, and Compromises to Strengthen the Relationship

We thought, for example, that our communication skills were wonderful since we could talk comfortably about almost anything. Yet, we hadn't had a major disagreement during the time we dated or were engaged. However, once we were married, we learned that many of our communication skills were weak and ineffective, as was evident when the conflicts that weren't supposed to happen became a reality. We were unaware of the significant influence our past family experiences had on how we approached and reacted to situations. Our families had handled such issues as responsibilities, traditions, and conflict in their own ways. One wasn't necessarily better than the other, but they were different.

We also thought that because we shared similar goals and values we were in for smooth sailing. We erroneously assumed that since our goals and values were similar, our expectations about our marital roles—who would do what, when, how, and where—would also be the same. Many of these expectations were based on our parents' marriages, and were unrealistic for the kind of marriage we wanted. So we had to make adjustments, choices, and compromises—and this was *before* we had children.

(Joe): *In retrospect I didn't have a very realistic idea of what the joys or demands of a marriage relationship would be. I knew I expected to share my life with someone very special, who shared my ideals, who would be my friend and make me a better person. That was a good beginning. However, I didn't know what was needed to nurture and develop that relationship. I had a few examples on which to base my ideal: my parents, the parents of close friends, and my colleagues who were married while I was in medical school. So when Cathy and I were married, I thought our relationship should be the sum of these marriages plus the characteristics that I understood would make our marriage loving, strong, and healthy. I thought our marriage would be marked by mutual love that flowed from mutual respect and admiration, as well as by the friendship we had developed. I knew we were both committed to this ideal.*

I expected my life to change once we were married; I would now have a loving companion to share my days and eliminate my loneliness. I expected to continue my pediatric training while Cathy would follow her professional pathway in education. We would be lovers and friends and everything would be wonderful. We hadn't experienced any true conflicts thus far in our relationship, and that was fine by me. I didn't handle conflict well. That is probably why I was such an easy person to deal with—I avoided conflict. So our married life began as two very happy people in Houston, although I was probably happier than Cathy since we were living where I had already established a niche.

In the year prior to our marriage, my life in Houston revolved around my training at the various Baylor College of Medicine teaching hospitals. I had so much time on my hands (nothing was waiting for me at my empty apartment) that I spent ten to twelve hours a day at the hospital taking care of patients. More important for me, I received such positive reinforcement from the faculty, my fellow residents, nurses, and patients. I was considered a very knowledgeable, dedicated young physician who was always available and ready to help. Most of my colleagues were married with responsibilities at home. They tried to get home as soon as they completed their hospital duties. In retrospect, the hospital served as a source of professional acceptance and praise, as well as providing much personal gratification. When I did go home, there was very little to keep me occupied other than catching up on much needed sleep (our night-call schedule was very rigorous).

Marriage changed my life. I now shared my life with an individual I truly loved and for whom I wanted to be a good spouse. However, I expected to continue to function as I always had at the hospital. I did want to come home and be with Cathy after my long hours and assumed that she would be understanding of my time demands. How could anyone complain about a doctor spending time taking care of his patients? I also thought Cathy would stay busy pursuing her own interests—we would travel parallel professional paths and just meet at home for mutual support and sharing. **I expected to have the best of "both" worlds. It doesn't work that way.**

Cathy was alone for long periods of time waiting for me to complete my daily hospital duties. (How quickly I had forgotten the loneliness of an empty apartment.) She had started teaching and wanted to share those experiences with me, but I was usually at the hospital or asleep. Our relationship had flourished in a special way before we were married because of our sharing. I realized this way of life was not going to work if we were going to have a marriage that would be as healthy and loving as we both knew it could be. This marked the beginning of my "maturing" as a spouse and a physician. I had to rethink the expectations that I had of my role as a physician. What really makes a physician a good physician? Long hours in the hospital? Availability to the hospital even when I wasn't on-call?

Dedication to research and academic advancement at the expense of our relationship? Did my patients' medical needs dictate this time commitment or did I need to spend those long hours at the hospital? It became increasingly evident to me that my long hours were driven by my need to be accepted and lauded. When I realized my patients would do well after my shift was over and under the management of my colleagues, I concentrated on working hard during my required rotations and nights in the hospital. Cathy supported these choices, even though it still meant extra work for her and time alone. Cathy's support and my confidence in my skills as a physician supplanted my drive to please. I matured as an individual and as a physician.

(Cathy): *The first year of our marriage was a huge adjustment for me: I began my life with Joe, I moved to a new city where I knew few people, and I started my career as a first-grade teacher. Joe's hours as a pediatric intern were horrendous, on-call in the hospital every third night and getting home the other nights after nine o'clock. I was more alone during this time than I'd ever been in my life, yet, I had never thought loneliness would be a major part of my day-to-day life when I was married. I'd always had a lot of people around, whether it was my four sisters or a dorm full of friends. Spending hours and hours alone was hard for me, not only during the week but especially on weekends. I wanted and needed to share time with Joe, to talk about what was happening at school and at the hospital. I wanted to go places and do things together. Every time there was a school social activity Joe seemed to be on-call. I often wondered if my colleagues thought my husband was simply a figment of my imagination.*

*Teaching and related activities filled most of my time. As a first-year teacher, preparation for class consumed many long, late hours. I was amazed at the after-school hours needed to organize for the next day. Spending my days with a classroom of first graders, although challenging, was a joy; I loved what I was doing. (I owe a debt of gratitude to those students for enriching my days as much as they did.) But as we all know, **you can't build a marriage by fulfilling most of your needs outside of the relationship. Time together allows the relationship to develop and mature.** Yet, with two more years of residency (and unbeknownst to me at the time, two years of a neonatal fellowship), I didn't see much hope for better hours. I began to understand what a priest had tried to tell me* *during a couples retreat we had attended before we got married. He said it takes a person with a lot of love and determination to be married to a doctor, because of the unique demands and pulls of the profession. I wish I'd had enough insight at the time to have pursued his comment further. I was totally unprepared for the experience and the demands—and I considered myself a strong, independent person.*

Other factors, too, entered into my frustrations. We owned only one car during our first four years of marriage. I dropped Joe off at the hospital in the morning and picked him up in the evening at whatever ungodly hour he finished. The morning routine wasn't a problem, but my evenings revolved around his hours. Since beepers and cellular phones were not readily available in the mid '70s, I needed to be where Joe could easily contact me when he finished his work—which usually meant home. The lack of freedom to come and go or just relax at the end of my day was difficult after the independence of my college years. The inconvenience grew even worse after Tony was born. Money was extremely tight during Joe's residency and fellowship, but if I had to change anything about those early years, I would have bought any running jalopy.

Another area of frustration involved Joe and the television. Before we were married, Joe would come home from the hospital and with no one else there, vegetate in front of the TV. Now when he came home and sat in front of the TV, I resented it. I wasn't a big television watcher, and since we had so little time together I didn't want to share it with the television. Although I "tolerated" the priority of medicine in his life, I was determined not to play second fiddle to the TV or other activities. Expressing my frustrations, though, was difficult. Conflict wasn't supposed to happen, especially this early in the marriage. I also had to deal with the pent-up anger I was beginning to feel about the television, Joe's long hours, and the lack of freedom to come and go.

Joe sensed I was upset, but didn't understand why. We fell into the trap of not expressing our feelings, either because we assumed the other knew how we were feeling or because we were afraid of the reaction. In addition, we are both very sensitive people and neither of us wanted to hurt the other. Joe took the lead in resolving our communication stalemate. He encouraged me to open up so he could better understand what I was thinking and feeling. I realized if I wanted anything to change I needed to tell Joe what was on my mind, for good or for bad.

Sharing my feelings and needs with Joe was an important step in strengthening our relationship. We learned that what may have worked for us individually before we were married and what may have worked for our parents wasn't always conducive to our growth as a couple. Joe respected my need to share my day with him and dramatically changed the amount of time he watched television. Initially, he didn't have much control over his hours at work. When he finally did have more control over his hours, I didn't experience any shift in his time commitments. Ultimately, I pressed for a more reasonable balance between his commitment to medicine and family.

In The Art of Loving, *Erich Fromm states,* **"To love somebody is not just a strong feeling—it is a decision, it is a judgment, it is a promise."** *Joe's decision to be an integral part of my life, and eventually the boys' lives, while continuing to practice good medicine, demonstrated his commitment to our relationship. I worked hard, and still do, at understanding the demanding hours and pressure that Joe is under. That doesn't mean it became easy for me to be alone or to go places alone, but since our time together became so much more rewarding, I more willingly accepted Joe's need to spend time with his patients and their families.*

Joe and I laugh at our early stabs at dealing with conflict and developing effective communication skills. Joe often teases he wasn't prepared for my eventual forthrightness; he will tell you, I "express" myself very well today. He sometimes wonders if he didn't open Pandora's box. **It's important to remember, too, that once we had the conflict in the open, we had to face the problem and resolve it. We learned to compromise and find solutions we were both comfortable with.**

Developing Effective, Respectful Communication Skills

A marriage must have effective communication in order to thrive. The communication skills we bring into a marriage are those we developed over the years and learned from our own families. Many of these skills, regretfully, are poor and actually hinder the growth of a relationship: avoiding or ignoring a problem, pouting, withdrawing, giving in, ranting and raving, manipulating, or fighting. **If you disliked the way your family communicated or dealt with conflict, be determined to change that pattern for your spouse and children.** We suggest examining your communication skills and developing new ones where necessary.

Respect is at the core of effective communication. The way we speak to and treat our spouse is a sign of respect: It's not only the words that matter. Learn to honestly share your thoughts and feelings with your spouse and in return listen to his or hers. Listening, truly listening, is so very important. Be accepting of what your spouse has to share—it may not necessarily reflect your own feelings—and do so with a loving heart. Even though Joe and I know what the skills are, we still fall into old patterns: Joe may avoid the conflict and I may withdraw. **Be realistic and acknowledge that good communication requires practice, constant effort, a determined spirit, understanding, and trust. We've noticed that the way a couple communicates with each other is often the way they communicate with their children. Thus the benefits of effective communication between spouses are many.**

Accepting and Adapting to Changes in Your Life

After we strengthened our communication skills, did all our problems evaporate? We don't think so. Marriage is continuously changing. Change weaves its way through a marriage and family, whether it's a new job, a lost job, new responsibilities, children, an illness, or death. All our experiences haven't been rosy. We've dealt with a sick child, Cathy's detached retina and the fear of losing her eyesight, as well as changes in personal and professional responsibilities and demands. We can't avoid life's uncertainties, but we can learn to adapt and grow with them to gain positive results.

Dealing effectively with change is imperative to a relationship. **When we face a new situation, we determine how it will affect each of us as individuals and also as a couple and a family.** Our willingness to compromise, adapt, and accept change enables us to grow from the experience. We've learned to temper individual goals with couple and family goals. Our strength as a couple has evolved from all our experiences—"for better or for worse." With each transition, we learn a little more about each other—and realize how working together strengthens and enriches our love. In his book *Unconditional Love*, John Powell, S.J., says, "Weathering the storms of the love process is the only way to find the rainbows of life."

(Cathy): *During our second year of marriage, I decided to return to school to work on my master's degree in education. Along with a full day in the classroom with thirty active first graders and hours of preparation for the next day, I attended grad school and studied. At home, I shouldered most of the responsibilities, similar to the roles of our parents. (I appreciate now how many people do all of the above* and *have children.) Before too long the days became overwhelming—too much to do, too little time. When I approached Joe with the problem, his initial solution was that I should either teach or go to school; it appeared I shouldn't do both. Frankly, I saw it differently. If Joe would shoulder some of the at-home responsibilities, I could successfully do both. He had juggled doing laundry, grocery shopping, and bill paying before we were married, there was no reason why he couldn't do it once in a while now. The situation necessitated Joe and I sitting down and working out a shared commitment, and a relearning of what was appropriate and realistic for each of us. Adjustments were made. Although I prepared dinner, Joe now helped me clean up so we could* both *relax or do whatever we wanted. When needed, Joe took the clothes to the laundromat, bought groceries, or paid the bills. Making these adjustments in our early years of marriage ultimately prepared and strengthened us for the many other events in our lives we were yet to face.*

Joe's willingness to compromise and adjust in the early 1970s when household responsibilities were viewed as "woman's work" reinforced his commitment to make our relationship succeed and demonstrated his respect for me, my needs, and my time. Recently another mother told me her husband felt they each had certain responsibilities to fulfill: He had "his" and she had "hers." If it took her until midnight to complete her work that was her problem, not his. He had completed his work. Joe, thank goodness, doesn't share that attitude. If he did, my days would be miserable, and I'd be frustrated, resentful, and angry.

A Balancing Act: Caring for Self and Others

(Cathy): *During this early period of our marriage, I recognized that although we now had a life together, I still needed to foster my own interests and friendships. Even today, with a husband and ten children, I am* Cathy *first.* **Having self-respect and self-love enables me to respect and love others.** *The greatest commandment Jesus gave us was to love the Lord your God with your whole heart, with your whole soul, and with all your mind; and to love your neighbor as yourself. Jesus doesn't instruct us to love our neighbor (family, friends, etc.) more than ourselves or to love ourselves more than our neighbor. And, in order to love God (and others) with my whole heart, soul, and mind, I* must *take care of my physical, emotional, intellectual, and spiritual needs. When I deprive myself of any of these, I struggle as a wife and mother. I'm not talking about being selfish, uncaring, or putting my needs first.*

In his book Moving in the Spirit, *theologian Richard Hauser, S.J., summarizes these thoughts beautifully: "True self-love is different from selfishness. Selfishness ends in the self; true self-love is integrated with a desire to love and serve God and others. And Jesus commands us to love our neighbor as our self. Jesus understood that if we loved ourselves because of our dignity as God's children, this love would naturally affect our attitudes toward all other people who are also God's children. True self-love is based on a desire to better serve God and others."* **The key is finding a balance between taking care of myself and those around me and, most important, distinguishing between my needs and my wants.**

I can hear the questions now, as I'm often asked, "When does a mother of ten children find time to fulfill her needs?" I have to make the time. *And I assure you I am an expert at taking advantage of every opportunity and minute available. For example, after I had Matthew, our fifth son who weighed more than ten pounds, I desperately needed to get back in shape: My shoulders were rounded, my abdominal muscles were* flabby, and my weak perineum caused incontinence. Matthew was born in March. As soon as summer arrived and I found young girls in the neighborhood to baby-sit, I enrolled in an aerobics class two mornings a week. After the first week of exercising, I felt like I had been hit by a truck; I could barely move as I shuffled around the house. Within a couple of weeks, though, I felt 100 percent better. I had improved muscle tone and more energy, and I found it easier to handle the stress associated with caring for five boys under the age of six. I made the time to take care of myself. Although I regretfully don't attend an aerobics class anymore, because of scheduling conflicts with the boys' hours, I walk whenever I can and use exercise tapes at home. (I exercise when the boys are not around to avoid the giggles and imitations.) **By addressing my physical needs, I feel better and am convinced I have more energy, more tolerance, and an improved mental and spiritual outlook, all of which benefit my marriage and family.**

Along the same lines, I made an effort to fulfill my spiritual needs. In 1980, shortly after Joe Pat, our fourth son, was born, our parish church established a perpetual adoration chapel, open twenty-four hours a day. The pastor asked for an hour commitment every week from the parishioners. Joe and I signed up for an hour on different nights of the week. Every week we had uninterrupted spiritual time. Talk about a boost! The hour didn't replace the daily prayer/spiritual time; it enhanced it. Joe noticed the sense of peace that one hour provided me. We still visit the chapel whenever we can.

Components That Influence a Marriage Relationship

For fourteen years we have worked with engaged couples in our church's marriage preparation program. We meet one night a week for five weeks with each engaged couple, sharing our insights and experiences. The sessions focus on the components that affect a marriage relationship: the influence of our families and past experiences, marital communications, intimacy, and spirituality. Each person answers a set of questions individually, followed by the couple sharing their answers. Then we come together to talk about that evening's particular topic.

The program familiarizes the couples with the realities of married life and the potential areas of marital difficulty; these issues vary from couple to couple. We help each couple understand how their individual strengths and weaknesses, family backgrounds, assumptions, and expectations of each other impact their day-to-day decisions. We discuss healthy communication skills, compromise, acceptance, and respect. We stress that the relationship should empower each partner to reach his or her full potential. And, we strongly encourage them to weave God into the fabric of their marriage.

One of the marriage preparation programs ends with the following important query: Name three ways you have demonstrated your love for your fiancé(e)/spouse this week. The first night that the couple is asked to respond to the query, they usually have to ponder for a few minutes and often can't recall three instances. But knowing this question will be asked every session encourages them to thoughtfully express their love to each other during the upcoming week. **The lesson learned is that strengthening and maintaining a marital relationship is an active process. Passivity and complacency will not allow a marriage to nurture and grow. It takes continuous effort, but we reap what we sow.**

Our experiences with engaged couples refresh our own marriage. With every couple we learn a little more about each other, reinforcing why we love each other as much as we do. We also realize the impact understanding, compromise, and respect have had on our relationship.

For example, while we share similar values and goals, **our individual personalities, strengths, and experiences determine how we handle various situations.** When faced with a task, Cathy gets it done as soon as possible; Joe prefers to take all the time allotted. A perfect example is filing taxes. Cathy wants them done early; Joe's quite content having them done the night before. Although Cathy prepares most of the records, there are certain areas pertaining to Joe's work that he must prepare. For years, Cathy would have everything done and still be waiting for Joe's information. Now to make Cathy's efforts easier and reduce her frustrations, Joe completes his information in a more timely fashion. A little compromising makes the experience easier for both of us, even if we owe the IRS.

We have learned to balance our strengths and weaknesses, our likes and dislikes, to our family's advantage. There are times Joe's calm nature is advantageous over Cathy's more excitable personality—dealing with a teacher or coach. Then there are times when Cathy's determination is a strength—when she refused to be rerouted through Chicago in the dead of winter with five small children and six additional travel hours. Whereas Cathy may get more excited and involved in an activity than Joe, it doesn't mean he's any less committed or successful.

Our ability and willingness to compromise and change enriches our relationship. Compromising may be on a large scale—Joe's helping out so Cathy could attend graduate school—or a small scale—Cathy taking the time to get the car repaired. We don't get hung up on the simple things. If Joe prefers Colgate to Cathy's Crest, we buy both instead of arguing. If Joe prefers going to see *Independence Day* to Cathy's going to see *Sense and Sensibility*, we choose one movie for that night and try to catch the other some other time. Our decision may rest on who needs the break more. **We constantly give and take—not "give in."** When one spouse feels he or she is always "giving in," resentment builds up, a signal that respect is lacking in the relationship.

When we do hurt each other, whether intentional or not, over something major or minor, we ask for forgiveness and grant forgiveness for our relationship to again be at peace. **The process of forgiving is difficult, but it is essential in a loving relationship.** When we ask for forgiveness, we are admitting we have done something wrong. The loving response is to forgive with tenderness and empathy.

Trusting in each other's love enables us to open our hearts and ask for forgiveness. We know we don't have to regain the other's love—we never lost it. We love unconditionally, reminding ourselves neither of us is perfect. We wonder if Jesus wasn't thinking of marriage when Peter asked Him, "How many times do we need to forgive another?" and He answered, "Seventy times seven times."

Accepting and balancing our differences, as well as caring for ourselves and each other, focuses on the importance of placing our marriage at the forefront of our priorities. We make a constant effort to keep our relationship in top working order. Children and careers are demanding and consume an enormous amount of time. When couples don't make their own relationship a priority, everything else suffers. We have miserable days when our relationship isn't in sync. It's harder dealing with the children at home and it's harder dealing with situations at work.

Keeping Love Alive

We take time to express our love with phone calls, cards, notes, favorite meals or desserts, flowers, helping each other with responsibilities, and listening to the other's concerns and needs. Talking to each other during the day keeps us connected and allows us to share our ups and downs. We empathize with the other, even if we're unable to "fix" the other's problem. We want to emphasize that it doesn't take money to show your love for a person. We met while Joe was attending Tulane Medical School and Cathy was at Loyola University. Neither of us had much money, yet, we had wonderful fun and loving times together going to the university plays, dances, athletic events, picnics, and pick-up football or softball games. **Sharing your time and your heart are what matter in the long run, not the dozen roses.**

Being friends and laughing together are integral to our marriage. After twenty-three years, we *still* enjoy each other's company. And although we love our times with our sons, we relish our time alone. It ties our life together and makes all our experiences that much more rewarding.

When the boys were small, we set aside Friday evenings for ourselves. **We didn't have to go to a fancy restaurant or spend a lot of money to renew ourselves and our relationship.** Running up to a neighborhood restaurant and having dessert and coffee provided us time to talk, laugh, and be together as a couple. Taking walks together gave us time to share.

Fortunately, we had wonderful young people who baby-sat for us. Our first baby-sitters were nursing students from the Texas Medical Center. When we moved into our present home, young people in the neighborhood baby-sat. Annemarsh (the boys always ran her first and last name together), Eric (referred to as the "giant" by the boys because he was 6 feet 6 inches), and Danielle (often referred to as our borrowed daughter) were gifts to our family, enabling us to enjoy our time out because we knew the boys were in loving hands. (They are still friends of our family, sharing in birthdays, baptisms, communions, confirmations, graduations, and eventually, we assume, marriages or ordinations to the religious life.) Now our older sons baby-sit; Timmy doesn't know any others. When Tony was old enough to watch his brothers, we appreciated the flexibility his baby-sitting provided. We remember all too well having to arrange for a baby-sitter two weeks ahead of an activity; a last minute dinner or movie was usually out of the question. People ask if we had to hire two or more baby-sitters. We never did, because the boys were well behaved and we had them bathed, fed, and ready for bed before the sitter arrived.

During a Marriage Encounter weekend, a retreat for couples wanting to renew and strengthen their marriage, we heard an interesting phrase, *married singles*. The term describes what too often occurs in marriages: Married couples doing their own thing, spending little time talking, listening, and being with each other. The marriage encounter experience stresses the significance of communication within the marriage relationship, emphasizing the daily need to "dialogue" with our spouse, not just about who went where and what happened, but more important, how you're feeling and what you're thinking.

When we're communicating well, all areas of our marriage are enhanced, including the physical. Is it really lovemaking when one or both persons doesn't feel loved and respected in the other areas of their relationship? **Our sexual relationship is an outpouring of our love and mutual respect.** We've learned how important it is to provide time and attention to the sexual dimension of our marriage to strengthen the entire relationship. We're convinced hugs, kisses, and some loving early in the morning are more warming and invigorating than any cup of coffee for getting your day off to a good start. And what better way to end your day than with those same feelings.

In the midst of our hectic schedules, **we make time for each other.** The love, time, and attention we give our marriage is invaluable. This love, respect, and commitment to each other carries us through the low days and tough times while at the same time increases tenfold all the joy and satisfaction we experience in our lives.

There's a saying: "The greatest gift a man can give his children is to love their mother." Conversely, the greatest gift a woman can give her children is to love their father. Our strong marriage forms the foundation of our family. The elements that foster a happy marriage—love, respect, and commitment—are the same elements that strengthen a family and each of its members. Building on that concept and taking advantage of the skills we learned in strengthening our own relationship, we began our parenting years.

Chapter 2

Becoming a Family: Enriched by the Uniqueness of Each Individual

Whatever the times, one thing will never change: Fathers and mothers, if you have children, they must come first. Your success as a family, our success as a society, depends not on what happens at the White House, but inside your house.

−Barbara Bush

The feet find the road easy when the heart walks with them.
−Anonymous

Family! All of us are part of a family. Each family has its own characteristics, personality, strengths, weaknesses, joys, and sorrows. The Garcia-Prats family is no exception. Our family is made up of a mother, a father, and ten sons. Our sons span eighteen years: The shortest span between the boys is 360 days and the longest span is three years, nine days. We are twelve individuals working together to make our family life a loving, joyful experience. And we are not ashamed to admit we *are* a happy, loving, caring family with each of us better because of the others. Did this happen by chance, the luck of the draw? We assure you, we've never relied on luck. Love, respect, commitment, hard work, and our faith in God provided the wanted results—**We are "richer by the dozen."**

Our strong marriage is the cornerstone of our family. We reiterate: The elements that foster a happy marriage—love, respect, and commitment— are the same elements that strengthen a family and each of its members. **Children must grow up in a home filled with love, respect, and commitment in order to mature and reach their full potential.** Therein lies the challenge: To make sure each member of the family develops and matures according to his or her individual talents and needs, yet at the same time, to mesh all this individuality into one unit—a family.

Decisions Made Before Starting Our Family

As we made the move from a couple to a family, we had new choices and decisions to make. We decided being financially secure before we started our family was not one of our priorities. Financial security would take more years than either of us cared to wait. For Cathy, Joe's "time" became more of a concern. Joe originally intended to complete his training and join a pediatric practice. But one day Joe came home and said he wanted to specialize in neonatology, which entailed two more years of training. Cathy remembers crying: The hours would continue to be dreadful and the financial compensation minimal. The residency years had not been easy—she was ready for a change. Yet, after all those years of schooling and working long hours, Joe deserved the opportunity to pursue his dream. Cathy would expect Joe to be understanding if the roles were reversed. However, neither of us wanted to wait two additional years to begin our family.

(Cathy): *The next big decision was whether I would continue to teach or stay at home. The decision was as controversial and difficult in the mid-1970s as it is today. I loved teaching and felt that with each year of* *experience I became a more effective teacher. Yet, as a teacher, I had observed how stressful and difficult it was for families, parents and children, when both parents worked outside the home. So, although I would miss the students and challenges of teaching, and financially we would struggle with only Joe's fellowship salary, I decided to stay home. My decision to stay home was not to become the 1990s version of Ozzie and Harriet or Leave It to Beaver. We both grew up in the 1950s, and the only thing our families had in common with these TV families was a stay-at-home mom. Mothers of the 1950s were expected to stay home, but today women and men have more choices. I don't regret my decision. I believe whenever possible parents should be the primary caregivers for their children. At the same time, I realize that it's often unrealistic. Socioeconomic conditions have changed since the 1950s, and now often both parents are required to work. Although, at the same time, these socioeconomic changes have enabled those who want to work to do so. **It's important to remember that parents aren't good or bad depending on whether they stay at home; they are good or bad depending on whether they meet the needs of their children and fulfill their parental responsibilities.***

Respecting the Individuality of All Ten Sons

The challenge of blending each family member's talents and needs never ends. Because of our individual imperfections, we work continuously as a family to keep the benefits flowing. Although we share similar values and goals, each of us has a different personality and different needs and experiences. Can you imagine how boring our lives would be if we were all the same?

The boys expressed their individuality from the start. Each of their labors and deliveries was a unique and exciting experience. **Tony,** our first, was probably closest to the textbook labor and delivery, although with an extra touch of concern when one of the nurses believed Cathy was carrying twins. Not until Cathy had delivered *one* Tony (8 pounds 1 ounce) was the nurse convinced there weren't twins. It would've been a pleasure, though, to have had two Tonys. **David** (8 pounds 2 ounces) arrived without a hitch, until the placenta wouldn't expel. So, after an anesthesia-free delivery, Cathy was given Demerol to deliver the placenta. David's still full of the unpredictable and is wonderfully easygoing. **Christopher** was our first son delivered in a birthing room, to the sounds of Willie Nelson's "Stardust" album. Cathy still remembers the words from the song "All of Me." And like the song, she was beginning to want them to take all of her as she delivered a healthy 9 pound 12 ounce boy. Christopher still favors country music. We didn't think **Joe Pat** (9 pounds 10 ounces) would ever arrive. Overdue by two weeks, Cathy was induced, only to wait another eleven hours to see Joe Pat face-to-face. He was definitely worth the wait. **Matthew**, weighing a whopping 10 pounds 9 ounces, was the talk of the hospital: "This little bitty mom (5 feet 1 inch, 105 pounds) had this HUGE baby." People assumed Cathy was married to a linebacker, but anyone who knows Joe realizes Cathy outweighs him when she's pregnant. One friend commenting later on Matthew's delivery said, "I prayed a decade of the rosary for a safe delivery. If I had known you were going to have a ten pounder, I would've said the whole rosary." Cathy's dad teased, "I know how Cathy spelled relief: M-A-T-T-H-E-W." **Mark** (8 pounds 6 ounces) emerged "sunny-side" up (facing up instead of down), looking like his brothers had already gotten to him—bruised and scratched from his difficult delivery. Our little raccoon healed quickly and is still doing things his way with a sunny disposition. On the night of **Tommy's** delivery, Joe and the three older boys had gone to a Houston Astros game. Joe called home at the end of each inning to check on Cathy, since she had felt contractions on and off all day. When he called after the sixth inning, she told him she had called the obstetrician, Dr. Thomas Strama (a wonderfully caring man who has delivered nine of the boys and holds a special place in our hearts). Cathy's Mom, who was visiting from Virginia, was relieved when Joe arrived home; she had no desire to deliver the baby. Tommy's delivery was a flash; he weighed 7 pounds 14 ounces, little by our standards. Tommy was easy then and is an extremely gentle, good-natured child now. **Danny's** delivery took an interesting turn when labor stalled at 9 centimeters. His brothers expected to hear the verdict, boy or girl, before they left for school. No such luck. Even the pediatrician, Dr. John Curtis, who was in the hospital making morning rounds, kept poking his head into our room joking, "Isn't that baby here yet?" Danny finally arrived, 9 pounds 6 ounces, full of creative energy and life. On the day of **Jamie's** delivery, Cathy had a one o'clock appointment with Dr. Strama. She'd been emotional most of the morning, but attributed it to leaving Danny at his first day of preschool. When she was examined by Dr. Strama, he announced she was 5 centimeters, in active labor with her bag of water ready to burst. He wanted to admit Cathy to the hospital on the spot, but in typical fashion, she wanted to go home and get organized. She rationalized that she needed to get the car home so her mom, in town again from Virginia, could pick up the boys from school. Cathy went home and made it back in plenty of time for Jamie's delivery at 8 pounds 8 ounces—a joy to behold. With **Timmy's** delivery (9 pounds 8 ounces), Cathy was 8 centimeters, thank goodness, when she arrived at the hospital. Timmy was delivered shortly after by Dr. Strama, who arrived from a gala wearing a tuxedo! Talk about a first-class delivery. There was so much electricity in the air that night as we waited to see whether we would have a "perfect 10"—ten boys, that is. (We have never found out the sex of the baby beforehand.) The laughter, shrieks, and amazement that followed Timmy's delivery will always be remembered, especially the phone call home to tell his nine brothers.

As you can see, each of our sons had a unique beginning. And each had his own style of nursing, sleeping, and playing. Tony was a voracious eater, while David couldn't be bothered with food his first year of life (although he has more than made up for it since). Joe Pat needed absolute silence to sleep and woke up from the slightest noise; Chris fell asleep easily and slept through anything. Some of the boys loved to be carried around in a snugglie, and others preferred the swing or their crib. Two of the boys sucked their thumbs, two liked the pacifier, and the others wanted neither.

From the earliest moments, we treated each son as an individual with his own personality and needs. If a parenting method worked for one but not for the next, we didn't force the baby to adapt; we adapted. Although many aspects of parenting were repeated, the experience unfolded differently with each son.

Adjusting to Life with Children

Tony's birth day, November 17, 1975, was probably the most exciting day of our lives. (Fortunately, we experienced that excitement nine more times.) With the excitement and joy of a new baby came all the new responsibilities and adjustments. **Our lives were changed forever.**

(Cathy): *My days especially changed, as they do for all women who have a baby. I was amazed at the time one little fella could consume and the fatigue associated with childbirth and new parenting responsibilities. I don't think new parents can be completely prepared for the changes they will face when they come home with their first bundle of joy. The experience did get easier, though, with each child. Although we experienced new challenges with each son, because they had different temperaments, the overall adjustments were less. The major adjustments were made with our first two sons.*

With our families living out of town, my friends working, and Joe's hours worse than they had been even during his residency, I found it difficult to be alone with a baby for so many hours. I missed adult conversation, stimulation, and involvement, and I had little time for myself. Tony's happy disposition did make it easier, but finding time to meet my needs seemed impossible. I laugh now about not having time when there was only Tony. If I had seen the future at that point I think I would have collapsed.

I learned, though, some important lessons that have guided me through the other nine sons' early months. **I learned to use the time the baby was asleep to meet my needs first, instead of always trying to catch up on housework.** *When I did housework first, the baby usually woke up before I had that important mental and physical break. Instead of being eager to face the next challenge, I was tired and frustrated. I also learned to take advantage of the time my mom visited. When the new baby slept, I rested and stopped feeling guilty about my mom taking care of the house. Although once we had four or five children, she spent most of her time keeping up with her grandsons.*

I realized that it is virtually impossible to accomplish anything in one sitting. I learned to avoid frustration by gearing activities

around the boys' schedules. I found that the jobs that required concentration—for example, business phone calls or balancing the checkbook—were best accomplished during nap time or in the evenings when the children were asleep. I could fold clothes, iron, and shop for groceries when they were awake. **I learned that being realistic about what I could accomplish made my days easier, and in the end, I actually could get more done.**

Becoming involved in activities where I met other young mothers helped a lot—I had other adults to talk to. *Mothers Day Out programs were just starting when I had Tony. They were a lifesaver later on with the other boys, providing me a morning or two with a less hectic schedule. (I usually had a new baby at home, so I wasn't totally free.) Mom told me her "mother's-day-out" was the one day a week her mother watched my sisters and me so she could do some of the things she needed and wanted to do. She stressed how important it was for me to take that time, especially with no family in town. Later, as I got to know other moms, we helped each other out as needed.*

Parenting as a Shared Responsibility

(Cathy): *During those first months after Tony was born, Joe realized he needed to provide me with some relief when he was home by sharing in the parenting responsibilities, even though he was tired after working at the hospital for thirty-six hours. (When Joe's on-call, I'm on-call in a sense, too, because I have to handle all the home responsibilities alone.) Joe's help, especially at this demanding time in his life, demonstrated his love and commitment to Tony and me.*

Joe still walks in the door after work and immediately helps in any way he can. He looks at parenting as a shared responsibility. Although I don't work outside the home, the importance of what I do all day, taking care of our sons and our home, is tremendously valued. **Joe never makes me feel less of a person, less of a woman, less intelligent, or less important because I am not contributing financially to our family.** *He realizes, as I do, my contributions are beyond monetary value. He supports me in every* *way he can. He also realizes being home with children, as good as they are, is demanding, physically and emotionally. He would never think of walking in the house and questioning or wondering why I hadn't completed a certain task. He knows with children, your time often is not your own.*

*Joe's love, commitment, and respect for me and the boys are obvious to people who know us. People ask, "How do you do it, Cathy? I only have three children and I'm going crazy. You seem to have it together." I let them know **we** do it. I doubt seriously whether I would have had ten children without Joe sharing the parenting effort. With both of us committed to each other and the boys, parenting and family life are a joyful experience, in spite of our fatigue.*

(Joe): *My willingness to take on responsibilities at home evolved out of my love and respect for Cathy and the boys, and the very important realization that these are my duties as well. Although I had helped Cathy before the boys were born, it was minimal compared with after. At first, I performed these duties out of sheer need due to the nature of our days and the fact that I had made a commitment to make our relationship work. In the beginning, my head was way ahead of my heart in accepting this "new role" at home. Initially, I felt coerced and unhappy when called upon to fulfill home responsibilities. I remember, however, the Saturday morning eighteen years ago I was standing at the kitchen sink cleaning the breakfast dishes and wondering, "Why am I doing this?" I felt as though I was probably the only male in Houston having to do household tasks. **Then it struck me like a strong wind—powerful and moving—I'm doing this because I love Cathy and the boys.** My heart, finally, caught up with my head.*

*I think many men are intimidated by household duties and/or totally underestimate the time, effort, and organization required to "get it all done." It is truly an awesome feeling when one individual (a male even) can negotiate the logistics of the many responsibilities of the daily household routine—alone. The real trick is being able to provide caring touches to your children while coordinating the washing, cooking, and homework. **We can handle the logistics, but it's handling the logistics and lovingly***

handling our children that makes us good parents. *One has great respect and empathy for one's spouse when one has to fulfill the other's role.*

I feel strongly that family must be a shared responsibility. ***I'm often amazed at husbands who expect their wives to do it all, and then wonder why their wives are frustrated, tired, angry, and unaffection-ate.*** *One evening, several years ago, our family had gone to the subdivision pool. A young couple with two small children was there. The mother was leaving to attend a meeting and asked the father to bathe the children before putting them to bed. The father looked at his wife incredulously, turned to me—wrong choice—and asked indignantly, "Do you ever have to bathe your sons?" I answered quite simply, "Sure. I do it all the time. It's actually kind of fun." Not the answer he expected or wanted.*

(Cathy): A few years ago, when Tony, our oldest, was in high school, he and I were chatting with several women. A couple of them complained that their husbands didn't help out around the house, something Tony couldn't identify with. In the next breath, though, they admitted they wouldn't be caught dead mowing the lawn or washing the cars. Tony didn't miss the dichotomy, and realized our family was different. These women wanted their husbands to help them around the house but didn't feel they needed to help with lawn care or "male" work. The older boys and I often mowed the lawn during the week so we could have more time to do fun things on the weekend with Dad. I didn't miss the opportunity later to tell Tony, "If your Dad's willing to fold clothes or fix dinner, then I should be willing to mow the lawn or wash a car."

This shared responsibility continues today, whether it's bathing chil-dren, supervising homework, reading to the boys, washing dishes, folding clothes, making car repairs, shopping for groceries, doing yard work, participating in a car pool, or doing the banking. **Neither of us considers these tasks or responsibilities exclusively his or hers. Whoever has the time or the talent to get the job done, does it.** We refer to this as our "divide and conquer" philosophy. It works beautifully, reduces conflict, helps our marriage and family run smoothly, and is an outward sign of respect and love.

Our sons see us sharing responsibilities and doing what it takes to make the family function successfully. Joe's helping out at home and Cathy's acceptance of his professional responsibilities are signs of love and mutual respect. Joe's willingness to participate fully at home has also provided opportunities for Cathy to be involved in the boys' schools and our community. If Cathy had a 7 A.M. board of trustees meeting at The Woman's Hospital of Texas or a 7 P.M. school board meeting at St. Francis de Sales School, for example, Joe would handle the home routine, not because he had to but because he wanted to. We've learned "the feet find the road easy when the heart walks with them."

Our Mantra: Love, Commitment, and Respect

Our family's strength is grounded in the three principles of love, commitment, and respect. All three are intertwined. One does not exist without the others. When we, as parents, say we love our children, our actions and our attitudes must send the same message. Just as it takes more than love to make a strong marriage, **it takes more than love to be a good parent.**

We have made choices, some difficult and some not so difficult, and we have established priorities that have enabled us not only to have our large family but also to enjoy our large family. Many people tell us we're lucky. But, again, it's not luck that got us where we are today. It is our commitment, love, and efforts. Have we been blessed with each other? Sure. But luck hasn't made our marriage strong. Luck didn't raise our children to be responsible, caring individuals. **People are successful at the things to which they devote most of their time and effort. It's a question of deciding what's important in your life and working hard to achieve it, whether it be marriage, family, career, or anything else.** "Remember where your treasure is, there your heart is also" (Matthew 6:21).

The respect we have for each other is the respect we share with our sons: We treat them and talk to them with respect. Just because they're younger than we are is no reason to speak unkindly, rudely, or in a demeaning, belittling manner. Since we treat our children with respect at home and they are expected to treat each other with respect, it has become second nature for them to treat people outside the home the same way, whether they are teachers, coaches, friends, neighbors, or people they've just met.

Showing affection has also become second nature for our family. Both of us—Cathy with her Irish and Italian background and Joe with his Spanish and Mexican heritage—grew up in families where hugs and kisses were the norm. And the gentle touches, warm hugs, and kisses don't stop when our sons grow out of diapers. We continue to express our feelings to them in outward ways. It's rewarding to have a sixteen-, seventeen-, or eighteen-year-old son come up to us at a high school function and give us a hug and peck on the cheek. They aren't ashamed or embarrassed to show their feelings. Teachers and friends are amazed at how close the boys are to each other. They are not only brothers—but also chosen friends. It's quite natural for them to go places and do things together. They support and encourage each other and share in each other's triumphs and disappointments, right along with us. We remember how empty David felt when Tony left for college. He not only missed his brother, he missed his *best* friend.

Respect and love can be taught. **Right from the beginning, our touch, our voice, and our attentiveness tells our sons they are loved.** As they grow and develop, we continue to meet their physical needs and treat them with respect and kindness. We reinforce the naturally good qualities in each son (and we do believe children are born naturally good) by our gentle words of encouragement and praise and by our example.

When dealing with our children, we remind ourselves **there is no substitute for our love, time, and attention.** These elements are just as important in parenting as they are in our marriage. **Children need to feel they are important in their parents' lives; the time and importance we give parenting tells them this, fostering self-esteem and a sense of security.** At times the demands of parenting are overwhelming, but as Erich Fromm says in *The Art of Loving,* "When you truly love, you want what is best for that person, sometimes at the expense of what is best for yourself."

(Joe): *Early in my medical career, I recognized that in addition to the long hours spent at the hospital doing patient care, I must be prepared to spend time working on research projects that could be published. Success in academic medicine is often predicated on producing numerous scientific publications. I wholeheartedly desired that type of recognition and advancement. Two years into my career, I had the opportunity to talk to a well-published, highly respected neonatologist who had been invited to Houston to present a conference. As our conversation shifted from medicine to more casual topics, I mentioned how much it was appreciated that he had taken the time to present this conference. The neonatologist said that to do so meant missing his two sons' hockey games (which he rarely had time to attend) and that he missed seeing his sons now that he was divorced. This physician had paid a high price for success. I realized I needed to rethink my career goals and how I measured success.*

(Cathy): *When I taught school, I observed many parenting approaches. There were those parents who obviously enjoyed their children and the parenting experience and those who clearly felt parenting was an inconvenience and a burden. For the latter, giving to their children, whether of their time or their finances, was an obligation—not a loving gift. I feel sorry for these parents, but even more so for their children, for what they're missing.* **Children know when "something" is done out of love.**

In St. Paul's first letter to the Corinthians, Chapter 13:1-3, he states, "If I speak with human tongues and angelic as well, but do not have love, I am a noisy gong, a clanging cymbal. If I have the gift of prophecy and, with full knowledge, comprehend all mysteries, if I have faith great enough to move mountains, but have not love, I am nothing. If I give everything I have to feed the poor and hand over my body to be burned, but have not love, I gain nothing."

Loving Your Children—No Strings Attached

Successful parenting entails giving of ourselves to our children out of love. How disappointing to hear a parent say, "I sacrificed to send my son to school and look at the appreciation he shows us," or "I provided my kids with everything and look at the gratitude I get." **The "parent provides—the child owes" philosophy** *stinks*. This philosophy reflects a lack of heartfelt giving on the parent's part and too often the child's response mirrors that lack of love. Both younger and older children sense when parents act out of love versus self-interest. Our love to our sons is a gift—no strings attached.

We are educating our sons, for example, not for what they will do for us in the future, but for the opportunities that education will provide each of them. Not only is it our parental responsibility to educate our children, it's a true gift—whether in a public, private, or parochial school. Look for schools that will best meet the needs of your children and family. The choice may be determined by where you live, and the interests, talents, or intellectual abilities of your children. We chose to have our sons attend parochial schools early in the boys' schooling. Although many public and private schools offered academically challenging programs, we wanted our sons in an educational environment that reinforced the values, especially religious values, we had established at home. The boys know it's financially demanding to attend parochial schools, yet they know we are committed to this goal and it's given with love.

When Tony and David were little and attending a Catholic elementary school, people would ask us where we intended to send the boys to high school. We would say Strake Jesuit College Prep. They would raise their eyebrows and ask, "How will you ever be able to afford that?"—and we had only five sons at the time. We knew, though, from our own experiences, Joe at El Paso Jesuit High School and both of us at Loyola University, New Orleans, that we wanted to provide our sons with an education that focused on strong intellectual development while fostering the spiritual dimension in their daily lives. We wanted our sons to learn that their most valuable gift is the giving of themselves to others, a tenet of Jesuit education. We realize other parents may have a different focus or goal for their children. Again, we encourage parents to find the best educational experience for their children. Education is so important, and a true gift when provided with love.

Establishing Priorities and Differentiating Between Wants and Needs

Education was, and still is, a priority. We both established this goal, as we do all family goals. People assume we are able to send our sons to parochial schools because Joe is a physician. However, his decision to remain in academic medicine versus a considerably more lucrative private practice meant making significant choices if we were to fulfill our desire to have a large family and educate our children in Catholic schools. Academic medicine provided Joe the opportunity to practice neonatology, do research, teach interns, residents, and fellows, *and* have hours more conducive to family life. We have chosen to live a simpler lifestyle—the boys sharing bedrooms and wearing hand-me-downs, and the family eating out infrequently, repairing items versus buying new ones, having one television without cable (not merely a financial choice), keeping cars as long as possible (Joe just traded in his fifteen-year-old car), saving for needs (and wants), and not accruing debt. **We have learned to live within our means.** We realize we are blessed and that Joe's income, along with our chosen lifestyle, affords us the luxury of providing our sons the education of our choice, as well as other educational, cultural, and athletic activities.

An added benefit of our choices and goals is the effect on other areas of our lives. We often feel having ten sons keeps us focused on what's really important in our day-to-day lives. **For our family to accomplish its goals and be successful, we have to prioritize our time and our needs.** Meeting the financial responsibilities of a large family keeps us, and the boys, from getting caught up in the materialistic "I have" game so prevalent in our society. **All of us are learning the difference between wants and needs.** For example, one of the boys may need a pair of shoes, but prefer a pair out of our price range. It may be our responsibility to provide the shoes, but not to buy what we consider unnecessary or frivolous. We tell the boys what we're willing to pay for the shoes, and if they want a more expensive pair, they must make up the difference. What's interesting is how often they'll choose the reasonably priced item versus the fancy brand. One year when David and Chris needed new winter jackets, we found some on sale at a local department store. The next day while shopping at a discount warehouse, we noticed some jackets, not quite as nice but of good quality, costing half of what we had paid for the others. Both boys willingly agreed to exchange the jackets, realizing the substantial savings.

Even when it comes to groceries, we are selective of choices and of where we shop. We're not ashamed to use coupons or shop at the less expensive, less fancy store. It's not unusual to find the boys scrutinizing the grocery store ads—they know we buy Blue Bell ice cream, a Texas favorite, only when it's on sale.

As we prioritize our needs, **we also prioritize our time.** We reiterate that there is no substitute for a parent's love, time, and attention. We are often asked, "How can you possibly give each one of the boys the love and attention they need or deserve?" "Don't the boys feel slighted with so many brothers?" We even had a parent tell us she had only two kids so she could provide the attention they needed to place them both in the top reading and math groups. We had five of our boys in school at the time and they were all doing well. It didn't have anything to do with two versus five. It had more to do with our willingness to commit the time needed to each of our sons.

How we decide to spend our time is our choice. We can choose to watch "Monday Night Football" or we can choose to review homework or read stories with our sons. We can choose to go shopping on a Saturday or attend the boys' soccer games. Cathy can choose to stay home and clean the house or attend a school play or program. Joe can choose to go to a Rockets game or attend his own son's basketball game. In every instance we have to make a choice. **When it comes to how we spend our time, we *choose* to be involved with the boys' lives and activities.** And, at the same time, we have to admit, we enjoy being a part of their lives. It usually means that if we attend a school program or a sports event, we'll be folding clothes or doing paperwork late at night.

Something has to give, but the trade-off is well worth it. Our sons have enriched our lives! We may get behind, but over the last twenty years of parenting, we still seem to accomplish the essentials while providing our sons with the time and attention needed at a precise moment. No one will ever convince us that children, whether six or sixteen years old, don't care if their parents are involved with their activities, whether it's school, music, sports, dance, or debate. **Children care, want, and need their parents to be a part of their lives**.

(Cathy): *When David was in seventh grade playing basketball, his team had a game after school 20 miles across town. I usually attended his games, as did Joe whenever his schedule allowed. This particular afternoon one of his brothers had a doctor's appointment. I explained that I would make the game if we finished soon enough with the doctor. David understood, but I sensed his disappointment. The doctor's appointment went quickly, so I headed to the game. As I entered the gym, David was running down the court in my direction. When he saw me, his eyes lit up expressing how pleased he was I was there. David knew by my making the effort to attend the game he was important to me. And parents have the nerve to think it doesn't matter if they're there or not.*

I also remember the time Joe Pat was in second grade and performing in a Thanksgiving program for Grandparents Day. It was the November following the birth of Danny, our eighth son. The play was scheduled for 9 A.M., which would give me plenty of time to get to the school. The night before, I was up with the baby several times. Joe, trying to give me a few extra minutes of sleep, turned off my alarm clock; he had forgotten about the program. When I awoke, it was already 8:30. Panic ensued. I have never thrown myself and a baby together faster than I did that morning. Joe Pat had been very excited about the program; there was no way I could miss his performance. I was late, but did make it in time to hear Joe Pat proudly announce, "I am Chief Massasoit, and these are my people."

(Joe): *One afternoon at the hospital, a young secretary and I discussed our children's after-school activities. She told me how much she had enjoyed her experience on a pep squad when she was in seventh grade. She had worked hard to be chosen for the squad and practiced many hours to be the squad's best member. Then she sadly recounted how neither of her parents had ever come to see her cheer. Here was a grown woman still hurt* that her parents never considered her important enough to see her perform. *I've never forgotten her disappointment.*

Obviously, attending all the boys' activities isn't easy. **It takes a lot of coordinating and cooperating by the entire family to make it work.** *Several years ago, Cathy's dad was describing our family to a man with a military background, explaining how organized our day-to-day operations were. "Real sergeants," the amazed man said. "Sergeants nothing," her dad replied. "They could run the whole darn Pentagon"—though sometimes it does seem we need several spreadsheets and Colin Powell to make it work.*

One weekend we had more than the usual number of activities. Chris had a varsity soccer showcase 35 miles away, Joe Pat had a freshman soccer tournament at the high school, Matthew had a middle school prep bowl competition, Mark had soccer practice, and Joe was on-call for the weekend. David, luckily, was still home from Creighton University and pitched right in. Cathy attended the freshman tournament and prep bowl—fortunately both were at the same location—with Joe Pat, Matthew, Timmy, and Mark, and David headed north to Chris's games with Tommy, Danny, and Jamie. When we have a commitment for one of the boys, his brothers willingly help because they appreciate our support, and want the same for their brothers.

In the evenings with schoolwork, this shared commitment continues. If you were to peek in the den window, you might find one of the older boys calling out spelling words or drilling flash cards with Tommy and Danny, another reading a story to Jamie or Timmy, Joe working on a science project with Matthew, and Cathy reviewing for a social studies test with Mark. **The "divide and conquer" technique is again at work.** Even the boys have learned how valuable a tool it is, not only in our family but also when they are involved in other activities.

Quality Time: Any Time You're with Your Children

Our commitment to and love for the boys flows to all areas and stages of their development. Parental commitment begins at birth (actually, it begins during pregnancy by taking care of yourself). When we're feeding the baby, giving him a bath, or changing a diaper, the manner in which we interact with the baby—our touch, our tone of voice—sends the message that he is loved. *Quality time* is a term used over and over again when discussing good parenting. **Quality time should be any time you're with your children, and not some designated time in your day or week.** But it's also important to ask yourself, How much quality time can there be if there's little quantity time?

(Cathy): *I was talking to a young mother who was in a quandary about postponing finishing medical school in order to stay home with her toddler. Another mother had told her leaving her son with a babysitter was not that "big a deal": "Anyone can feed or change a baby." What that mother hadn't learned was that, sure, anyone could do the physical caregiving, but not necessarily the emotional mothering. I tell this story not to weigh the benefits of staying at home versus working, but rather to emphasize that **it's the interaction with our children that's important.** If this mom feels that way about taking care of her child, she is missing golden opportunities to plant the seeds of love and learning in her child.*

I find quality time all around us: washing clothes, changing diapers, raking leaves, making puzzles, reading stories, preparing dinner, and even riding in the car. I listen to many a tale while preparing dinner each night. Our kitchen counter is set up with stools on one side and a work area on the other. While I'm shredding a head of lettuce for the salad or peeling a dozen potatoes, Danny may be sitting on a stool relating one of his real or imaginary adventures, or Mark may be telling me about the Houston Hotshot soccer players that visited their school that afternoon, or I may be calling out spelling words to Tommy.

Celebrating Each Child's Uniqueness

Playing with our children—building blocks, play dough, cars and trucks, puzzles, swings, big wheels, games, swimming, kicking or throwing the ball—shows them we care about them *and* enjoy being with them. When we are asked, "Doesn't it get old and boring after a few kids?" we have to admit playing Candy Land does get old, but we remind ourselves that it's the first time playing the game for this particular son.

When we visited the high school open house with Matthew, our fifth son, people asked and wondered why we were there again since our older sons either attend or attended the school. We remind them that it may be *our* fifth time for open house but it's Matthew's first. **One of the reasons each of the boys feels special, and not slighted, is because we make the effort to make each experience special as it happens for that particular son.** We've discovered that because each of the boys is different, usually the experience is different for us.

We respect each of the boys, too, for who they are, not for who we may want them to be. We teach certain principles and values to all our sons: to be responsible, caring, loving, well educated, and respectful of God and His world. We also emphasize that their success and self-worth is measured by who they are, what they do, and how they live their lives. We do not pressure them to be a doctor, play a certain sport, or march to a certain drummer. They each have God-given talents and must find their own path to follow. The boys know they are loved and respected for who they are. When Joe Pat was in middle school, he wrote an autobiography. In it he stated, "I have a good relationship with my parents. They understand my needs and things other people don't. I am not as talented as my brothers in academics and they understand. They support me and love me." **How rewarding as a parent to have your children understand they are loved unconditionally.**

Tony decided to major in pre-med at Saint Louis University, and many people assumed David would do likewise at Creighton University. But anyone who knows David realizes he tolerates math and science; his strengths are writing and the social sciences. And when people used to comment, "Wouldn't it be easier if they all swam?" (because Tony was a swimmer), we'd respond, "Sure, it would be easier, but the other boys only enjoy swimming; they *love* soccer."

By respecting each son's interests, abilities, strengths, and personality, we foster strong self-esteem in our sons. They see themselves valued by us as individuals. We may face scheduling challenges due to their individual interests, but we are rewarded over and over again by their continued successes and self-fulfillment. In his book *Unconditional Love*, John Powell, S.J., refers to the words of Viktor Frankl: "True self-esteem and a true sense of identity can be found only in the reflected appraisal of those whom we have loved."

Chapter 3

Positive Parenting
Produces Positive Results

I *am only one; but still I am one.*
I cannot do everything, but still I can do something.
I will not refuse to do the something I can do.
                                    –Helen Keller

Learning to Be Adaptable, Flexible, and Prepared

Each day in the Garcia-Prats household is different from the next. When we wake up in the morning, we are never quite sure what the day will bring. The night before, we usually have a pretty good idea of the activities planned and how we'll accomplish them: six loads of wash, the usual housekeeping responsibilities, four soccer practices in four different locations, school open house, and an orthodontist appointment—all in one day.

We set our alarm a few minutes earlier than we need to get up. These few minutes allow us to gather our thoughts, and think about what needs to be done and what we want to do. It's also at this time that we ask God for the grace we need to get through the day, and remind ourselves that with His guidance, there is nothing we can't handle.

And so the day begins. We have already chosen to wake up and have the best day possible. We could, just as easily, wake up and bemoan the fact that we have ten sons and the work associated with a large family. But since we truly believe our sons are blessings, **we choose to make the best of what the day has to offer.**

Parenting is not always easy, and sure, the frustrations and disappointments creep in. It's usually the unexpected events that throw a wrench into our day's carefully mapped out schedule and routine. These unexpected events happen to all of us—whether we have children or not, whether we have ten children or one. But to moan, groan, be angry, or self-pitying only ruins the day for you and most likely for your children.

(Cathy): *When Tony was in second grade, his class had tickets to attend the Broadway musical* Annie *that was touring in town. His teacher, knowing my love of musicals, invited me to accompany the class. It all sounds easy enough until you realize I had several schedules to manipulate in order to attend. But I creatively managed to have all our children not yet in school taken care of. I was really excited—it was rare that I had this kind of opportunity. Well, the morning of the field trip one of the boys woke up with a fever and sore throat. There went the plans for the day. All my efforts instantly undone. Instead of sitting at the Music Hall watching* Annie, *I sat in the doctor's office with an uncomfortable child and a few other energetic children to boot. It happens! Was I disappointed? Of course. Was I angry? No.* **When we have children we must be prepared for the unexpected and be willing to accept this reality.**

On another occasion, a Sunday evening, we looked forward to relaxing after a hectic weekend. While eating dinner, Joe Pat, then three years old, blurted, "I almost choked today."

"What do you mean you almost choked?" asked Cathy.

"A battery was in my mouth."

"What battery—and where is this battery now?" Cathy quizzed him.

"In my tummy!" Joe Pat answered, explaining, in his words, that it was a small nickel-sized cadmium battery from his older brothers' hand-held game. We glanced at each other, and Cathy decided to call Poison Control (an essential phone number to have handy in a home with children, especially ten boys). The kind soul on the other end of the line, in as calm a tone as he could muster, said, "Ma'am, call your doctor and get to the nearest emergency room immediately."

What was supposed to be a relaxing evening was spent in the emergency room taking X rays of Joe Pat's "electrified" stomach. When Joe Pat found out he would get to see his buddy, Dr. Curtis, and lots of ambulances, he was thrilled. Dr. Curtis assured us, after viewing the X ray, that yes, a battery had been swallowed.

Each morning at 7 A.M., until the battery passed through his system, Joe drove Joe Pat to the hospital to check the status of the battery. Although it was extremely inconvenient, we counted our blessings, because the recommended procedure not too long before had been to remove the battery through abdominal surgery. The incident still lives on for Joe Pat when he is teasingly reminded, "Had your battery charged lately?" "Is your charge low?" or "Joe Pat can take a lickin' and keep on tickin'."

The point of these stories, and there are many more, is that with children, one or ten, you never know what will happen. **It's how we deal with these snarls in our day that makes the difference.** You can get "bent out of shape" or you can try to relax, accept what's happened, and move on. **We need to learn to be adaptable and to be flexible, two all-important words in a parent's** *modus operandi.*

Maintaining a Positive Attitude and Approach

A positive attitude is essential to parenting. It's important even if you don't have children, but a must if you do.

(Cathy): *When I was ten years old, my Dad taught me the Serenity Prayer: "God grant that I may have the serenity to accept the things I cannot change, the courage to change the things I can, and the wisdom to know the difference." At the time, the prayer didn't completely make sense, but as I grew older and confronted various situations, I understood its meaning, and was grateful for this enduring gift my Dad had shared.*

We are not a couple or a family without problems. We realize, though, that our approach, our attitude, has to be positive and uplifting. It affects our marriage and it affects our family. **We often find that difficult situations become learning experiences when approached in this positive fashion.**

The old maxim, "Positiveness begets positiveness" is so true. Nowhere is it more important to practice than in the home, where we must look for and emphasize the positive in all areas of our lives. Though being positive sounds easy, too often, it is not practiced on a day-to-day basis. To be positive with each other and our children, we must as individuals be positive and love ourselves. We truly believe God gave us our unique gifts for a reason, just as He gave unique gifts to each of our sons. God did not make any two of us exactly the same, and it is nice to remember, "God don't make junk." **We have learned to recognize our individual strengths and our weaknesses, and we have been willing to make the choices and changes necessary to improve ourselves and stretch and grow.** We are not, we assure you, the exact same people we were when we married twenty-three years ago.

(Cathy): *Since I was twelve years old, I would save little sayings that were inspirational, encouraging, or set a standard I wanted to attain: "To belittle is to be little." "It's nice to be important but it's more important to be nice." I was inspired by books I read and courses I took in college that helped develop my approach to life and guided me in a positive mind-set about who I was and how to lead my life. In his book* Living, Loving and Learning, *Leo Buscaglia says, "We're teaching everybody everything there is except what is essential, and that is how to live in joy, how to live in happiness, how to have a sense of self-worth and personal dignity. Those things are taught, and they are learned."*

I'm grateful beyond words that my parents, my Church, some teachers, and my Jesuit education taught me these essential truths. But I haven't stopped learning. I continue to read inspirational, positive materials today. I believe what we read, what we hear, and what we see makes a difference in who we are: Junk in, junk out; positive in, positive out.

How can you read The Power of Positive Thinking *by Norman Vincent Peale and not feel like you can accomplish most anything? Peale emphasizes the positive mind-set: "I can do all things through God who strengthens me." I was drawn to read* The Power of Positive Thinking *several months after the birth of Matthew, our fifth son. There were so many people who, although very helpful and giving, left the impression they felt sorry for me and my "lot in life." I better understand their perspective now than I did then. Tony was six-and-a-half years old when Matthew was born. That's five sons in six and a half years, three in diapers. Although people meant well, their comments were often in a negative vein: "How are you possibly going to take care of them?" "You need help." "You should consider getting your tubes tied." "Can't Joe leave you alone?"—as if I had nothing to do with having the boys. After a while you start to question yourself. Here we were, feeling blessed and content, and yet there was this negative barrage from the outside. Reading* The Power of Positive Thinking *gave me the boost I needed to "bunk the junk" that we were hearing and feeling.*

Positiveness encompasses our approach to situations, our language, and our actions. **It's important to remember that *what* and *how* we say and do things makes a difference. We try very hard to think before we speak and consider how our words will affect the other person, whether it is to our spouse, our children, or others.**

Avoiding The "Negative" Traps

Many people don't realize they are sending negative messages. They get into the habit of using negative words and practicing a negative approach.

(Cathy): One summer, when I was pregnant with our eighth son, Danny, I went to the neighborhood pool with the boys. A young mother with three small children arrived shortly after. Seeing me in the wading pool with the two youngest boys and pregnant, she lamented how having

a third child had been a rude awakening for her and her husband. "Two kids was easy," she said, "but the third one has thrown everything out of kilter." The negative comments continued, and I said nothing. Then the older boys started calling for attention: "Mom, watch my dive." "Mom, look at my cannonball." One of the boys walked over to the wading pool to play with his younger brothers. The young mother looked and asked, "Whose kids are those?" When I answered, "Mine, I have seven children," the woman's face turned red. Not only had I surpassed three children, I seemed to have survived quite well.

Cathy turned the tables in this situation, seeing a golden opportunity to share the joys and blessings of having three or more children. The young mother was feeling overwhelmed by the responsibilities of motherhood. We often tell people our first couple of years of parenting were our hardest. We had much to learn, much unfamiliar territory to face, and many adjustments to make in our lifestyle. Parenting did become "easier" in the sense of our being able to adjust to the day-to-day challenges. We are convinced, too, that we made the necessary choices that enabled us to enjoy parenting and our growing family.

We avoid letting the routine activities (laundry, cooking, cleaning, homework, and so forth) wear us down. We accept them as part and parcel of raising a family. One evening a few years ago, at a high school function, a mother of two sons grumbled on and on about how much wash she had to do all the time. It was funny sitting there listening to her. After the mom walked away, a father turned to us and said, "Doesn't she know that you have ten sons? You *have* to have incredibly more wash than she has. Why didn't you say something?" We answered, matter-of-factly and from experience, that people like her don't understand—to them their life and problems are always worse than anyone else's.

We count our blessings often, realizing many other families have very difficult situations in their lives: serious illnesses, mental or physical handicaps, deaths of family members, unemployment, and so on. We are inspired by how these families handle their difficulties. Friends tell us that on unusually busy days, they think of us and feel less overwhelmed, knowing we probably have even more on the docket than they.

Starting the Day in a Positive Way

We, the parents, set the tone in our family. We believe it is important for mornings to get off to a good start—not just for the parents but especially for the children. The Garcia-Prats mornings, much to the amazement of many, run very smoothly. We have established a routine that provides a calm, fresh start to the day. Each of our sons knows his individual responsibilities and his family responsibilities. Clothes and schoolwork are taken care of the night before, and in the morning schoolbags are packed, lunches prepared, beds made, dishes rinsed and put in the dishwasher, and our dog, Princess, fed. Chaos ensues if one child can't find his shoes, science book, permission slip, or whatever. Thus, a calm morning turns into bedlam and everyone's day begins with an edge. With a little forethought, instead of yelling and constant coaxing, we have time to talk about the plans for the day, wish the boys success in their schoolwork, laugh, and feel warm together.

This routine started when Tony and David were little, and has become second nature for each of the boys. When Danny began kindergarten, he was eager to be a part of the morning school routine. The first day of school he wanted to know what his "job" was in the morning. Picking up the newspaper and shutting off the outside lights became his prideful morning tasks. Because his older brothers were accepting and positive with their responsibilities, Danny also wanted to contribute.

The positive approach builds on itself and makes our day easier. We remind the boys it takes all of us working together to make it work well. By encouraging the boys, respecting their efforts and contributions, we foster a positive home, positive feelings, and positive self-images.

As parents, we know it's often easier to do things ourselves; many times we can complete tasks in a more "perfect" manner. **But by not allowing and encouraging young children to do things themselves, we squelch their desire to help out.** To rekindle the desire in later years is difficult and the source of much friction. Little Timmy, age two, is already learning how to dress and undress himself. We start with the easier items first and gradually move to the harder ones. It definitely takes more time right now, but with our support, within a relatively short period of time, he will learn to dress himself. All of our sons felt proud when they accomplished this skill.

The same principle applies to making beds in the mornings. At a young age, children like to help "Mommy" make the beds. Eventually, they want to try to do it themselves. If children see us remake the bed to our standards, it sends the message that their work wasn't good enough. Work with your child, provide hints on making the bed, but don't expect perfection or you will soon have a child unwilling to make the effort. **The more positive reinforcement we provide and the more we involve our children with helping at an early age, the more likely they will share in the responsibilities as they grow older.** (Sometimes college-aged kids need "gentle" reminding that beds *are* made each morning!)

(Cathy): *My first direct experience with applying positive techniques was during my teaching years. I saw the rewards of positive attitude day after day. When attending Loyola University, New Orleans, Professor Mary Fitzgerald emphasized the difference positive comments and "good" notes home to parents could make for students. Each week I would write a note home to a few parents, praising their children for something they had accomplished during the week: "Paul was a math wiz this week." "Tommy's reading has shown great improvement. Thanks for reading with him at home." "Beth's poems have been marvelous. We are all enjoying her creativity." These simple notes made parents feel good about their child and were reflected in the student's daily attitude. I actually had a class of poets after praising Beth for her poems and allowing her to share them with the class. Parents who had older children told me they had never in all their years of parenting received such notes. I was amazed that something so simple could have that much effect.*

(Joe): *Teaching young residents (physicians in training), usually in the context of a busy intensive care unit, calls for close supervision and a positive approach. I endeavor to teach and encourage the young physicians to reason through the management of their patients. During a resident's discussion of a case on patient rounds with three to four other residents, I first emphasize every well-thought-out concept. Then I focus on the concepts that were missed. We review the analysis of the patient together, using any mistakes as an opportunity to discuss and clarify other concepts.*

If I harped on each mistake made by the resident during his or her analysis of the case, the resident would not venture into the unsure ground of inexperience, never developing his or her talent for medical reasoning. The opportunity to advance the young doctor's medical aptitude and experience would be lost.

Our discussions are always done in an atmosphere of positiveness, never intimidation. Intimidation only causes stress. It's more important to have the resident remember the lesson and grasp the knowledge needed to take care of the next patient with that particular disease than it is to remember the amount of sweat and tears engendered by the "teaching rounds." **Positive approaches promote the atmosphere of willingness to explore without the threat of failure or loss of self-esteem, especially in the presence of one's peers.**

Children respond in a similar fashion. Our attitude toward the boys allows them to be happy at home and "try things safely" with Mom and Dad. Thus they'll be ready to "try them" with their teachers at school.

In shaping my "style of managing" at work, I was fortunate to observe individuals whom I considered good bosses. I have known and worked with very intelligent and famous people in the Texas Medical Center. Not every one of them, though, was a good boss. The distinguishing characteristic of good bosses was not that they were easy or that they paid the best salary, but that they were positive toward those around them. They were demanding but fair. Most of all, they looked at a situation in the best possible light. They showed resilience in all situations, and their offices reflected their attitude.

I apply this approach not only at work but also with my family. My encouragement and support of Cathy and the boys influences how they approach their daily challenges. Just as I face many little struggles and hassles at work, so do they in school, sports, extracurricular activities, and childrearing responsibilities. **A parent must be prepared to honestly be** *the "cheerleader" for the family. Think about what wonderful individuals you have to cheer for.*

The positive mind-set applied at home gets the same positive results. **If we praise our children for their accomplishments and encourage them in their efforts, our children will be happy and confident in who they are and what they do.** Our influence on our children is incredible, perhaps overwhelming at times. Our tone of voice and our choice of words have quite an impact on our boys. Once again, what and how we say and do things makes a difference for our children. Just as adults can detect from the tone of voice what someone implies, our children can do the same. If you tell your child, "That's great," but without enthusiasm in your voice, he'll never believe it's great. If we constantly point out how many are wrong on a work sheet, instead of how many are right, the child feels more like a failure than a success.

Danny, seven, is doing a lot of creative writing, both at school and at home. He has an extremely creative mind. Many of the words are spelled phonetically, and so not correctly. If all we or his teachers emphasized was the incorrect spelling, we are convinced Danny would soon lose his love of writing. Correct spelling is important, we know, but so is developing his written expression. With both school and home encouraging him and working on spelling in other ways, Danny feels confident about his accomplishments.

Providing Children with Positive Role Models and Positive Environments

Since our children spend a large portion of their time outside the home as they grow older, we are concerned with the environment they are in and the people they are with. **We expect their teachers and coaches to be positive and to live and reinforce the values we teach and live at home.** Our sons have been blessed over the years with some wonderful teachers and coaches, too numerous to name. Many are close friends and individuals our family admires. Of course, we've experienced the opposite side of the coin, too. We've had to deal with those times when a teacher's or coach's attitude and approach have not been beneficial to one of our sons.

You can imagine how upset we were when one individual, who had coached a few of the boys, told one son he was the "black sheep" of our family. This coach did not respect our son's individuality. Instead, he expected him to be a carbon copy of his brothers, talent-wise and personality-wise. When our son did achieve, the praises were not there. Yet, when a mistake was made, the coach quickly pulled him from the game. If this coach had worked with our son differently and respected his individuality, he would have been amazed at what they could have accomplished together.

Coaches (and teachers) have a unique responsibility to provide direction and be good role models for their players. With ten sons, we've had the opportunity to observe quite a few coaches over the last fourteen years, in soccer, swimming, basketball, and baseball. **We define a successful coach as that rare individual who not only knows the sport and the skills and techniques required to field a strong team but also has the ability to work with kids, helping them develop, excel, and grow from their efforts.** Being a winning coach does not necessarily classify them as "winning" in our eyes, since many coaches sacrifice their principles and their athletes for a win.

One of our favorite soccer coaches, Glenn Davis, Director of the Hurricane Youth Soccer Club, shares our feelings on the approach to athletics (and other endeavors). He expresses to his players more pleasure with the improvement of their skills and their effort as a team than a game won that was poorly played and/or without effort. Swimmers coached by Tony's high school swim coach, Jamie La Rochelle, not only improved their times and techniques but also grew as individuals because they witnessed Jamie living his values day in and day out. Jamie realized his influence extended beyond the pool. Adults involved with children, whether in the classroom, extracurricular activities, or sports, must understand the impact their words and actions have on the young people with whom they are entrusted. Coaches and teachers had positive effects on us growing up, so we realize the important role they play in our sons' lives.

We remember a soccer tournament several years ago where Chris's team had just lost their first two games. The players felt down, blaming each other for the losses. Their coach, David Moore, whom we really admired because of the way he understood and treated young athletes, took control. The boys and parents expected a "deserved" tongue-lashing. Instead, David lowered his voice as he prepared to address the team. He then calmly reiterated the strengths of the team and the individual talents each player possessed. Each player, he reminded them, needed to play hard using those talents: "If we do that, then we will win the rest of the games in this tournament." The young men realized what the coach was asking of each of them. Every player walked away with a feeling of renewed confidence in his ability. And they *did* win the rest of the games in the tournament. A positive coach using a positive approach received a positive response from his team.

(Cathy): *At last year's field day at St. Francis de Sales School, I was asked to help with the kindergarten activities. The kids lined up to do the crab crawl down the gym and back. One precious boy struggled with the awkward movement and was discouraged his first time down. Noticing his discouragement, I stayed at one end and cheered him on. Each time he came down the gym he improved the skill. By the fourth time, he had a huge smile on his face and wanted to do the crab crawl the rest of the afternoon. A little encouragement went a long way. He won my gold medal for the day.*

We often witness the "I can" philosophy working for our sons. The more confident they are, the more likely they are to succeed. We could usually predict the outcome of one of Tony's swim meets by his mental readiness. Mental readiness and confidence are often as important as the physical or academic ability.

When attending our sons' sports events, we remind ourselves we're there to cheer them on; we're not there to coach them or be their number one critic. Attend any children's sports activity and you'll be dismayed by the reactions of many parents to their child's performance: The upset mom at the swim meet chiding her daughter for not getting the time the mom expected, as if she swam slowly on purpose or had a bad dive in order to lose an extra second or two; or the overzealous dad at the basketball game demeaning his son for missing an important free throw, as if his son stepped up to the line to deliberately miss the shot. The child is disappointed enough and needs support and encouragement, not a parent's criticism and personal disappointment.

As adults we experience these same concepts at work. If your boss constantly rides you and points out your weaknesses and flaws, you begin to doubt your abilities and lose your self-confidence. Children aren't any different. All of us have our weaknesses and characteristics we need to improve—nobody is perfect. **Our efforts need to focus on becoming better people, encouraging, not discouraging, our children to grow and mature.**

Using Positive Language to Encourage Your Children

Parents who have attended Cathy's lectures tell her that *not* using positive language is probably their greatest weakness. Too many parents have gotten in the habit of saying or yelling commands such as "Put those toys away" or "Take out the garbage," instead of politely saying "Please put your toys away" or "Will you, please, take out the garbage?" **If we ask, not order, our children to do things, we'll see better results.** We use please and thank you with our sons. In the Garcia-Prats home, politeness extends to everyone, between mother and father, parents and children, and brother and brother. **The way we talk to each other and treat each other signifies respect.**

We're especially disturbed when we hear parents call each other or their children names or speak unkindly to or about each other. Children imitate their parents' behavior—to their parents, siblings, and others. Last summer, Cathy observed a mom with three young children leaving the grocery store. The mother was frustrated with her children, pushing them along and snapping at them to hurry and get in the car, calling the younger boy "stupid." The older child proceeded to push his younger brother into the car and yelled, "Hurry up, stupid." The mom then reprimanded the older son for calling names. Like mother, like son.

We want our sons to realize they are wonderful gifts from God. It's up to us to convey that truth. We speak to them with words that are honest and loving. We believe they are precious, funny, creative, and bright—and we tell them so. When they act kindly, we recognize their kindness. When they have helped us or their brothers, we express our appreciation. **If you praise your children honestly, they'll feel special and loved.** They know, of course, when the praise is false or unearned. If they played an awful basketball game, don't tell them they had a great game, because they know otherwise.

Learn positive words and phrases to show your support and encouragement: "I knew you could do it." "You're special." "Great job." "Thanks for all the help." "How creative!" **Don't be afraid to hug and kiss your children, at any age, to show your love, pride, and understanding. They need to hear and feel your love.** You'll discover that positive words and actions quickly make a difference in your child.

Remember that it's important to sing your child's praises. Our children need to know we are proud of them. You can talk about your children's accomplishments without being boastful. Speak highly of them and take pride in their achievements. If you don't, how can your children expect others to? So much of our self-esteem is determined at an early age by parents. **Build your children up; don't tear them down.**

We are our sons' loudest cheerleaders—their advocates, not their adversaries. We share with them positive comments people make about them, individually and as a family. When someone asks how one of the boys did in a particular activity, we share his accomplishments. Often the other parent wants information to make a comparison with their own child. We find that inappropriate and rarely share a grade or score with someone else. Even in our own home, grades and scores are private for each of our sons. We are comfortable saying, "Our son did well," or "Yes, we're proud of him," or "Isn't it wonderful. He worked hard."

The Positive Approach Catches On

(Cathy): *Over and over again, we experience the effectiveness of the positive approach. On one unusually hectic afternoon, when many things needed to get done, I walked into the kitchen to find someone had cleaned the counter and straightened up after snacks. When I found out it was nine-year-old Tommy, I thanked him and praised him for helping, especially without being asked. Within earshot, coloring, was Danny, age seven. The next thing I knew, Danny put away the silverware from the dishwasher. He was all smiles, too, when he received similar praise. Being positive with one affected the other. In our home, we call it the "trickle down effect."*

The trickle down effect flows from brother to brother, too. It's not uncommon to hear one of the older boys encouraging a younger brother in his efforts, whether it be swimming, soccer, reading, computer, or drawing. We think it's wonderful that they receive extra doses of positive reinforcement. Since the boys admire and look up to each other, younger to older and older to younger, it means so much to them to have the praise and encouragement of a brother or two. People often ask, "Aren't they jealous of each other?" We can honestly say no. They respect their brothers' talents, are proud of their brothers' achievements, and share in their disappointments. **Again, because we as parents have reinforced that each has been blessed with unique gifts from God, they understand that each will excel in his own special way, if he develops the gifts he has been given.**

Discipline as a Positive Learning Experience

One of our responsibilities as parents is to assist our children in all areas of their development. When one of the boys acts or speaks inappropriately, we don't say, "It's just a phase," or "That's the way boys are," or blame someone else. We deal with the situation up front and right away. If they have been unkind or acted out of line, we let them know how disappointed we are and what we think needs to be done. We express that disappointment in a positive manner, never giving the impression that they are unloved.

We describe our discipline style as gentle, firm, consistent, and age appropriate. Patting a shoulder, calling a son's name, or sending a piercing look reminds them they are acting improperly. Chris asked recently, when one of his younger brothers was fooling around in the car, "How is it, Mom, all you do is *look* at him and he stops?" The boys know when we "ask" them to change their behavior, we mean it.

We follow through with our discipline, determining appropriate consequences for their actions. When one of the boys "falls apart," he is asked to go to his room and get himself back together. "Time-out" is effective when not overused. If we're at church and one of the younger boys fidgets, we'll pat his shoulder or scoot him over closer to us. The touch reminds him where he is and how he should behave. If we've asked them to put away their clean, folded clothes and we find them on the floor of the closet they will be responsible for washing their own clothes for a determined amount of time. If a responsibility has not been fulfilled, they lose a privilege. Years ago, when they fussed about where they were going to sit in the car, we assigned seats. When they were uncooperative in the car, they rode the bus.

Our sons understand that consequences may be imposed by us or by someone else in authority. When Chris was in eighth grade, he elected to take a high school entrance exam preparation class being offered after school. One day he and several friends decided to skip the class and go across the street to the park. Some teachers noticed them, rounded them up, and brought them back to the school. The school notified the parents, informing us of what happened and that the students would not be allowed to participate in any after-school activities for two weeks.

A few of the students were not actively involved in an activity at the time, but the rest of the students were involved in sports or cheerleading. Some parents of the athletes and cheerleaders protested the discipline, claiming it was unfair to those who were involved in activities at the time. Our approach was to support the school, and in addition, deal with Chris at home. **We expressed our disappointment and discussed the importance of making good choices, because life is about making choices, day in and day out.** We also explained that as a member of the soccer team he had a responsibility to his team and now he couldn't play for two weeks. We tell the boys, "If you're going to gamble, you must be prepared to lose." This time around, Chris's pockets were full and he had a lot to lose, whereas his classmates' pockets were not as full.

In disciplining our sons, we want them to learn from their mistakes, learn that their actions affect other people, and learn to make appropriate choices, thinking before they act or speak. We could have ranted and raved when confronted with the above problem—and accomplished little. By being positive, working with our son through the problem, it became a learning experience.

Once we have dealt with a discipline situation, we don't dwell on it. The slate is clean and the boys know, very importantly, that we love them. We remind them that if we didn't love them, we wouldn't care or provide them with the guidance they need. It's important to point out that we handle each situation individually. The way we resolve a problem at one time with one son may not be the same way we resolve a similar problem with another son, only because each child is unique.

(Joe): *I recently attended a medical conference that discussed childhood behavioral problems. The child psychiatrist presenting the topic quickly focused on the importance of positive parenting. He cited research that found* **for every negative experience a child was subjected to, seven positive experiences were necessary to undo it.** *That's a tremendous responsibility—knowing that one negative comment or one negative reaction I make can have that much effect on my sons.*

As parents then, we must choose to have a positive attitude, to use positive language, and to discipline in a positive manner. We've seen the benefits of positive parenting with our family. "Try it—you'll like it"—and so will your children.

Chapter 4

To Be the Garcia-Prats
Not the Garcia-Brats:
Raising Disciplined,
Responsible, Caring Children

A nd the beginning, as you know, is always the most important part, especially in dealing with anything young and tender. That is the time when the character is being moulded and easily takes any impress one may wish to stamp on it.

–Plato

Learning How to Parent

Parenting is one vocation in which no training is required before you receive the official title of parent. Each of us has to learn and develop good parenting techniques. Although our past experiences greatly influence us, on-the-job training describes the way most of us learn to parent.

Both of us took child development courses in college. Cathy baby-sat since she was thirteen years old, volunteered in the nurseries at Charity Hospital in New Orleans, and taught school; and Joe specialized in pediatrics. Children definitely played an integral role in our lives. However, having our own child was different—exciting, scary, and, often, overwhelming.

Even with all our experience with children, we were still unsure about our ability to parent. Since Joe spent every day holding and caring for babies, he was more comfortable than Cathy handling Tony those first few weeks. (Joe's still more at ease than Cathy in the early weeks—even after ten children.) As we experienced new successes and learned from our mistakes, our confidence surged. **We weren't embarrassed to ask questions and seek advice from our parents, our friends, and, especially, our first pediatrician, Dr. Richard Plessala.**

As Tony grew, we were fascinated by his every new move and milestone. *The First Twelve Months of Life* by Frank Caplan became our parenting bible as we anticipated each stage. The book described developmental guidelines in motor, language, mental, and social skills, and provided practical and playful suggestions on ways to interact with Tony. Caplan's positive tone encouraged and enlightened us as we grew in our role as parents. The book stressed individuality, constantly reminding us that each child will accomplish developmental skills on his or her own timetable. Parents shouldn't feel guilty or frustrated when their child isn't sitting up, drinking from a cup, or walking as early as another, even a sibling. Caplan also emphasized *enjoying* your child. Although most parents expect to enjoy their child, too many other stresses can interfere with that ideal becoming a reality.

The Building Blocks of Effective Discipline

What did we do to make enjoying our sons an integral part of our parenting? We knew establishing guidelines, rules, boundaries, and standards was essential, not only to allow each member of the family to develop and mature but also to avoid chaos and frustration. Neither of us wanted to spend most of our parenting time disciplining. What fun is that? And we are not by nature or upbringing hard-core disciplinarians. **We view discipline as a way to teach our children appropriate behavior with our ultimate goal being *self-discipline.***

After twenty years of parenting, we know there are several reasons for our success in raising responsible, caring, and disciplined sons: We begin disciplining when they are young and we are consistent, loving, and fair. We acknowledge their different developmental and moral stages. We talk, listen, and empathize with our sons. We prevent and avoid potential problems, and we implement consequences for their behavior. Does this sound like a lot of effort? It is, especially in the early years, but once we started reaping the rewards of our time and effort with our older sons, Tony and David, we knew the effort was a worthwhile investment. We had fun exploring museums, feeding the ducks, having picnics in the park, and visiting the Galleria. We could go almost anywhere because they were well behaved. At home, they would play together for hours without a disagreement. They learned to give and take and help each other. In fact, in nineteen years, we can remember only one time Tony and David had a physical fight—and they were more devastated by the incident than we were. The time we now spend disciplining our older sons is minimal—they are self-disciplined.

We teach our sons right from the beginning what is appropriate and acceptable behavior, imparting our values and morals as we discipline. We are gentle, firm, loving, consistent, and constructive in our approach. We do not discipline the two-year-old, the eight-year-old, and the fourteen-year-old in exactly the same manner because they are at different developmental stages, especially morally. **It's important to have age-appropriate expectations of your child as well as age-appropriate consequences.** We discipline each son according to his age and his needs.

Understanding the boys' physical, emotional, and moral developmental stages guides us in our approach and reaction to situations. If you understand a child's need for independence at a certain age or a child's indecisiveness at another, you'll patiently tolerate his or her need to exert control over the littlest decisions. Each morning Timmy may select five different cups before he's made his final choice. Each of the boys, in turn, has wanted their sandwiches cut a certain way. One liked a triangle; one preferred a rectangle. One wanted it open (no bread on top); another wanted it closed. Jamie wants us to "bump" his cereal in the morning—a new one even for us; he wants the Cheerios pushed under the milk. Our flexibility in handling the day-to-day activities prevents the minor, and sometimes major, confrontations that frustrate and wear parents out. Just as we don't argue about which toothpaste to buy, we don't argue with the boys about which cup to use or the validity of "bumping" cereal or, as they get older, the length of their sideburns or hair.

If one of our sons wants to have something, do something, or go somewhere, we determine whether it is appropriate based on his age, the time of day, who is going, and the location. Our decision is determined by what we believe is right. **If we want our children to learn what is right and wrong, appropriate and inappropriate, we must** *teach* **them the difference.** We establish standards, rules, and consequences. Then we implement and enforce them. If you begin early when your children are ages two, four, and six, it's easier when they're twelve, fourteen, and sixteen, because you've established the foundation.

Timmy—our "terrific" two-year-old—exemplifies how the system works. Timmy is a strong-willed, energetic, curious, loving, happy child—not unlike most two-year-olds. He is loved by his mom and dad and adored by his nine older brothers. Timmy has learned to say *please* and *thank you* and even surprised us one day by saying *excuse me* when he needed to interrupt our conversation. Timmy didn't learn to use the words *please* and *thank you* overnight. He heard them over and over again when we or his brothers spoke to him, even before he said his first word. Timmy also loves to help, whether he's emptying trash cans, adding soap to the washing machine, or doing anything involved with water. We reinforce his willingness to help by letting him help. Too often parents take over tasks ourselves—and we wonder why our children say "I do it myself." **Encouraging and praising Timmy's efforts, teaching him how and what to do so he can do it himself, builds self-confidence and self-esteem at even this early age.**

When Cathy shared this approach at a conference she attended, one skeptic doubted that Timmy's positive behavior would continue. "It's natural for a two-year-old to want to help, not a six-year-old," she argued. We disagree. If children are made to feel loved and accepted and if they receive the right signals from their parents, we find the behavior continues. As they grow older, we may use a somewhat different type of encouragement or approach, but the same philosophy of love and acceptance holds true. Children need to understand that their contribution, even if it's just picking up their toys each night, is important to the family. **We emphasize over and over again that it takes all of us working together to make it work.** Just as Joe helped clean up the kitchen in the early years so we could have more time together, the same holds true as a family. When each of the boys does his part, we have time to read stories or play a game of Sequence, instead of Mom and Dad feeling exhausted and frustrated from doing everything themselves. **Our children have learned that our time is important too and that we like to have time to do the things we enjoy, just as they do.** That's not possible if Mom and Dad do everything.

Just as consistency worked in teaching Timmy to say *please* and *thank you*, consistency works effectively when discouraging negative behavior. Timmy is presently going through the whining stage. It drives all of us crazy. Instead of asking for a glass of juice, for example, he'll whine for it. We all want the whining to stop. So he doesn't get what he wants unless he asks appropriately. If he continues to whine, we put him in his room until he decides to ask properly or stop whining. He's learning whining doesn't pay. All the boys went through this phase, and each of them learned the same lesson. We don't have to yell or scream to change the behavior. **Consistently following through with our actions produces the desired results.**

Disciplining Requires Respect

At the core of our discipline is respect. It's amazing how we keep coming back to that one word, that one concept. Yet, it influences most areas of our lives. Our eight-year-old nephew, Dan, came home his first day in third grade at a new school excited to tell his parents, "Linton Hall has only *one* rule—respect. And you know, Mom and Dad," he said, "that covers just about everything. When you raise your hand and talk in turn—that's respect. When you are kind to your classmates—that's respect. When you take care of the school—that's respect." The same truth applies at home.

If we want our children to learn appropriate, acceptable behavior—which means respecting themselves, others, and property—then we must teach them correct behavior. **We teach them primarily through our own speech and actions, not only with our children but also with anyone we encounter.** We are polite to our sons at all ages. We ask them to do things—we don't demand! There's a huge difference between saying, "Clean up that room or you'll be sorry" and "If you intend to go to the concert tonight, you will need to clean your room first." And saying, "Take care of your brothers" is very different from saying, "I need to finish filling out these forms. Would you please help me by watching your younger brothers for a while?" Our choice of words and the tone of voice makes a difference in our sons' responses and willingness to help. When a boss speaks to you in a belittling manner, your self-esteem and confidence, and eagerness to help are diminished. Children are no different. **Be conscious of the words you say and how you say them.**

When you're outside the home, be aware of how you treat other people and the example you set. One afternoon, while in a bakery buying some chocolate rum balls for a "Christmas in August" party we were having, several adults spoke very rudely to the teenagers working behind the counter, demanding specific breads and pastries. When one young boy, obviously new on the job, brought the wrong bread, a woman lambasted him in front of everyone. (And adults complain about the behavior of our youth.) After witnessing this abuse, a few customers demonstrated to these young people, by the way they spoke and treated them, that not all adults are rude. The teenagers' appreciation showed in their smiles. **Think about what lesson you are teaching your children or other young people through your words and actions.** Your children notice your behavior.

Our sons are expected to treat each other with respect. Although the boys tease that "seniority rules," that doesn't imply that they may belittle or demean anyone younger. We teach the boys that each of us has our weaknesses, faults, and distinct physical characteristics. Just as they don't want their lesser qualities constantly pointed out or laughed at, neither do their brothers. **Being sensitive to others' feelings is essential in a loving home. Each of us must experience this unconditional love, security, and acceptance in our own home, by *all* members of a family, in order to develop into a secure, loving, and accepting individual.** We explain to our sons, for example, that if they're teasing their brother, it must also be funny to their brother. If their brother is hurt by their comment, it is *not* teasing. Behavior that is belittling, mean, unkind—basically, disrespectful—is unacceptable. We remind them that "to belittle is to be little."

Along the same lines, **we expect our sons to use appropriate language.** We don't tolerate "shut up," "stupid," or any other name calling, and we certainly don't accept foul language. One afternoon thirteen years ago, our family was outside working in the yard. All of a sudden, Chris, who was four years old, yelled at the top of his lungs, "I need to go piss." We knew Chris didn't realize he had said anything wrong, and we knew that he hadn't learned that phrase from us. We firmly explained to Chris that he was not to repeat those words, and *then* we took Tony and David aside. They may not have been guilty of saying anything wrong at the time, but they had obviously used inappropriate words in front of their brother at another time. If we wanted to curtail foul language in the future, now was the time to make an impression. Tony and David were disciplined! **By setting the standards early and with the older boys, we established what is acceptable in our family—allowing the "trickle-down" effect to work in our favor.**

We want our sons to learn that they are responsible for their brothers. They have a powerful influence on each other! They need to understand that they are accountable not only to us, for what they do or don't do for their brothers, but also to God. If they provide strong guidance they will reap the rewards, just as if they lead them astray, they will be held accountable. Some say it's a heavy burden to place on our sons, but **we strongly believe we are all ultimately responsible for each other.** In the Garcia-Prats home, **we strive to make each other better individuals.**

Adapting Discipline as Children Grow

Discipline the first year and a half serves to protect our children. Children at this age don't do "bad" things, but they can get into trouble. We teach them by persistent reinforcement what they can and cannot do. For example, they cannot crawl upstairs, play with lamp cords, put objects in their mouths, run into the street, or throw toys. We also minimize the "no's" we have to say by arranging our home to accommodate their growing curiosity and mobility. Breakables are on higher shelves, sockets are covered with safety caps, bathroom doors are kept closed, and cabinets and drawers we want left intact have safety locks. Since we've had a toddler in the house for the last twenty years, our house is child-proofed. Yet, each child discovered different things to "investigate." With Timmy being especially curious, we added locks on drawers we hadn't had to in the nineteen years we've been in the house. And we key-lock all the outside doors so he won't wander outside. His brothers didn't do that.

With a child's growing independence, setting guidelines and enforcing them is essential. **We take a positive approach, emphasizing what they *can* do, rather than what they can't do, and following through with consequences when the rule is broken.** One rule, for example, is that we eat in the kitchen. We don't allow the boys to eat all over the house. If they take food into the den, then we firmly remind them to eat in the kitchen, and if necessary, take the food away from them or restrict snacks for a couple of afternoons to reinforce the concept.

Another rule is to clean up their rooms before going to bed. We want them to learn that it's to their benefit to organize and clean their rooms so they'll know where their things are the next day. Cleaning up can be overwhelming to a young child. Ten blocks and trucks strewn across the floor look like a major undertaking to a toddler. With assistance from one of us or a brother, and the jingle "Clean-up, clean-up, everybody, everywhere, clean-up, clean-up, everybody do their share," the room is quickly tackled. **We keep our expectations realistic and *help* him accomplish the goal.** (When our children see us helping them, it reinforces the concept that it takes all of us working together to make it work well.) When they don't clean up, we may take the blocks or trucks for a couple of days.

As our sons grow, we adapt and change the guidelines as appropriate. The ten-year-old may stay up later than the five-year-old. The seventeen-year-old may watch movies that are inappropriate for a twelve-year-old. Our college-aged sons may have different hours than our sons in high school. Yet, there are rules that remain constant, such as cleaning up their rooms, eating in the kitchen, using appropriate language, and above all, respecting others.

Implementing Relevant Consequences—It Isn't Easy!

(Cathy): *Rules and guidelines without relevant consequences when broken are ineffective. **Since we make our rules for a reason, our sons** know **that we will enforce them.** Being fair and finding appropriate consequences takes time and effort. When the children were younger, I depended a lot on the advice of Dr. Plessala, our pediatrician. He was not only an excellent doctor but also a great teacher. He was the father of six children, and I admired and trusted his advice and approach to parenting. His suggestions were practical and the results attainable. When I would ask how to deal with a situation, he would, in his own way, help me solve my own problem. "What do you think you should do?" he'd reply. My answer was usually what he would've recommended. My hesitation to implement the specific* consequence was usually due to my lack of confidence, my reluctance to be inconvenienced, or the fact that the solution just seemed too simple.

An example that comes to mind is of Tony and David, three and a half years old and two and a half years old, urinating wherever they wanted: in the bathtub, on the rugs, in the trash cans, or outside. When Dr. Plessala asked me what I thought I should do, I replied, "Put them back in diapers?" He agreed. Yet, I didn't want or need two kids in diapers again with Chris due in another month. Dr. Plessala assured me they wouldn't like wearing diapers and would quickly learn to "pee" only in a potty. He was right—it took one day. **The solution may be obvious, but because of the inconvenience it may cause, we, as parents, choose not to act. I've learned that the long-term benefits are well worth the temporary inconvenience.**

Another example of accepting inconvenience to obtain a desired result concerns nap time. Young children need a quiet time during the day. However, they usually resist this interruption in their freedom. What a difference, though, in a rested three-year-old at four o'clock in the afternoon versus one who has been active since dawn. Since we realize the impact on their behavior, our sons through the age of five rest every afternoon. Some sleep; some just rest quietly with a book or a couple of play figures. Many parents forego quiet time prematurely because of their child's resistance—and pay the price in a grouchy, difficult child. When the two-year-old is confined to his crib, putting him down for a nap is fairly easy. When he's in a youth bed and has mobility, the experience creates new challenges. But, since we know it's in our child's best interest to rest, we place him back in his bed every time he gets up. The quiet time not only affects the child's behavior, the moments of silence rejuvenate a tired parent, physically and mentally. The inconvenience and resistance is a hassle at the time, but the benefits of a well-rested child and a renewed parent make it worth the effort. Many behavior problems are due to a child's lack of adequate sleep. **By ensuring our children receive enough sleep, we avoid the problems associated with a tired child.**

We teach our sons early in their development that there are consequences for their actions—good and bad, depending on what

they do or don't do. When Timmy throws a two-year-old temper tantrum, we promptly deal with it. The problem almost always arises because he wants something and we have said no. (Children, at any age, don't throw a fit when you say yes or give them what they want!) When Timmy acts this way, we first try to interest him in something else. If we can't distract him and the behavior continues, we put him in his room. Time-out when used judiciously is effective. Timmy also knows by our tone of voice that we're displeased with his behavior. However, doing this once isn't going to solve the problem. It means putting him in his room every time he has a temper tantrum or acts inappropriately. He needs to learn that we won't tolerate this type of behavior and that it's not to his benefit to act this way. If we gave in to his demand, we assure you, the behavior would continue. Children learn that concept very quickly, **so teach them very early that negative behavior is ineffective.**

When out in public, a temper tantrum is an even greater challenge. How embarrassing to have a screaming, misbehaving child in public. We've all been there. Cathy remembers the morning she went into the local Savings of America and Timmy started crying and carrying on, for no apparent reason. It's unpleasant having people criticize you with their eyes. (The tellers knew this was out of character for Timmy, but the customers didn't.) Cathy zipped through her transactions, went home and proceeded to put Timmy in his room. At times like these, **it's important to remember that although the child loses self-control, the parent shouldn't follow suit.** How many times in the grocery store have we seen a child yelling, "I want some candy" and the parent yelling right back, "No! You can't have any." **Our children need us to stay in control—verbally and physically.**

As our sons grow older, we continue to determine consequences for their actions. When David was in second grade, he couldn't find his uniform vest one morning. (The boys are responsible for having their clothes ready for school the evening before.) By the time David located his vest, the car pool had left. In addition to arriving late to school, he had to explain to the principal, a towering, 6-foot figure, what happened. Mrs. Johnson listened patiently and then, suppressing a smile, proceeded to revoke his beloved recess time to complete missed class work. We probably could've helped him find the vest in time for the car pool, but David needed to learn to fulfill his responsibilities. **Parents too often rescue their children from negative consequences. Yet, if we want them to learn responsibility and appropriate conduct, sometimes we have to let them feel the pain.**

Following through with consequences in the long run makes our days easier because we aren't hassling with the same problems and concerns repeatedly. When the boys argued about where they were going to sit in the Suburban, Cathy assigned seats. Loading everyone in the car is no longer a fiasco. When the boys continually bickered in the car on the way home from school, Cathy explained that being picked up from school was a privilege, not a right. After they rode the city bus for a period of time, the bickering in the car stopped. When the high school boys were visibly annoyed the afternoon Cathy was late picking them up, she reminded them that the city bus was a viable alternative, and they became more appreciative of their mom's time and effort. When Mark and Tommy left their clean, folded clothes on the floor of the closet instead of placing them in their drawers, they folded their clothes the next week. When the boys kicked a soccer ball through the upstairs window after being told not to kick the ball against the house, they paid for the window repair. When the boys lost a school book, they bought the replacement.

We don't argue with the boys. We don't nag the boys. Neither is effective. When we ask them to do something and they don't do it, they lose a privilege, whether they're seven or seventeen years old. For a seven-year-old, it may mean not watching a movie on Friday night. For a seventeen-year-old, it may mean not driving the car for the weekend.

Too many parents are afraid to impose consequences because of the inconvenience to themselves or the reactions of their children. If one of our older sons loses his driving privileges, it means we have to drive the boys to school for that period of time. Having the older boys drive their brothers to school in the morning is a tremendous help. But, if we want to make an impression on the boys, we have to be willing to follow through with our actions, despite the inconvenience. A frustrated mother told us how she had decided to assign new responsibilities to each of her teenage sons. She was tired of doing everything. The first night her son was responsible for cleaning the kitchen, he vehemently complained, left the table, and never returned to help. At ten o'clock she finished the dishes to avoid a confrontation. Her son learned that with enough complaining and resistance, he could do what he wanted.

In the Garcia-Prats household, that scenario would play differently. If our son refused to do the dishes, he would pay a dear price for his refusal. Our sons don't jump for joy on their kitchen cleaning night, but they do accept the responsibility. They realize if Mom's cleaning the kitchen by herself, it delays or eliminates bath time and story time for the younger boys. The older boys cherished the time we spent reading stories to them, and want their younger brothers to experience that treasured time, too.

Enforcing consequences can be tough. Parents want to protect their children and make life easy for them. Yet, understanding that our actions have consequences is an important life lesson. As our sons are involved in more activities outside the home, we encourage them to make good choices—in what they do, where they go, and who they are with. Knowing the difference between right and wrong means nothing if it's not applied. And just because they can get away with something, doesn't make it right. We know they'll make mistakes and poor choices from time to time, but our role is to help them learn from the experience. They need to understand that consequences are imposed not only by a parent but also by a teacher, a principal, a coach, a boss, or a law enforcement officer.

Recently, a friend, Kelly, shared a story about two young men who worked for her husband. Her husband was extremely frustrated by the young men's failure to fill out their time cards on time. He couldn't complete payroll without them. Constant nagging hadn't solved the problem. Kelly, remembering a discussion we'd had on nagging, told her husband, "Stop badgering the young men for their cards. If it's their responsibility to fill them out each week and they don't, then don't pay them. They'll learn their lesson."

The Father's Role as Disciplinarian

(Joe): *There are probably many anthropologic reasons why the father has been expected to be the disciplinarian for the household. Each of us may or may not have experienced this growing up. The threat by mothers and/or siblings— "Just you wait till your father gets home"—implied dire consequences for some deviance of behavior that we had committed. Dad seemed to be the one who meted out the punishment. I can remember that Mom was fairly lenient about some issues of discipline but you didn't mess with Dad. There continues to be some macho tag or "ruler of the house" idea that men have when it comes to discipline. I guess if one's bigger and yells louder, it scares the kids (or anyone else) into doing what is demanded. However, after a while, the kids can yell just as loud and puberty can be a great equalizer regarding size. Practically, the "I'm bigger so do what I say" approach doesn't work for long. Besides, it's really out of place in church or a restaurant, even McDonald's.*

One Sunday morning as I was leaving church with five of the boys (ages two through eight), I was approached by a very prim and proper elderly woman who commented to me that she had been observing the boys over the past several Sundays. "Your sons are so good in church," she noted. "How do you get them to behave so well?" I was feeling a bit feisty that morning and replied, tongue-in-cheek, "The threat of physical violence works very well." That's not what the woman expected and looked aghast with my answer. I certainly didn't want her to faint, so I quickly explained that we were a close family and had high expectations of our boys and guided them through good examples. She liked that answer better.

Two things make a father, or a mother, a good and effective disciplinarian. First, the "rules" of the family are held wholeheartedly by both parents. They support each other in disciplining their children. Second, there must be a consistent approach to a child's misbehavior with reasonable and appropriate consequences. Threatening a child with a consequence that is unreasonable and unlikely to be enforced, only worsens the ability to discipline in the future.

A quiet voice that earnestly relates to the child the consequences if misbehavior occurs is quite effective if that child knows that you, with your spouse's support, will follow through with the consequence. That captures a child's attention!

Establishing Rules and Standards to Show You Care

By establishing rules, standards, and consequences, we demonstrate to our sons that we care, even if they aren't always pleased with our decisions. Cathy's sister Patrice shared a story about her son Douglas when he spent spring break with a friend. While they were at the beach, the two boys, only fourteen years old at the time, were allowed to come and go as they pleased. The boy's parents weren't concerned where they went or when they returned. Douglas was amazed at his friend's freedom and expressed to him how lucky he was. (Patrice has set limits for Douglas.) This young man turned to Douglas and said, "No, Douglas, you're lucky. Your mom *really* cares about you." This young man felt his parents' lack of rules expressed their lack of interest in his well being. **We strongly believe children want and need guidelines; and they need us, their parents, to establish and enforce them. If you love your children, do what you know is best for them, not what is easy.** The word *no* is often the loving response to a child's request.

We prevent and avoid many problems and confrontations by setting limits. With five teenagers in the house at once, our home would be in a constant state of chaos without some semblance of order. Our teenage sons know what they can do, where they can go, and when to be home—and what happens when they don't abide by the agreed upon time, place, and activity. We try to be reasonable with the boys and explain the reasons behind our decisions. We talk about why we think an activity is appropriate or not. And we don't hesitate to share our views on morals and values.

Establishing Lines of Communication–Early!

Our ability to sit down and talk with our sons didn't happen overnight. We've been talking to the boys all along. **Although we don't reason or argue with a two-, five-, or eight-year-old, we do explain why we allow or don't allow them to do something.** For example, we'll say, "We wear seat belts in the car at all times because you can get seriously injured if we're in an accident; we love you and don't want anything bad to happen to you" or "We don't play on the stairs because one of you will fall and get hurt" or "No, you may not have ice cream now. It's almost time for supper."

As they get older, we continue to explain our reasons behind our decisions. We don't argue about whether they can or can't do the activity. For instance, we may say, "You may not watch that program. The way the characters conduct themselves is inappropriate and immoral" or "We don't want you going to the party because we don't think twelve-year-olds are ready for boy-girl parties. Your time will come."

We establish lines of communication early. The communication skills we learned as a couple are employed with our sons. We encourage them to be open and honest, first with themselves and then with us. Since we want our sons to be comfortable sharing their problems and concerns with us, we create the environment that allows them to do so. **By being understanding, accepting, caring, and loving, we reinforce that we are here for them.** Ranting, raving, and blaming them or others doesn't solve a problem or teach anything constructive. If our sons are afraid of what we'll say or do, they'll slam the door on our help.

Keeping On Track with Family "Meetings"

Whenever we have concerns or want to share some good news, we gather the family together. If the family's not in "sync," we use this time to discuss what we're observing and what can be done to get us back on track. Reminding the boys that it takes cooperation on everyone's part to function successfully, helps refocus all of us.

We adapt to changes in routines and the boys' outside responsibilities. **In order for them to participate in their individual activities and fulfill their home responsibilities, we often rearrange schedules to accommodate everyone's needs.** The boys have a schedule they work out for cleaning the kitchen in the evening. However, as soccer practices change, so does the schedule for cleaning the kitchen. We have to sit down and work out a new system that allows the boys to participate in their individual activities, yet fulfill responsibilities at home.

Our family meetings are also the times we share good news, such as announcing we're expecting another child. We had quite a chuckle, the summer we went to Italy, when a friend told us the older boys assumed another baby would be on the way following our two-week trip. When we called the boys together a week after returning home, they were convinced an announcement was forthcoming. They had this "routine" down pat. But much to their surprise, nothing was mentioned about a baby.

When one of the boys has an individual problem or concern, he will usually ask if we can talk. It may relate to a problem with a teacher, a low grade, a situation with a friend, a request to go somewhere, or a decision to be made. It varies. We calmly discuss the issue and work through a solution—together. If we feel we need time to think it over, we take that time.

And when *we* have concerns, we approach them in a similar manner. We must also be open and honest with them. It's not always easy telling a son we are concerned about his friend, his schoolwork, or maybe his attitude, but **it is our responsibility as a parent to guide them through these various situations and for them to understand our point of view and values.**

During Chris's junior year, he carried a number of commitments: group leader for the high school freshmen retreat, club soccer, high school soccer, assistant coach for the middle school soccer team at St. Francis de Sales, weekly cleaning of the neighborhood pool, home responsibilities, plus a heavy academic load. We worried that these commitments would interfere with the quality of his schoolwork. We shared our concerns with Chris. He assured us he would stay organized, balance the commitments, and maintain his grades. We trusted him. When we received the first quarter grades, we were impressed with all he had accomplished.

Likewise, when we were concerned about David's financial planning, we reviewed with him his financial responsibilities and the implications of his choices. We didn't demand he do it our way, and we didn't ask to see his checkbook or statements; but he did learn where we stood and the consequences of his choices.

Putting Yourself in Your Children's Shoes

We try very hard to understand their position or the circumstances surrounding a situation. We'll put ourselves in our son's place, remembering what it was like at his age under similar circumstances. **When you empathize, you often react differently than you would otherwise.** Chris wound up in an awkward predicament his sophomore year of high school. He asked if he could drive a group of friends to the homecoming dance. Since he had been driving only a few months, we agreed, but with stipulations: We didn't want him driving in unfamiliar parts of the city or after one o'clock. His friends agreed to meet at a restaurant and proceed to the dance from there. Following the dance, the girls had decided to spend the night together, and some of the boys were doing the same. This meant only two stops in an area of Houston Chris frequently drove. Everything went according to plan until two of the girls decided not to spend the night. Instead of calling us to find out what to do, Chris felt obligated as the driver to take them home. They lived forty minutes away in a section of Houston Chris was unfamiliar with. Not only were we worried, we were upset at the turn of events. Chris was upset, too. He had an early soccer game the next morning and had planned on being home earlier. When Chris arrived home tired and upset, we opted to postpone any discussion until the next day. Our primary objective was for Chris to learn how to handle a similar situation in the future. We explained that when there's a change of plans he needs to call us. If he had called us after the girls had decided not to spend the night together, we would've suggested alternatives to his driving them across town.

Teaching Your Values and Beliefs Without Hesitation

Our sons know we have their best interests at heart. We're not trying to control or inhibit their development, but we are trying to lead them along the right paths. We understand the power of peer pressure—it doesn't end when you move out of the teenage years—and the social influences bombarding them from all sides. If we don't teach them our values and beliefs, someone else will teach them theirs. **We must live, teach, and stand up for what we believe.**

(Cathy): *When Joe Pat was seven years old, he was invited to a friend's birthday party. The invitation indicated the party would begin at a pizza parlor and then proceed to the movie* Indiana Jones and the Temple of Doom. *We felt the movie was an inappropriate choice for Joe Pat, and probably most seven-year-olds. I called the friend's mom to see whether she minded if Joe Pat attended only the pizza party. The mom assumed the reason Joe Pat couldn't stay for the movie was scheduling logistics and offered to help. I explained the reason, indicating only the inappropriateness for our son. The other mom grew defensive and tried to justify her movie choice. I knew, though, that Joe Pat could not handle certain frightening scenes and stuck with my decision. Joe Pat accepted the decision better than his friend's mom; he knew we had his best interests at heart.*

Societal pressures bombard us. It's not easy saying no when so many other parents are saying yes. **But if we want our sons to stand up to peer pressure, we, as parents, must also stand up to the peer pressure around us.** When David graduated from eighth grade, the school sponsored a graduation dance. It was the last evening the students would all be together, since they would attend different high schools in the fall. The dance ended at eleven o'clock. One set of parents decided to continue the celebration and invited the students over to their house for an after-dance party. We felt the evening had been designed appropriately.

Thirteen- and fourteen-year-olds don't need to be out until one o'clock in the morning. When David asked to go, we told him no and explained why. Other parents asked us what we planned to do and we told them. Although they felt the same, they bent to the pressure and allowed their son or daughter to go.

It wasn't that the party was "bad"; we felt it was inappropriate for that particular age group. Children grow up fast enough. We don't need to hurry the process or allow them to be in situations they aren't ready for or are uncomfortable with. The titles alone of two of David Elkind's books, *The Hurried Child: Growing Up Too Fast Too Soon* and *All Grown Up and No Place to Go*, remind us to let our children be children and participate in age-appropriate activities.

Consider the message conveyed to our children when we allow them to stay out to all hours, see violent or sexually explicit movies, listen to vulgar music, or watch television programs that undermine our values or are beyond their level of comprehension. By not taking a stand, we condone the behavior. We become desensitized to what is right when we are repeatedly bombarded by what is wrong. Although most of us would agree our children are influenced by what they see and hear, many parents continue to let their children see and hear what *they* want.

When *The Simpsons* cartoon premiered several years ago, the boys asked to watch the program on a nonschool night. We had read conflicting reviews on the program so we hesitatingly agreed. Five minutes of the Simpson children talking back to their parents was enough for us. When discussing the show with another mother, she tried to rationalize watching the show by pointing out the moral provided at the end. Oh great! We have to listen to twenty minutes of garbage to receive a moral. We choose to teach our sons in a more constructive manner.

Our older sons understand the value of our decisions, especially now that we ask them to help evaluate movies for their younger brothers. Before the movie *Jumanji* premiered, the hype was mind boggling—the younger boys couldn't wait to see the movie. We were familiar with the story; most of Christopher Van Allsburg's books are in our home library. Tony and David saw the movie and determined that Mark and Tommy could see the movie but Danny and Jamie should wait. They considered Danny's vivid imagination and felt he might not be able to distinguish between reality and fiction. We had made a similar decision a few years earlier when *Jurassic Park* hit the theaters. Although most of the younger boys' friends saw the movie when it came out, our sons saw it a few years later (and some still haven't seen it). With movies available on video, we can delay watching a movie until they are old enough.

The Teen Years–A Time When You're Needed More Than Ever

While influencing the moral development of our sons is essential at all ages, **our involvement in our sons' lives becomes crucial during the preteen and early teen years.** These are the years our children are stretching their wings beyond the home. The middle school years are exactly where this age group is—in the middle. They're not young kids anymore; but they're not young adults. Intellectually they are in transition from concrete to abstract thinking. They need their parents' love and guidance, and want to be accepted by their peers. Their bodies are changing, and their emotions are confusing.

What can we, as parents, do to help our children through these difficult years? Remember what these years were like for you; and in remembering, **be there for your child.**

(Cathy): *I remember being skinny, having acne, wearing coke-bottle thick glasses, being excessively shy, yet, having lots of friends and doing well academically. I remember the times I acted without thinking, though not to be mean or malicious—I just didn't think. I made good choices. I made poor choices. I stood up to some pressures, and I succumbed to others. Through it all, my parents and sisters were the strongest influence in my life. Their love, guidance (they did set limits), and acceptance of me—Cathy—carried me through these tumultuous early teen years.*

The Five L's of Parenting

During Tony's freshman year in high school, Fr. Francis Huete, S.J., Principal of Strake Jesuit, gave an opening school address entitled "The Four *L*'s of Parenting: **Love, Laughter, Liberty,** and **Limits.**" (We've added a fifth—**Learning**—suggested by a cousin in Italy, Joseph Musco, a professor in English and American History.) Fr. Huete told the parents our children need all four *L*'s throughout their lives. He'd seen parents who didn't give enough liberty to their children, and parents who didn't give enough love and whose homes were not filled with laughter. But, more commonly, he saw parents who didn't set *limits*. Father used the analogy of a young man lifting weights, an analogy appropriate for a boys high school. "Kids love to [lift weights]," he said, "but to be effective, as they push, gravity must push back. If there is no resistance, they would never grow, and the exercise would be fruitless. When they push us, we must provide resistance—limits—or they will never grow. When people lift weights, they often grunt and groan and make noises. When your sons push, they make a lot of noise. But most of it has no more real meaning than noises made during weight lifting." He told us that our sons would not stop loving us because we had set limits. **And in closing, he reminded us that another *L*—loot—was a poor substitute for any of the others, and frequently makes matters worse.**

We heed Father's words and apply them to our family. We love the boys for who they are. We don't try to make Matthew into a Chris, or Danny into a Mark, or Tony into a Mark Spitz, or David into Hakeem Olajuwon. Our acceptance of who they are encourages them to accept themselves. Self-acceptance, or self-love, helps them to cope with peer and societal pressures.

A loving home is filled with laughter. If we didn't laugh at our many joys and mishaps, we'd be spending a lot of wasted time crying. Our dinner hour is usually lively and filled with colorful stories of the day. If it's a quiet, peaceful dinner you're looking for, the Garcia-Prats home is not the place. Even dinner prayers add humor to our day, especially now that Timmy adds his requests. We never know what to expect, but when he solemnly asked, "Please, pray for my girlfriend," we roared.

(Cathy): **Laughter and humor can often diffuse difficult or uncomfortable situations.** *David's senior year in high school, he had offered to pick up Chris from school following his exams. Jamie went along for the ride. They arrived home, ate lunch, and then went outside to shoot baskets. Later that afternoon, I left to pick up the younger boys from school. Jamie again came along for the ride. Driving to school, we saw a police car and I pointed it out to Jamie. Jamie declared very matter-of-factly, "David talked to a policeman today." "What?" I said. "David talked to a policeman today," he repeated. Now why would David be talking to a policeman, I asked myself. The answer seemed obvious. When we returned home, David was still outside shooting baskets. I nonchalantly remarked, "David, I understand you had a nice conversation with a policeman this morning. Anything interesting?" David was rather amazed that I already knew he had received a speeding ticket. I teasingly reminded him he had a little brother in the car who, using Chris's terminology, "ratted" on him.*

We strongly believe that our support, encouragement, and understanding during the preteen and early teen years provides our sons with the tools they need to handle their new freedoms and responsibilities. While allowing our sons increased independence, we are still responsible for teaching them appropriate behavior, and right from wrong. **We make decisions they may not like but that are in their best interests.** We still have rules and enforce those rules. They have responsibilities and are expected to fulfill them.

We sound like really tough parents. In essence, though, we are gentle and loving, yet firm in our beliefs and tireless in our efforts to guide our sons. Our strong love, guidance, and support over the years has proved invaluable. We look at our sons and are extremely proud of them—not because of what they have accomplished, and they have done well, but for *who* they are. We are proud of them and we enjoy them. What wonderful people to be around!

Chapter 5

Recognizing and Fulfilling
Our Parental Responsibilities

O*ur children will rise to the level of expectations we have of them.*

–From the movie Stand and Deliver

None of us is perfect.
It is better to have crooked legs than a crooked spirit.
We can only do the best we can with what we have.
That, after all, is the measure of success: what we do with what we have.
        –Marguerite de Angeli, The Door in the Wall

Contrary to the opinion of many, having more than two children does not denote irresponsibility. Responsible parenting isn't determined by the number of children in a family, but by how parents love and teach those children.

Our approach to teaching responsibility to our sons focuses on fulfilling our own parental responsibilities. **If our children aren't responsible, caring, well-educated young people, we are to blame—not them.** Before we can ensure that our children are responsible individuals, we have to examine our consciences and determine if we are living responsible lives. "Remove the plank from your own eye first, then you will see clearly to take the speck from your brother's eye" (Matthew 7:5).

Responsibility and Self-Respect

Cathy shared her beliefs on self-respect and self-love in an earlier chapter. In order to love others, you must first love God and yourself. Loving yourself entails accepting who you are and the responsibility for your physical, emotional, intellectual, and spiritual well being. **We need to strive to be the best we can be before we expect the same from our spouse and children.**

(Cathy): *In the 1980s I was actively involved with The Woman's Hospital of Texas Research and Education Foundation. The Foundation provides educational materials and programs on women's health issues. I learned that many women's health problems are preventable or controllable: osteoporosis, ovarian cancer, breast cancer, and heart disease. Our diet, exercise routine, and lifestyle choices all affect our health. Yet, I was amazed at how many of my friends had not seen a doctor since the birth of their last child, which for some friends was several years. These women weren't taking advantage of the preventive health care measures available: for example, Pap smears, mammograms, cholesterol screenings, and blood pressure readings. In a November 1996 issue of* Time Magazine, *an article stated that 80 percent of women who die of cervical cancer in the United States hadn't had a Pap smear in five years. Early detection of a breast lump, a cervical cell change, or high blood pressure improves the long-range health outcome. I can't stress enough the importance of taking care of yourself, male or female. A healthy lifestyle benefits you today, as well as in the future. You're not being vain or selfish by meeting your physical needs.*

Annual visits to my ophthalmologist detected a detached retina in my right eye and tears in the retina of the left eye. If the detachment and tears had gone unnoticed, I likely would've lost partial or total vision in one or both eyes. What a different direction our lives would have taken.

Accepting Who You Are

(Cathy): **Another facet of responsibility is accepting who you are and the special gifts God has given you.** *While I'm 5 feet 1 inch, have poor vision, a less than perfect complexion, a flat chest, and a mediocre singing voice (I love music), and am demanding and intolerant of laziness and incompetence, I'm also well educated, optimistic, organized, sensitive, compassionate, and fun loving, and have a slender figure, thick hair, and, according to an unbiased Joe, nice legs.* **I accept the things I can't change and work hard to improve the things I can.**

I apply the same philosophy to Joe and the boys. Our sons are unlikely to reach 6 feet in height. So what! Joe's not 6 feet tall either, but few men can measure up to his love, dedication, and fullness of heart. If we're accepting of who we are, and in turn accepting of our sons, they are more likely to be accepting of themselves. **We want our sons to understand that it's what's inside the person that matters—who they are, not what they look like or what they have.**

Our society places excessive emphasis on perfection. If we expect our sons and daughters to be the perfect physical specimen or the perfect student or athlete and convey that desire to them, we do them a great disservice. How can we expect our children to feel good about who they are when mom or dad is clearly dissatisfied with them? If we continually comment on their "inferior" attributes, what message do we convey? We are amazed at the insensitive comments made in front of children, as if being short, overweight, or an average student implies you're a person of poor quality.

A mother shared a story about a lesson her daughter learned in high school after losing weight. When the daughter became a slim size 2, people who had avoided her friendship suddenly found it acceptable to be her friend. Yet, she told her mom, she was no different inside. These people judged her only by her outward appearance.

The old saying "Beauty's only skin deep" rings true. Big breasts and long thin legs aren't going to make me a better person. Thirty extra pounds and rippling muscles aren't going to make Joe a better husband, father, or physician. Additional height, weight, and muscles won't make our sons responsible and loving young men. **We should invest our energies and the energies of our children in what really matters—a healthy body, mind, and soul.**

Taking Responsibility for the Physical Well Being of Your Children

Responsible parenting was defined earlier in the book as providing for the physical, intellectual, emotional, and spiritual needs of your children. Are we accepting that responsibility and the work that accompanies it?

Are we assuring our children receive appropriate health and dental checkups? Protecting our children from childhood diseases, for example, is a parental responsibility. Are your children immunized? Many cities provide programs for childhood immunizations. Take advantage of available programs, if necessary, to obtain the care you need. When Cathy was in college and finances were tight, she availed herself of the excellent, low-cost dental care provided by the dental school.

As a responsible parent, are you and your children wearing seat belts *every* time you ride in a car? We're amazed at the parents who don't require their children to wear seat belts. We hear every excuse in the book: They fight putting them on, it takes too much time, or they're uncomfortable. **Yet, if we love our children, isn't protecting them from potential injury a loving, responsible gesture?**

Our older sons had a car accident in which the Suburban flipped and landed upside down. To the amazement of the emergency medical technicians who arrived on the scene, nobody was injured. All four teenagers wore seat belts. The young woman in the car later lamented to her mom,

"Why do I always learn the hard way? I don't usually wear a seat belt, but Tony asked all of us to put our belts on when we left Astroworld." We're convinced wearing the seat belts protected them from serious injury.

When we drive car pools to school, games, or other activities, we insist everyone wear a seat belt. We tease that the GP cars don't run unless all the seat belts are clicked. Our children rode home from the hospital in an infant car seat. And early on, they got in the habit of buckling their seat belts as soon as they get into a car. Because our sons have always worn them, they accept the practice as part of riding in a car.

Along the same lines, do your children wear protective head gear when riding a bike or in-line skating? With all the information on the head injuries that could be avoided by wearing protective equipment, we can't imagine why loving parents would allow their children to ride a bike or go in-line skating unprotected.

Nurturing and Developing the Intellectual Abilities of Your Children

Are we being responsible parents regarding the intellectual development and education of our children? Parents continually blame teachers and schools for their children's poor performance. Although schools share a portion of the blame, we believe the bulk of the responsibility falls on parents. Are we supporting the efforts of the schools and teachers by being involved? Are we providing an environment at home conducive to learning? Do we expose our children to new ideas and activities? Do we talk with our children about current events in the world and in *their* world? Do we turn the TV on every evening or spend that time reading to our children or helping them with their schoolwork? One of the boys' principals urged parents at every opportunity to "*read, read,* and *read* some more to your kiddos." Reading to children at an early age has proven to be the most important factor behind successful students. **The time spent reading to your children provides intellectual stimulation, but, more important, reading with your children nurtures the emotional closeness on which children**

thrive. We find reading with the boys also provides a quiet, restful respite from the hectic hours of the day.

We read to the boys even after they have learned to read by themselves. We've just finished reading *Hatchet* and the sequel *The River* with Mark and Tommy. We're now reading *Across Five Aprils*. Reading to the boys expands their world and provides opportunities to discuss all kinds of issues, including the Civil War (*Shades of Gray*), the Holocaust (*Number the Stars*), death (*A Taste of Blackberries*), and racism and injustice (*The Well*).

Many of the activities we engage in with our sons fulfill multiple purposes. Tossing a ball, fixing the chain on a bike, baking a cake, or feeding the ducks develops their physical and intellectual abilities while also enriching the emotional dimension of their lives. The loving time we spend with our children tells them in a special way that we care about them. If we don't spend time with our children, how can we expect them to understand our values? During these activities, we garner the opportunity to share our goals and our feelings with our sons. We want the boys to see us not only as parents but also as individuals with feelings, struggles, and dreams like themselves.

Developing Your Children's Talents

We are also responsible for developing the individual talents of each of our sons. **We begin by respecting their individual gifts, interests, and abilities.** One son may excel in science and math, and another may excel in creative writing. Tony's a successful swimmer; his brothers excel in soccer.

Once Tony decided to pursue swimming, we found a United States Swimming program to develop his skills. We supported his efforts by driving him to practices and swim meets. Tony accepted the responsibility of working hard to achieve the times he realistically felt he could swim. Eventually, his goal was to continue swimming competitively in college at the Division I level. He had also decided to pursue a pre-med academic program. Because he had done extremely well in high school and was a National Merit Scholar, he felt confident he could compete academically at most universities. He needed to have realistic expectations, though, about where he could swim successfully at the Division I level. He looked for a university that would provide strong programs in both areas. Tony chose Saint Louis University. There he balances a demanding pre-med curriculum with his love of swimming. Fortunately, under the direction of an understanding, realistic coach, Doc Beeson, Tony excels in both areas, maintaining his high level of academic achievement while breaking a twenty-year school record in the mile his freshman year. To have expected similar athletic success at such swimming powerhouses as The University of Texas or Stanford would have been unrealistic for Tony.

We follow a similar routine with our other sons: We find strong soccer programs and summer training camps while supporting their efforts and future goals. We do this not only for athletics, but for all areas of interests and talent. When we realized Danny was artistically gifted, we purchased art materials for him to use at home and provided opportunities for him to attend classes. **Our encouragement and pride in the boys' individual interests and successes increases their self-motivation.** How exciting to have Mom and Dad as excited about your interests as you are.

Sharing Your Faith with Your Children

We also openly share our faith with our sons. Parents are responsible for the spiritual development of their children. We are their first teachers; **it is through our example they learn the importance and relevance of God.** Have we incorporated God in all aspects of our lives or do we just find time for God on Sunday or Easter or Yom Kippur? Responsible parents don't find excuses for missing religious services or shirking involvement in their religious community, but instead find ways to participate more. Do we pray with our children? Our family prayers teach our sons to praise God, to thank Him for our many blessings, and to seek

His loving guidance in our daily lives. **Our children won't learn the importance of God by osmosis, but by our commitment to live our faith in both words and actions.**

Making Responsible Parental Choices

Responsible parenting entails making choices in the best interests of our children and family. Are we caught up in the materialistic goals of our society? **Are we providing more and more "things" to our children in the guise of love, when what we responsibly should be providing is more of our time and talents?** During a parent-student session at a freshmen retreat held at the Jesuit high school, the six boys in our group voiced their desire to spend more time with their parents. They wanted to share their aspirations and fears with their parents but felt the desire wasn't mutual. One freshman said, "My parents always say there's not enough time. But we're in the car a lot. Why can't we shut off the radio and spend that time talking?" The group leader, a senior, later commented, "I leave in a few months for college. I regret not spending more time with my parents." He encouraged the freshmen to make the effort to involve their parents in their activities, rather than wait for their parents to take the initiative. Both sides, though, have to be willing to work at enriching the relationship.

In the summer of 1995, Cathy attended a conference, "The Family in the American Context," held in Houston. Robert Bellah, the keynote speaker and author of *Habits of the Heart,* spoke about the forces in our society causing the disintegration of the family. He claimed that one of the negative forces is consumerism. He said that the American dream is defined in economic terms: money, career, and power—having "more, bigger, and better."

Are we making responsible financial choices that are enriching the happiness of our family, or are we convincing ourselves that we are happier, and making our children happier, because we own the fancier car, the 52-inch television screen, or the latest fashions? Are our children demanding more and more things because they observe us wanting more and more? Are we confusing *success* with "more, bigger, and better"? **We need to evaluate our stand on materialism and its effect on our children.** We need to learn to differentiate wants from needs.

Demonstrating Responsibility for Others

Are we demonstrating responsible sharing of our financial treasures and our talents outside the family? Are we preoccupied with having more at the expense of those less fortunate? **We want our sons to learn that they are responsible for others.**

(Cathy): *Reading just one letter from the Columban Fathers, a missionary society, puts our many blessings in perspective. When I read about the women of Corn Hill, a settlement on the outskirts of Lima, Peru, who live in primitive shelters on barren rock without water or sewerage, I appreciate even more our home and the blessings I too often take for granted: running water, sewerage, electricity, and food. Is our family willing to go without dessert for a week so we can share our resources with the families of Corn Hill? Am I willing to forego that new dress to send a donation to the women of Corn Hill? These indomitable women, described as "big in their littleness, rich in their poverty," struggle each day for their basic needs, yet find joy in living. I find myself better able not only to forego the dress but also, and more important, to place the inconveniences of my day in perspective because of these valiant women. They touch my heart, because in their struggle to improve their lives and the lives of their families, they continue to love and have hope.*

When our family opened our home to young pregnant women in the 1980s, many people openly criticized our decision. Some felt it was irresponsible to give these girls our time and love when we had five children of our own who needed our attention. Others felt we were condoning the choices these girls had made—what kind of an example was this for our sons? We knew we could provide these girls with a loving home while helping them cope with a pregnancy under less than ideal circumstances.

We certainly understand the tremendous physical and emotional demands of pregnancy. When a woman experiences these demands *alone*, it can be overwhelming. Knowing someone else cares eases the discomforts and concerns.

As for neglecting the needs of our sons, we believe the experience enriched their lives. Although young, the boys knew they were fortunate to have parents who loved and cared for them. They also learned that we are responsible for people outside our family. **We may not approve of what others do, but we are still responsible for loving them.** When people questioned us, we explained that the command to love others did not include exemptions. Nowhere in the Bible does it say that because we have two children or ten children, we aren't responsible for feeding the hungry, clothing the naked, or visiting the sick. **If we want our sons to learn to accept responsibility for those less fortunate, we must set the example by our choices to share our time, our talents, and our resources.** We don't feel guilty about opening our home to others or sharing our resources with the women of Corn Hill. Our sons may not drive their own cars or dress in the more expensive brand-name clothes, but they are well fed, well educated, and dearly loved.

As our sons mature in their faith, responsibility for others is readily accepted. Both the high school and the elementary school that the boys attend encourage students to share their God-given gifts with others. St. Francis de Sales has a service organization, the Micah Club. The students are involved in service activities that improve the lives of others, sometimes in the parish community, but more often outside the community. They organize parish baby showers, donating the gifts to women in need. And each Valentine's Day the Micah Club sponsors a candy-gram project. For fifty cents the students order candy-grams to send to friends, teachers, and staff. The project raises nearly $1000 each year. The money is donated to a soup kitchen in the Houston area. The middle school students spend hours organizing and making the candy-grams; and they feel tremendous satisfaction when they personally present the check to the soup kitchen's director. In addition, the Micah Club sponsors a Christmas party for less fortunate children—complete with Santa and Mrs. Claus. The children can make their requests and pose for a Polaroid shot with the Clauses—the first for many of the children. The students plan games and activities. After watching the faces of *all* the children, it's hard to determine who's having more fun—the eighth graders or their guests.

The motto at our son's high school is, "A man for others." All Strake Jesuit students are required to perform one hundred hours of community service in order to graduate. Many students begin their projects reluctantly only to find the experience so rewarding they continue to volunteer their time. It's rewarding to see our sons involved in social service activities. Tony volunteered as a counselor at a Muscular Dystrophy Association camp. David counseled boys at a Big Brothers camp. One summer, David accompanied Dr. Maria-Teresa Garcia, a dentist in our parish, to Ocotlan, Mexico. Dr. Garcia returns to her hometown for ten days every summer to provide free dental care. She affectionately told us that when David wasn't needed in the clinic, he organized soccer games for the children at the neighboring orphanage. His love of children (and soccer) and their love of him were obvious. The boys gain an appreciation for others and their needs when they are involved in volunteer activities.

Teaching Responsibility

Teaching responsibility to children should begin at an early age. Our career backgrounds and our two decades of parenting experience have taught us that instilling responsibility entails understanding the different levels of moral development, so that our expectations, of our children and of ourselves, are realistic. **Ultimately, we want our sons to conscientiously choose to do what is right because they understand the principles of right and wrong.** First, though, children move through other stages, from doing what is right to please us, to doing what is right to avoid consequences. In the beginning, they want to look good to others and live up to others' expectations. Gradually, if parents guide them, they move away from a more self-centered approach to feeling obligated and responsible to do what is morally right.

Understanding the stages of moral development helps us to focus on ways to teach each of our sons at every age what is appropriate and inappropriate, right and wrong. **Learning to accept responsibility for their own actions is imperative.** Whereas Timmy, the two-year-old, cleans up his room to please Mommy and Daddy, Matthew, the fourteen-year-old, cleans the dinner dishes because he understands he has a responsibility to help out in the family.

Because we worked with the boys when they were two years old, they understand as teenagers that they have personal and family responsibilities to fulfill. They don't just wake up one Monday morning in their teenage years and decide to be responsible.

We teach our sons that responsibility is threefold: responsibility for oneself, responsibility for others, and responsibility to God. Accepting responsibility for themselves encompasses their physical well being, their belongings, their schoolwork, and their athletics. Responsibility for others involves family, friends, and society at large. Responsibility to God entails loving your neighbor as yourself and loving God with your whole heart, soul, and mind by living according to His laws.

Children first learn to be responsible by helping and being involved at home. We find appropriate chores for the boys at different stages of development. With an increase in age and ability, we increase the level of responsibility. As the boys mature, we also increase their privileges and freedoms, emphasizing that with these new freedoms there is responsibility. This approach works for our family because the younger boys see firsthand that as they get older they too will be granted more privileges.

For the two-year-old, we start with simple responsibilities, remembering to keep our expectations realistic according to his age and ability. These responsibilities include picking up his toys, dressing himself, putting his dirty clothes in the hamper, putting the silverware away (also a great lesson in sorting items), deciding on his next day's clothes the night before, and picking up pinecones outside in the yard so his older brothers can mow. Jamie, five years old, is responsible for the same personal items in addition to putting his folded clothes in his drawers, making his bed in the morning, setting the table for dinner, emptying the small trash cans throughout the house once a week, and picking up piles of grass or leaves his brothers have raked.

In the early school years, the boys wake up in the morning and are responsible for dressing, making their beds, gathering the items they need for school, and taking care of the dog. They are responsible for having their uniforms and backpacks ready the night before, bathing in the evenings, bringing home all assignments and books from school, and ensuring that homework and papers needing signatures are completed at night. They clear the dinner dishes, put away placemats, and wipe the table. They put their clothes away, keep their rooms clean, and sweep the sidewalks and curbs after their older brothers have mowed and edged the yard. When they have a sports practice or game, they keep track of their uniforms and equipment.

As the boys grow older, they continue to take care of their personal needs and the responsibilities of schoolwork and sports. In the mornings, a couple of the older boys straighten up the kitchen after breakfast and the others make sure their bedrooms and the upstairs bathroom are picked up. In the evenings the boys coordinate cleaning the dinner dishes and the kitchen. When they begin to drive, they help us drive their younger brothers to school on their way to the high school. And they willingly baby-sit their younger brothers when needed.

The boys understand their responsibilities and expectations at each age. **They realize the impact they have on the successful functioning of our family and the chaos that would ensue if everyone did their own thing on their own time.** The boys' acceptance of their responsibilities makes parenting considerably easier. They know what to do and do it, so we're not constantly nagging them to fulfill their responsibilities. There's also a shared feeling of accomplishment—knowing they too are responsible for our happy family.

We avoid a lot of chaos and problems because we provide our sons with responsibilities. At a soccer game one morning, a ten-year-old boy came screaming and demanding of his mom, "Where's my black jersey?" The flustered mom went searching for it, only to realize she had forgotten to put it in his soccer bag. The son was extremely angry and the mom felt embarrassed and guilty. Standing next to Cathy, this disheartened mom asked, "How do you keep it all straight with six sons playing soccer? I only have two kids playing." Cathy explained to her that the boys, all six of them, from eight to seventeen years old, are responsible for their soccer uniforms and equipment. We'll make sure it's clean and they have the required equipment, but they must prepare and organize their soccer bag.

A ten-year-old is capable of organizing his soccer paraphernalia, his clothes, and his schoolwork. If one of our sons had forgotten the black jersey, he would've been upset with himself. Mark arrived at soccer practice one afternoon and realized he had only one of his soccer shoes—the other was under his bed. With the practice field thirty minutes away, there was no running home to find the other shoe. He missed practice that day, disappointed but determined not to let that happen again.

We expect our sons to take care of their belongings, not only because they should but also because we hand down many items: clothes (never shoes—they wear them out first), schoolbooks, games, toys, and bikes. If we have to replace a lost jacket or sweater, it means we have less to spend on other things. As they get older, they replace the lost items themselves. **They learn to be more responsible for their personal belongings if they realize Mom and Dad won't bail them out each time they lose or ruin an item.**

When Cathy was volunteering at the high school book sale (books aren't provided by the school, but are purchased by the students), a mother grumbled that paying the tab (roughly $300) once was bad enough but buying the books again when her son lost them frustrated her. "You must go broke just keeping up with books, Cathy," she said. "Not I," replied Cathy. "Taking care of their books is their responsibility. If one of the boys loses a book, he buys the replacement." When a physics book costs $89 and you know you'll have to buy another one, you take care of it. Our sons would rather spend their hard-earned money in more exciting ways.

Teaching Financial Responsibility

Learning financial responsibility is important for children. We don't pay allowances, contrary to the teaching of most psychologists, because it just doesn't work for us. Since we don't promote the buying of lots of unnecessary items, we don't see the need for our younger sons to have excess cash. If they receive money from relatives or as a gift, we allow them to buy what they like with the money. This philosophy hasn't caused our sons to be "deprived" or financially irresponsible.

After the age of twelve, the boys begin earning their own money by mowing lawns, raking yards, baby-sitting, pet-sitting, painting, life guarding, coaching swim teams or soccer teams, teaching swim lessons, or working as a lab assistant. We teach the boys basic finances: saving, taxes (sales and income), budgeting, and reconciling a bank statement. As they grow older, we outline the different financial responsibilities we expect them to handle, depending on their age and income. When they are fourteen, for example, we expect them to pay for their own entertainment, unless they are going to a movie or activity with us. While we purchase their clothes and other essentials, they buy any additional T-shirts or hats they may want. If a particular piece of clothing costs more than we have determined reasonable, they choose whether they want to make up the difference or instead spend the money on a new CD, for example. In high school, the boys are responsible for paying school fees outside of tuition, roughly $250 each. Once they begin driving, they pay a portion of the car insurance.

Since we don't want the boys to work during the school year, we keep our expectations reasonable. Having financial obligations, though, teaches the boys the necessity of budgeting their money. If they spend all their money on CD's, they won't have money to go to the movies or a game with their friends. They learn to prioritize their needs and wants. When they want to attend an activity, such as a soccer camp, we may offer to pay part of the fees if they are willing to pay the balance. **We believe when you invest your own money or time, you appreciate the experience more than if it's handed to you on a silver platter.**

The boys aren't always thrilled about spending their money on school fees or car insurance. Living in Harris County, we pay the highest car insurance rate in the state. Tony, when one of his payments was due, grumbled about having to pay it. We informed him that we didn't like paying the insurance either and would rather use the money elsewhere, too. Having car insurance, though, is required and comes with the responsibility of driving a car. The decision, to pay or not to pay, thus to drive or not to drive, became his choice.

In addition to providing a source of income, working teaches our sons many lessons. It teaches them the importance of being dependable, how to define job expectations—determining what needs to be done in what time frame and for what pay—how to deal with adults and peers, and the value of an education. We both worked summer jobs that were less than exciting. You learn, though, that if you accept the position, you must fulfill your responsibilities, regardless of whether or not the job is boring. Knowing our education would provide additional opportunities for us later on motivated us to continue our studies. Each of our older sons has had a similar experience.

Augmenting Self-Esteem and Self-Reliance by Providing Realistic Responsibilities

Provide your children with responsibilities they are capable of handling. Doing too much for our kids doesn't benefit them in the long run. Teaching Timmy to dress himself, clean up his room, and put the silverware away is a help to us, but more important, they are skills he needs to learn. In addition, the sense of accomplishment he feels when he's finished with these tasks augments his self-esteem. Accepting responsibility for their soccer equipment teaches Mark and his brothers the importance of organizing their belongings and putting them in their proper place.

On the flip side, we must be careful not to have unrealistic expectations of our children. When Cathy taught first grade, one student's parents expected her to clean the kitchen *and* bathe her younger brother and put him to bed each night, in addition to her school responsibilities. The girl was exhausted most days and lacked that spark of childhood enthusiasm evident in the other children. She was seven years old— much too young to be responsible for that level of caregiving. She needed to be loved and nurtured herself. Instead she was fulfilling her parents' responsibility for the care of her brother. Her parents both worked, and told Cathy they needed their daughter to do these chores. **We cannot as parents let outside responsibilities take precedence over *our* responsibilities at home.** In this situation, the parents *irresponsibly* shifted their parental obligations to their young daughter.

We are careful not to shift our responsibilities for our younger children onto the older boys. We want our sons to enjoy each other and not view their brothers as a burden. We ask the boys to help with each other, but we remember we are the parents and their brothers are *our* children, not theirs. **When children are constantly *expected* to take on the role of parent, they begin to resent their siblings.** When we want to go out on a weekend, we first check with the boys' schedules; we don't assume one of them will be available for baby-sitting, and we don't demand they change their plans. The boys are willing to adjust their activities to accommodate our needs, just as we are willing to adjust our plans to fulfill our commitments to them.

Handing Down Responsibility Through Generations

We're both fortunate to have parents who taught us the value of responsibility. We could not successfully raise ten children if we were irresponsible. Our parents taught us to aim high and be the best that we could be. Now we are handing down these lessons in responsibility and expectations to our children.

(Cathy): *I remember so well the lessons my parents instilled in me regarding realistic, yet high, expectations. We were a family of five girls with varied intellectual abilities and personalities. When report cards were* distributed each quarter, my parents always looked at our grades in effort and deportment (conduct on today's report cards) first. They told us we could control our behavior and our effort. If our grades in those two areas were at the highest level, then the subject grades were acceptable. On the other hand, if our effort grade was low and so were our subject grades, we weren't working to the best of our ability. **My parents expected us, and our God expected us, to use the gifts He so graciously provided us.** One of my sisters struggled in math. My Dad would patiently work with her night after night, but she still made C's in math. I enjoyed and excelled in math. If I had come home with a C, my parents would've been very disappointed in my effort.

My parents accepted the fact that each of their daughters was stronger in some areas and weaker in others. They never expected me to perform at anyone else's level, and the same pertained to my sisters. That doesn't mean they lowered their expectations; they were just realistic.

I learned another important lesson in expectations from my favorite elementary school teacher, Mrs. Moerings. One day she assigned my seventh-grade class a two-page history report. When I received the paper back with a C, I was quite disappointed. A classmate sitting behind me was thrilled with her A; yet when I read her paper, I didn't think it was as good as mine. After class I approached Mrs. Moerings to ask about the grade in comparison to my friend's. She looked at me and said, "That was Theresa's best effort. She deserved an A. But Cathy, that paper was C work for you. That wasn't your best effort." You know, she was right. I learned an essential lesson that day—to do my best at all times in all ways. That's what was expected of me.

Now as a mom, I continue to work hard to be the best mom I can be for my children. That doesn't mean I'm perfect and don't have bad days. But having a bad day doesn't mean I'm a bad mom. I believe moms, more than dads, evaluate their parenting ability much too critically and harshly. There were days when I was teaching that I wanted to throw up my hands and cry, "Why am I doing this?" Yet I loved teaching, and a bad day didn't mean I was a bad teacher. Fortunately, the good days outnumbered the bad.

The same holds true at home. I have long, hard days just like everyone else. If I'm not feeling well, one or more of the boys woke up on the wrong side of the bed, or other circumstances outside of my control have made the day what it is, I do the best I can under the circumstances and move on. **Expecting more than I have to give or berating myself for not being the perfect mom is not healthy for me or our family.** *Years ago when we had only five children, I was upset with myself for getting angry with the boys. I shared my feelings with Fr. Rehkophf, a priest and dear friend. He took my hands and said so caringly, "Cathy, don't be so hard on yourself. Look at your sons and what you have done with them. They're wonderful children. I know God's pleased." It is hard, though, when I've been less than the perfect parent. When I've had that kind of day, I sit back and ask myself what went wrong and how could I do it differently next time.* **Just like I want my children to learn from their mistakes, I try to do it better the next time around.**

And it's okay to shed a sigh of relief when the children are finally all in bed. **I work hard all day, giving my love, time, and energy; I don't feel guilty and I'm definitely not a bad mom because I want and need a few minutes to myself.** *When Joe finishes taking care of a sick baby at the hospital, he's usually ready for a break too—that doesn't mean he's an uncaring or incompetent doctor. A parent's no different.*

We teach our sons to do and be the best that they can be—that doesn't necessarily translate into being *the* best. We remember a story we heard about Pablo Picasso. His mother told him that if he were to be a soldier, he should aspire to be a general. If he were to be a priest, he should aspire to be the Pope. He decided to be an artist and became Pablo Picasso.

Our sons may or may not end up generals or popes or Picassos. But, if we leave our children a legacy of responsibility, high standards, realistic expectations, and, above all, unconditional love, we'll be rewarded for our efforts. We are confident they will be the best they can be.

Inheriting the Moral and Emotional Characteristics of Our Parents

One catalyst for writing this book is the often asked question, What's wrong with kids today? We recognize that children are different today, but we believe that the source of that difference is the adults. Our young people are criticized for being rude, violent, irresponsible, selfish, materialistic, unmotivated, uneducated, and unethical. How did they get that way?

(Joe): *I have wondered what influence or influences could have affected our young people so negatively. I considered the effects of television, radio, the written media, contemporary music, computer games, the Internet, and the increasing acceptance of sex in every facet of media. Is it all of these influences combined? The answer seems obvious when one takes the time to observe the youth around us.*

At a hotly contested soccer game of one of our older sons, one of the opposing team's players injured his shoulder. He was in significant pain when he left the game and walked to the sidelines. He began to curse quite loudly as he was attended to by his coach and his father. As the pain subsided, he asked his coach to please let him back in the game. This request was followed by a similar round of cursing from the father. It became clear to me where the young man had "inherited" his propensity for cursing.

It makes sense that if a particular society has a very high proportion of individuals with blue eyes, the chances are very high the offspring of that society will reflect that inherited characteristic; that is, there will be a lot of kids with blue eyes. I believe this is the case with the moral and emotional development of our youth. Our young people have inherited the moral and emotional characteristics of our adults. The violence, sexuality, dishonesty, and unfaithfulness portrayed in the media permeate our evening entertainment, as well as our daily lives. Is it really surprising that our young people are in sad shape? When a child abuses his sibling or bullies younger children that is, most likely, what he experiences at home. Children have inherited unaccountability, selfishness, and disrespect for themselves and others.

How do we change this? We start by changing the character of the individual whose face we see in the mirror each morning. As parents, we should leave children a legacy of character that will give them the moral and emotional strengths to make them responsible and caring young men and women.

Chapter 6

Teaching by Example:
Living What You Want
Your Children to Learn

B*e what you want your children to be, and watch them grow.*

–Leo Buscaglia

In practicing the art of parenthood an ounce of example is worth a ton of preachment.

–Wilferd A. Peterson

We realized when we started this chapter on setting a good example for our children, that all the concepts presented in this book are taught by example: love, respect, commitment, responsibility, positive attitude, spirituality, and love of learning. As parents, we communicate our values by how we conduct ourselves each day.

Teaching Our Children What We Say We Want Them to Learn

Children are always watching us—the adults—and can easily spot hypocrisies and discrepancies. The old philosophy "Do as I say, not as I do" doesn't work—as much as we may wish it did. There's no pressure on us if we tell our children what to do but don't hold ourselves to the same standards. **Your children will do as you do!** If we want our children to be respectful, we must treat them and our spouse with respect. If we want our children to be responsible, we must accept and fulfill our responsibilities. If we want our children to be kind and compassionate, we must be sensitive and caring in our words and actions. If we want our children to be happy, optimistic, and hopeful, we must show them the way.

(Joe): *It's a sobering thought to realize that your children will become what you are. We, as parents, want so many wonderful things for our children, yet I believe we frequently forget this salient truth that **our children mirror what we practice. This fact should serve as a great incentive for each of us to become better individuals; to improve our weaknesses and develop our talents so that our children will embrace these attributes.** I'm a procrastinator and I always urge my sons not to procrastinate. I do this with much less vigor than I used to, since I can only urge them not to procrastinate while I work to improve on this weakness myself. To be a good parent means constantly trying to become a better individual. Likewise, we can better empathize with our children's struggles to overcome their weaknesses each day.*

Teaching Values by Living Them

Opportunities to teach *our* values to our children arise every day. Carpe diem—seize the day. One afternoon Cathy stopped with the boys at the grocery store to pick up discounted movie tickets. When she returned to the car, she realized the young girl working the service desk had given her an extra ticket. Cathy told the boys they needed to return the ticket. Annoyed, one of the boys said, "It was *her* mistake," and another added,

"It's only a three-dollar ticket, Mom." Cathy explained she hadn't paid for the ticket, so it was wrong to keep it. The girl had made an honest mistake, and in many stores, the salesperson or cashier is responsible for discrepancies in the day's tally. Cathy asked the boys how they would feel in a similar situation. It was a hassle taking everyone back inside and returning the ticket. But the boys learned firsthand a lesson in honesty, and gratitude—the young cashier was most appreciative. If we want our children to be honest, then we must be honest. Do we steal office supplies from work or pretend a child's under twelve years old to pay less at the movies? Minor discrepancies in the "rules" don't go unnoticed by our children.

Through our example our sons learn our values. **By stretching ourselves to be better people and learn new concepts, we teach our sons that educating and improving oneself is a continual process.** Cathy, shy and timid as a child, would never have dreamed of willingly speaking in front of a group of people. Yet today, she addresses audiences of various sizes and comfortably shares her parenting experiences. And originally intimidated by the computer, Cathy now can aptly handle word processing, thanks to the endless patience of her teachers—her sons. Joe couldn't boil water when first married. Because of Cathy's nausea and inability to even look at food during the early months of her pregnancies, Joe learned out of necessity to prepare delectable meals. (The boys actually prefer Joe's grilled chicken to Cathy's.) When we had only a couple of children, Joe could stop and pick up something for himself and the boys to eat. As our family grew, stopping anywhere for a meal cost a small fortune. Ask Cathy's Dad. On one of his visits, he decided to take the boys to McDonald's—against our advice. When he returned, he teased, "I could have flown your mom down here for what it cost me to feed your sons." We tried to tell him.

Our willingness to accept change (with ten kids, change is inevitable) and be flexible, teaches our sons to adapt and grow with new experiences. No one can go through life without some unexpected incident wreaking havoc in their day, whether it's an illness, a car that doesn't start, lost keys, or an overflowing toilet. How we handle life's little difficulties is a powerful lesson for our children. Do we rant and rave or calmly figure out how to solve the dilemma?

(Cathy): *Joe is a master at maintaining composure in the midst of disaster. He assesses the situation and formulates a plan of action—without raising his blood pressure. If the car won't start, he'll determine what's wrong and what needs to be done. Then he'll call the schools or his office to let them know what's happening. When one of the boys decided to flush little Matchbox cars down the toilet at seven o'clock in the morning causing the toilet to overflow, Joe calmly shut off the valve, pulled out the plumber's snake, and cleaned up the mess.* **Joe, by his example, teaches our sons and me to deal positively with the challenges of daily life.**

Developing Sibling Love, Not Sibling Rivalry

We teach justice and the ramifications of that truth at home in our dealings with each other. Our fair treatment of our sons is an expression of justice. People ask how we handle a common family problem, sibling rivalry. We can honestly say sibling rivalry is not a source of friction in our home. The boys take pride in each other's achievements—they're not jealous of them. **When we consider why rivalry isn't a problem, we realize the boys are comfortable and pleased with who they are and aren't striving to be a carbon copy of each other.** We don't compare one with the other or expect one to be like his brother or do what his brother does. Because we respect our sons' individual talents, abilities, and personalities, they are secure in who they are. They aren't competing to gain our approval and attention—they know we love each one of them unconditionally.

From the earliest moments, we have encouraged our sons to be a part of each other's lives. When we came home from the hospital with David, Tony, five days shy of a year old, played an integral part in our loving and caring for him. Even a one-year-old can share in the excitement of a new baby without feeling diminished in value or jealous of the time and attention we shower on the new member of our family. **Our attitude**

about the new baby and the way we integrate our other sons in his early days contributes to the positive feelings and love they have for each other. We aren't yelling "Don't touch the baby," "Get out of the baby's room," or "Get away, you'll make the baby sick." Negative statements such as these cause the older child to view the baby as a rival and a pain in the neck. Instead, we allow our sons to hold the baby, helping the youngest ones by propping pillows on their laps. Cathy reads stories to the boys as she nurses the baby or lets them sit on the bed with her and make puzzles or color pictures for their new brother. Our windowsill is plastered with the artwork the older boys created for their younger brothers. When you make the decision not to let the older siblings feel deprived, you are more likely to create a positive experience for the entire family. **We allow them to assist, making them feel like real big brothers.** They help by getting a diaper, soaping the baby during bath time, covering the baby with a blanket, and taking care of the baby's new stuffed animal. The new baby usually gives a small present to each of his brothers. Of course, as the boys got older, it became obvious who the present was really from. When they realized the gift was from us, they never squealed to their younger brothers.

Our goal is to make the experience positive for everyone and to disrupt their daily routine as little as possible. Cathy, after the first two boys, returned home from the hospital within twenty-four hours, although she would not have been comfortable doing so after Tony's delivery. It was all too new! Since then, though, she prefers being home in her own bed, on her own schedule, eating the foods she likes, and not having to wait to see the boys each day. Fortunately, Cathy's mom stays with us for a couple of weeks after each delivery, making it feasible for Cathy to come home early.

The boys enjoy the new baby as much as we do. After Timmy, our tenth son, was born, the boys would race through the house after school to our bedroom to love and shower him with kisses. How disappointed they were if he was sound asleep. If awake, we played musical baby for the next hour. We often tease, because the boys are so involved with the baby, that somehow our new little fella survives his brothers' love.

Sharing is another important component of developing sibling love. **As parents though, we often forget that we need to show our children how to share.** If we share our cookie or a sip of our drink with our sons, they learn to share what they have with their siblings. Timmy will actually ask one of us to "share" our drink, whatever it is. Cathy started drinking water and lemon one summer thinking the boys wouldn't enjoy the sour taste, but they did—and she continues to share.

Learning to share is a process that evolves over the first few years of life. A typical one-year-old doesn't comprehend the concept of sharing—everything is "mine." But always taking a toy away from the older sibling to give to the younger creates resentment. Instead, parents should make sure each child has a specific toy to play with and not allow one child to take from the other. Being younger, or older, shouldn't automatically give a child the right to have or do what he or she wants. When a younger brother wants an older brother's toy, we ask the older son's permission for his brother to play with it. The boys have learned, too, that little brothers tire quickly of playing with the same item, so they'll have it back shortly.

Set standards that are fair and workable. By treating everyone similarly, we avoid the cry "You're not being fair" or "You love him more." When we don't know who had a toy first and the boys can't agree on how to resolve the problem, we take the toy away from both of them. Trying to decide who had the toy first is a losing battle, and giving the toy to one over the other fuels sibling rivalry. When buying clothes or presents, we try hard to keep purchases similar in value and number. Is it possible to always be perfectly fair? Of course not. Tony, being the oldest, winds up with more new clothes than his brothers because we hand down clothes. But we always make sure each son has something new to wear. **When you consciously make the effort to be fair, you usually experience success.**

(Cathy): *My parents excelled at treating my sisters and me fairly and equitably. Because each of us feels special in our parents' eyes, we can tease about who's their favorite daughter. The beauty of the joke is that we can tease about what is so sensitive an issue in many families—favoritism. One* year my sister Michele sent me a Valentine's Day card that read, "Mom gave me a trip to the Bahamas for Valentine's Day. What did she give you?" I proceeded to call my Mom and joked, "I just received a card from Michele saying you gave her a trip to the Bahamas. Now we know who's your favorite."

Through their example, my parents taught my sisters and me the importance of being fair. When you're not fair, you send the message that one child is of more value to you than the other. Resentment builds and sibling rivalry surfaces. I remember one of Chris's and Joe Pat's soccer coaches who worked extremely hard to treat each player fairly. He told me his parents had always favored his brother, and he was determined not to repeat their mistake—he remembers too clearly the hurt feelings.

We are very conscious of treating the boys fairly and *not* comparing one with another. **Not comparing the boys with each other is *crucial* in avoiding sibling rivalry.** We **never, never** say, "Why can't you be like your brother?" or give the impression we *want* one to be like another. We enjoy each of the boys for what he has to offer, be it humor, extra sensitivity, creativity, or initiative. We take pride in each of their accomplishments; we're not looking for perfection or the number one position. Maintaining a 3.0 grade point average is just as impressive and satisfying to us as a 4.0, because we understand the effort that goes into both. Report cards are not shared, displayed, or compared in the Garcia-Prats home; they are private between parents and child.

The boys do compete with each other, but there's a big difference between healthy competition and unhealthy competition. **Healthy competition builds up the person, whether it's physical or character building.** During the summers, our sons swim competitively on a summer league swim team. The children are divided by age brackets for the competition. Each bracket encompasses two age levels, seven- and eight-year-olds, eleven- and twelve-year-olds, and so on. Chris, Joe Pat, and Matthew are sequential ages. Joe Pat, being in the middle, competes against either Chris or Matthew every year. People wonder if this frustrates Joe Pat. On the contrary, the competition makes all three of them stronger swimmers. When Joe Pat swims against Chris, he works hard to beat him, never assuming that just because he is younger, he should lose.

When he swims against Matthew, the incentive is the opposite—not to be beaten by a younger brother. When the younger brother does win a particular competition, there is no anger or jealousy; they are proud of the other, recognizing that their brother is stronger in that stroke. Just as in most areas, the boys prefer and excel in different swim strokes.

Watching the boys share in the pride of their brothers' achievements is heartwarming. Matthew received the highest honor, the Principal's Award, at his eighth-grade graduation. When the ceremony ended, all of Matthew's brothers rushed to be the first to congratulate him. The same emotion flowed the afternoon of Tony's graduation from high school. Tony received several honors, the most notable was salutatorian of his class. Following the graduation, Joe Pat came up to me and with a huge smile filled with pride said, "I'm *so* proud to be Tony's brother." We all felt "puffed" up that day sharing in Tony's accomplishments, just as we did the following year with David, who was awarded several scholarships.

We, the Adults: Living Examples of Responsible Behavior

We have worked hard to teach our sons the importance of setting a good example. Earlier in this book, we emphasized that we are each responsible for the other. We are held accountable for what we do and don't do for each other, and for what we teach and don't teach each other. **If our children live their daily lives with what's good and right, they will learn what's good and right.**

Children learn what they live. **If we want our sons to accept our values, we must be conscious of setting a good example in all areas of our lives: what we eat, where we go, what we do, what we read, and what we watch on television or in the movies.** Do we use appropriate language? Which movies do we choose to watch? We teach the boys that a PG-13 rating doesn't mean a movie is necessarily appropriate for a thirteen-year-old any more than an R-rated movie is necessarily appropriate for a seventeen-year-old. As parents we must discriminate in the movies we watch to set an example of what is appropriate viewing

material. The same holds true for reading material. Pornographic magazines and books have no place in the home if we want our children to
learn respect for the other sex. Do we drink alcoholic beverages responsibly or do we come home from a party obviously under the influence of
alcohol or drugs? Do we drive home under the influence of alcohol or
drugs, but tell our children not to drink and drive? Do we irresponsibly
and illegally provide alcohol or drugs to our children and their friends?
Do we drive responsibly or with disregard for the laws and for safety? Do
we run red lights or drive too fast? Do we wear seat belts? As our sons
grew closer to the driving age, we became even more conscious of our
driving habits. Driving is a perfect example of how children will do as
you do, rather than as you say.

We are careful about what we discuss in front of our children. If we're
upset with a teacher or a colleague, we'll wait until we're alone to talk
about it. Children will repeat what is said at home, not always understanding the implications of their words. If derogatory or demeaning
words are used at home, expect your children to follow suit. We're
amazed at the words that come out of little mouths. Cathy was thankful
she had only called the driver of the pickup truck an "idiot" when he cut
in front of her car one afternoon. As soon as she said it, Timmy, who was
behind her in his car seat, began yelling, "Idiot. Idiot."

We also want the adults in our sons' lives to understand the influence
they have on our children. When Fr. Brian Zinnamon, S.J., President of
Strake Jesuit, addressed parents at the beginning of the 1996 school year,
he emphasized that Jesuits don't accept mediocrity. He expected the
faculty, staff, and students to stretch and reach their full potential. **We
have found that young people are acutely aware when mediocrity is
acceptable.** When Tony was in second grade, he scribbled out his homework one night. When we encouraged him to rewrite the assignment, he
argued that it was fine. Much to our satisfaction, his teacher also found
the work sloppy and had Tony stay in from recess to rewrite it. Ms.
Renken sent a clear message to Tony on what was an acceptable quality
of work in her class. However, a similar incident in sixth grade produced
the opposite results. Tony wrote a less than adequate science report.

When we commented on the quality of the paper and reminded him he needed to do his best work, he flashed back, "Yeh, right. Just like the teachers." Unlike Cathy's own experience in seventh grade when she received a C for her mediocre paper, this teacher gave Tony an A for less than A work. The message was clear again, but not the message we wanted to communicate to our children.

We wish all teachers understood that yelling and speaking disrespectfully to students is inappropriate and sets a terrible example. We're convinced that disrespectful behavior doesn't solve the problem or create a positive learning environment, especially for students who aren't used to that type of behavior at home. Teachers should also strive to be fair in their treatment of individuals and the class as a whole. Students, from first grade through twelfth, recognize when they or their classmates are treated unjustly. One afternoon, an upset Joe Pat arrived home from first grade with a conduct referral, indicating a major infraction. The conduct referral indicated "destruction of school property." When we questioned Joe Pat about what had happened, he explained he had taken his finger and scribbled a design in the dew of the music room door. We called the school and set up an appointment to meet with the teacher the next day. (Joe went alone; Cathy was too furious to step in the door.) If the door was damaged, we expected Joe Pat to either clean it or work to pay for its repair. Of course, when Joe asked to see the damaged property, the dew had evaporated and there was nothing to show. The teacher was embarrassed, as she rightfully should've been. The consequence was way out of line for the offense, and we're not sure the teacher ever understood the impact it had on Joe Pat's year. He lived with the fear of doing something wrong from that day on, and children have a difficult time enjoying the learning process when they live in fear. (We transferred our sons at the end of the school year following the above incidents to a school more conducive to our philosophy of raising children. We want our children to be in a loving, nurturing environment that is academically challenging, yet realistic.)

Getting Involved and Showing Your Children They Can Make a Difference in the World

Exemplifying responsible behavior extends beyond the home. Are we fulfilling our civic responsibilities by voting and being involved in choosing our representatives at the local and national levels? Take your children with you when you vote, so they can witness firsthand your commitment to democracy. When they're little, let them place the completed ballot in the ballot box. With only half the eligible voters voting in the 1996 election, many adults aren't setting a good example of civic responsibility. Change will never happen unless each of us takes the initiative.

Get involved in your community. Our world will never improve if we all just sit around and complain. Our high school sons participate in a freshman retreat program. The theme of the retreats focuses on the difference *each* individual can make when we put our hearts into making a difference. We can make a difference by participating in schools, churches, nonprofit organizations, hospitals, and community activities. If the only commitment you have at your children's school is the car pool line, you're not acting responsibly. **Our sons see us actively participate in our church, the schools, and our community.** We volunteer our time to the school board, the booster club, school auctions, and fund-raisers. In our church community, we are sponsors for engaged couples, and Eucharistic ministers; we also chair a booth at the annual bazaar and support the activities of the various organizations. In the community, Joe serves on the executive board of the March of Dimes and lectures on the importance of prenatal care; Cathy has served on The Woman's Hospital Board of Trustees and The Woman's Hospital Research and Education Foundation. We don't juggle these activities all at once. As we finish a commitment to one organization we may choose to help another. Our sons appreciate the time and energy we give to improve their individual worlds and the world at large. They also witness our personal satisfaction in helping others. **We want them to learn by our example that each of them can make a difference.**

A family in our neighborhood, the Goetzes, embody the art of giving with unique birthday celebrations for their children. The theme of each child's birthday party focuses on giving rather than receiving. The children invited to the party may be asked to bring a toy or clothes to share with a homeless shelter or food for the local food bank. One year they raked an elderly neighbor's yard, following it up with games at the park. They invite community representatives to share their experiences with the children or to pick up the clothes or food in person. These parents have shown their children and their children's friends that making a difference in other people's lives isn't drudgery—it can be extremely rewarding and a lot of fun.

Respecting the environment is one way we teach our sons to appreciate God's world. We've been recycling since we first got married, more than twenty years ago. Rice University had recycling bins available to the public at the back of the campus. Every couple of weeks, we'd drop off newspapers, glass, tin, and aluminum. Cathy taught her first graders a unit on ecology and conservation, the terminology of the mid-1970s, even replanting an overgrown flower garden on campus. Our family mulches leaves and yard clippings to reuse in flower beds. With curbside recycling and our commitment to the environment, the Garcia-Prats household has less garbage than other families in the neighborhood who don't take the time to recycle. We support the efforts of Danny's second-grade class to raise money for an acre of rain forest by saving aluminum cans for the drives. Through these efforts, we are confident we are raising our sons' awareness of their responsibility to the environment.

Being Happy: Children Watching Their Parents Enjoy Life

For our sons to see us as happy people enjoying life teaches them that life is full of joy. All work and no play is unhealthy. **We work hard and find time to have fun, too,** whether enjoying picnics with them, country western dancing, or going to a movie or a friend's party. The boys were amazed the year we actually dressed up as Mr. and Mrs. Rabbit, complete with ears and fluffy tails, for a Mardi Gras party. Our friends at the party teased us the rest of the night, "It's not fair, Joe and Cathy didn't come in costume."

On a daily basis, our sons need to observe us enjoying who we are and what we do. They understand we have many obligations, but they don't hear us constantly complaining about them. Mundane, routine chores are enlivened by turning on the stereo and mopping the floor to the sound track of *Forrest Gump*, or dancing to *West Side Story* while ironing or folding clothes. Cathy is used to the "I don't believe she's doing that" looks of the boys.

The boys also need to see the sensitive side of us: for example, when a friend dies or is diagnosed with a severe illness, when people in Bosnia or Rwanda live with atrocities, or when natural disasters strike causing so much human tragedy. Even closer to home, our sons observe our sensitivity to each other's needs. When Cathy is feeling nauseated and tired during a pregnancy, Joe will lovingly pick up the slack. When Joe's emotionally drained from working with an extremely ill infant, Cathy will empathize with him. We want our sons to share their feelings and be sensitive to the needs of others. If we want sensitivity, kindness, and understanding to be a part of the makeup of our sons, we must let them know it's okay. Parents of sons are too often more concerned with their sons acting macho. **We emphasize in our family that sensitivity, kindness, and understanding aren't feminine traits; they're *human* traits.**

A Loving, Respectful Relationship: The Best Teacher of Responsible Sexuality

Setting good examples on basic family issues will make it easier for you to set a credible and authoritative example on larger, more critical issues that your children will encounter outside the family—from racism to sexuality.

Our example of respect for each other is the most profound teacher of responsible sexuality that we can provide our sons. **We can explain in detail the facts of life and talk until we're blue in the face about** morality, but if we aren't living a loving, respectful relationship, they are empty, futile words. Our loving gestures and kind expressions tell our sons we're friends and lovers. We value the sexual component of our marriage—the gift of each other and our fertility. Our sons have no doubt that they are our greatest treasures—the fruits of our love. Our example of healthy communication teaches them the importance of sharing their own thoughts, feelings, and dreams with someone they love. Our commitment to each other reinforces the importance of fidelity. Although the prevalent view in society is "If it feels good, do it," with whoever is available, that philosophy relegates the sexual act to nothing more than two animals copulating. **We want our sons to realize that when respect, love, and commitment are woven into the relationship, the sexual act takes on a deeper, more fulfilling meaning.** To share that unique experience without a total commitment by both individuals is emotionally and often physically harmful. Society is paying the price for irresponsible sexuality in the form of increased unwanted pregnancies, abortions, divorces, and life-debilitating and life-threatening sexually transmitted diseases. We tell our sons that *our* decisions regarding sexuality have eased our burden, not increased it. Maybe it's right to say: The truth will set you free.

Prejudicial Attitudes: Are They Inherited?

Our acceptance of people of all races, cultures, and creeds teaches our sons that we genuinely believe all people are made in the image and likeness of God. Children learn acceptance—or the opposite, prejudice—from their parents and other influential adults in their lives. **If we want our children to grow up in a society where everyone is judged by their character and not the color of their skin, the language they speak, or the traditions they practice, we must demonstrate that belief in our choice of friends and attitude toward others.**

Due to our Hispanic background and last name, we are victims of prejudicial comments and treatment. We don't experience this negativity to the extent of many other minorities, probably because we are fair skinned, speak English, and are well educated.

(Cathy): *The first week I was married, I applied for my Texas driver's license. I filled out the form writing G-A-R-C-I-A P-R-A-T-S in the space provided for my last name. When the state trooper behind the counter read the form, he looked at me strangely, probably because I was white with an Hispanic last name, and then said, "You can't put both names on your license. Take my advice—pick Prats." I was totally shocked by his comment. I had* never *considered Garcia to be any different from Musco— my Italian maiden name—or Johnson—my mother's maiden name. I explained that* Garcia-Prats *was my legal last name—not Prats. The trooper demanded I obtain legal documentation of my name, explaining he would hold my paperwork for future processing. When I returned with my documentation, the office couldn't find my paperwork or any record that I had previously applied. Fortunately, another employee remembered my case, and kindly processed my license. The experience was a rude reminder of the prejudices prevalent in our society. (Our last name, for clarification, is a combination of Joe's father's last name, Garcia, and his mother's last name, Prats. Contrary to what most people think, it's Joe's eighty-five-year-old mom who's the liberated woman.)*

Another incident I vividly remember was the year I tried to arrange a preschool car pool. I contacted a friend in the neighborhood to see if I could join hers. She was excited because it meant we would only have to drive one day a week. When my friend called back, she hesitantly told me that the other mom had no desire to car pool with me. My friend embarrassingly explained, "She's afraid her kids will get sick being around your kids." This mom assumed that because we were Hispanic, we were germ infested. I was flabbergasted by her ignorance. Months later, I met this woman walking down the grocery store aisle. It was obvious she didn't know who I was when she amiably asked, "Don't you have children at the preschool?" When I answered yes and stretched my hand out and introduced myself, she was extremely surprised—and embarrassed. My prayer for her was that she learn not to prejudge people.

Our acceptance of people of all races and creeds teaches our children what no textbook or lecture can—that God created all people equal. When a mother expressed concern about the growing diversity of our Catholic elementary school, I shared with her my belief that the multicultural diversity at our school was an asset. I went on to tell her that one of my dearest friends, Veronica, is Chinese, that Timmy's godfather, Mike, is Filipino, and that the eighth-grade class president, Gabby, is African American—an exceptionally talented young lady, chosen by her peers to lead their class.

Cathy's dad is Italian; her mom is Irish. Joe's dad is Mexican; his mom is Spanish. Our sons are gifted with the four rich, diverse cultures of our families and the cultures of our many friends. Our children value their heritage, as we do.

Young children are initially unaware of differences in color or race—their attitudes are learned. For a couple of years, Bryant, a friend of our family, carpooled to high school with the boys. Bryant and Chris played soccer together and our families became friends. Each morning, Bryant was dropped off at our home and while waiting to leave for school, played with our younger sons, especially Jamie. Jamie loved Bryant. One afternoon when Cathy picked up Chris and Bryant from school, Jamie eagerly slid next to Bryant as he got in the car. A few minutes later, Jamie looked at Bryant and, in a quizzical tone of voice, innocently said, "Bryant, you're black." And continuing to look at him, he added in amazement, "You're hat's black, too." We all roared. Jamie was three and a half years old; he had known Bryant from the day he was born.

We have many friends of different religious faiths: Protestant, Jewish, Muslim, and Mormon. **We share a mutual respect for the beliefs and traditions of these friends—not condemning what others hold true.** Our family has been enriched by this special sharing of traditions and teachings. Every year during the Jewish holiday of Succot, our neighbors, the Smolenskys, invite us to visit the succah (a small hut decorated with fruits and vegetables) their family constructs. During the seven days of Succot, the Smolenskys eat their meals in the hut. Randee, the mom, explained that the hut symbolizes the temporary dwelling places used by the Jewish people when they wandered in the desert for forty years following their exodus from Egypt and before they entered the land of Israel. What a wonderful way for our family to learn the traditions of our friends' faith and the role Jewish traditions play in Catholic religious practices.

Our sons share our belief in the dignity of all people, because they experience, along with us, the richness of our many friends. We hope the young people of today appreciate people different from themselves. We realize how much we learn from the experiences of others!

We defend this belief to our sons when we express our intolerance of prejudicial comments and actions, whether heard or seen on television or in person. During a high school soccer game against a predominantly Hispanic team, an opposing player made a dangerous slide tackle. A parent from our sons' school yelled, "Typical Hispanic. They all play dirty." Joe, tactfully but forcefully, corrected him. "Excuse me. *My* sons are Hispanic and they don't play like that. That kid's just a dirty player. It doesn't have anything to do with him being Hispanic." Other Hispanic parents in the stands were pleased Joe spoke up.

We parents have to realize the impact our prejudicial comments have, not only on the person they are directed to but also on our children. Such comments are distasteful, hurtful, insensitive, and unjust. **We must *think* before we speak and teach our children to do the same.**

(Cathy): *In the early 1960s I lived in Jacksonville, Florida, and attended a parochial school for the first time. My sisters and I took the city buses to and from school each day wearing our forest green uniforms. One day we came home and told my Mom that some ladies on the bus kept calling us "fish eaters." My sisters and I thought it was funny; we didn't particularly like fish and didn't realize these women were insulting our religion. The comments were directed at our church's teaching at the time to abstain from eating meat on Fridays. My Mom, though, was horrified that adults would speak to young children that way.*

While a cheerleader at Loyola University in the early 1970s, my squad traveled with the basketball team to Alabama for a game. Two of the

African American cheerleaders decided not to go; their parents weren't comfortable with the idea. Judith, the other African American cheerleader, decided to go. When we walked down the street to eat breakfast, car after car of adults yelled racial epithets at us. Returning to New Orleans after the game, we stopped at a restaurant to eat dinner. The owner refused to serve the black members of the team and Judith. Appalled, we left and found another establishment where we could eat. Is it any surprise that our children grow up with prejudice and insensitivity toward others?

Our influence as parents is beyond measure. The effort to be the best example for our children is inexorable but extremely worthwhile, especially when we see our older sons consciously making the right choices in order to set a good example for their younger brothers. Our hope and dream is that they are an example not only to each other but also to their friends and the people they meet along life's path. Living our beliefs and values on a day-to-day basis shows our sons, beyond a doubt, that we value those convictions. **"Be what you want your children to be, and watch them grow."**

Chapter 7

Instilling the Love of Learning

I had a Mother who read me the things
That wholesome life to the boy heart brings–
Stories that stir with an upward touch
Oh, that each mother of boys were such!

You may have tangible wealth untold;
Caskets of jewels and coffers of gold.
Richer than I you can never be–
I had a Mother who read to me.
    – "The Reading Mother" by Strickland Gillilan
    from *The Best Loved Poems of the American People*

One of the greatest gifts we give our children is an appreciation and respect for knowledge. When you have knowledge, it's yours forever— nobody can take it away. Instilling a lifelong love of learning in your children can be one of the most enjoyable aspects of parenting, *if* we approach learning as our total interaction with our children.

Educating our children to their fullest potential is a primary parental responsibility. Learning, though, is too narrowly associated with schooling and book work. Although schools are a major source of education, we wholeheartedly believe the process begins before a child goes to school and continues into adulthood. A parent's role in the learning process, therefore, is vital and fundamental. The child is with you from the first moments of life—that's when learning begins. **Our sons are unaware they are even learning, because we teach them as they experience their daily life.** Learning is a naturally evolving process.

Parental Interaction: Motivating Children to Learn

We acquire knowledge from using our five senses: touch, hearing, smell, taste, and sight. In newborns, all these senses are activated, and stimulated through interaction. The way we touch our newborn, whether gently or roughly, telegraphs our feelings to the baby. Studies abound on the importance of touch in a child's development. Children deprived of physical contact manifest slower rates of physical, mental, and social development. **Cuddling and holding a child doesn't spoil him, the touch stimulates him and lets him know he's loved.** With our belief in the importance of touch, our younger children have truly been blessed, because their older brothers, in addition to us, held and rocked them endlessly. Touch and physical contact shouldn't stop at a certain age. The hugs and kisses we continue to bestow on our sons reflect our love for them and foster an unspoken sense of security. **Being loved and feeling secure has a positive effect on learning and development.** Fortunately, we both grew up in families where physical expressions of love were acceptable. When we see our parents, brothers and sisters, aunts, uncles, and cousins, we shower each other with hugs and kisses. We wouldn't trade Aunt Bessie's warm embrace, Papa's firm squeeze, Grandma's gentle caress, or Aunt Pauline's tweak on the cheek for anything. As parents we wouldn't miss those special good-bye hugs in the morning as our sons rush off to school or the welcoming squeeze when they walk in the door at the end of the day. We express our love as a couple too, not only at home but when we meet at a soccer game or social function. A poem on our refrigerator espouses the benefits of a simple hug: "It reduces stress; is invigorating and rejuvenating; has low energy consumption and high energy yield; and is nonfattening, nonpolluting, and fully returnable—Caution! It is contagious." **We encourage all parents to find the time to hug their children.** Time's too short to let these golden moments slip away. So hug, hug, and hug some more. What your child will *learn,* money can't buy.

From the moment of birth, a child also learns from what he hears. **Your voice teaches your child about his world,** as small as it is at that moment in time. The age-old practice of singing lullabies soothes a restless child, and, we're convinced, relaxes a restless mom and dad, too. An infant recognizes voices early on. A baby will turn his head toward his mom when he hears her voice. The older boys were often frustrated if Cathy entered the room while they were holding the baby. As soon as the baby heard her voice, he wanted his mom.

Talking to our children from the earliest moments sets in motion the important wheels of language development. Children understand the meaning of words long before they are able to speak them. **It's through the repetitive hearing of words that children master language.** When Cathy nurses the baby, she talks to him; she knows full well he doesn't understand one word she's saying, but realizes the experience is richer than it appears. If she reads a story to one of the boys while she nurses, the baby hears her voice and language. Cathy often wonders if Tony acquired his strong command of language because she read out loud to him—*Time, National Geographic,* and novels—while she rocked him. Looking back, not having a baby swing was a blessing—Cathy spent extra time holding and reading to Tony.

The opportunities to speak to our children are endless. We take advantage of every moment: during the baby's bath, when he nurses, while he sits in the infant seat and we prepare dinner or fold clothes, and especially during the never-ending diaper changes. We sing songs, nursery rhymes, and the ABC's, count, and tell stories or jokes. The baby doesn't have to comprehend the words we're saying for the time to be meaningful and stimulating. The child's response—the smile, the giggle—rewards us time and again, just as our responses and interactions with the baby encourage and motivate him.

Playing music also develops a baby's hearing and language. We listen to music throughout the day. For the toddlers, we listen to children's music—Raffi, *The Lion King*—*especially* in the car. It makes the time in the car more fun, and the repetitive tunes and words help develop a child's memory, just as the counting and singing does during diaper time.

Learning, we want to reemphasize, is not a structured time in our day. **We don't sit down and formally teach our sons to talk, read, and write. Learning happens as our sons scurry through their day.** When we speak to the boys, we don't use baby talk. That doesn't mean we don't imitate some of the da-da sounds they make when we're playing with them, but we use correct terminology and sentence structure when talking with them. **If we never spoke to them with words above the first-grade level, their vocabularies would reflect that; children learn to speak and understand the words they hear on a regular basis.** The words Jamie and Timmy use often amaze us, but they're repeating words heard from us and their brothers. If they don't understand the meaning of a word or phrase, we'll explain it to them in language they do understand, then continue to use the word. Children don't know a word is too difficult for them to speak. Adults assume because a word's not typical for a particular age level that a child can't learn to pronounce and use it correctly. How wrong we are.

(Cathy): *During the first February I taught school, I realized the students thought their hearts were shaped like a Valentine's Day heart. Taking advantage of the opportunity, I contacted the American Heart Association and asked if they could provide any teaching materials on the heart. Fortunately, they had developed some wonderful materials appropriate for first graders: a model of the heart and hands-on materials for the children to manipulate. My students became fascinated with the circulatory system; and I was fascinated at how quickly they grasped the concepts and appropriate terminology. They weren't intimidated by the unfamiliar words:* circulation, arteries, veins, *and* valves. *They were proud of themselves when their parents expressed delight in their level of understanding. As a teacher, the experience was exciting because it reinforced for me how* **young children absorb knowledge like a sponge— we provide the information and they soak it up (a concept parents need to apply).** *From the circulatory system, we moved on to the respiratory system. Some very inspiring science lessons emerged from the simple Valentine's Day heart.*

Providing a Stimulating Environment for Your Children

When we were at Loyola University, we both had Mrs. Egan for child psychology. She used to tell us, "**Bombard the environment**"—provide stimulating surroundings for your children, constantly expanding the environment with new stimuli as they develop.

We hang a colorful mobile over the baby's crib, play soft music, and situate bright-colored toys and pictures where the baby can see them. Our boys loved a red plastic apple that wobbled and rattled when they touched it. We have pictures of each of them trying to mouth the apple, a simple, inexpensive toy that provided hours of entertainment over the years.

Children don't need expensive toys to play with. Cathy's dad gave Tony a truck when he was six months old. Tony preferred playing with the box the truck came in rather than the truck itself. Children are fascinated with simplicity; adults are the ones who like all the fancy gizmos. Young children love banging on pans, putting the juice can tops in and out of a plastic bowl, and stacking jello boxes or small cans. All these items are readily available in the home.

We also provide toys that develop the boys' mental and physical skills. Push toys and pull toys are great for toddlers. Shape sorters, puzzles, and blocks develop spatial relationships and can be played alone or with others. We make homemade play dough (see the recipe at the back of this book)—it's softer and more pliable, making it easier for small fingers to manipulate. Using cookie cutters and other small kitchen objects, the boys create an assortment of items.

We furnish art materials for the boys, enabling them to artistically "express" themselves while developing fine motor skills. We supervise the younger boys' use of nontoxic markers and glue. (We prefer markers to crayons at first because a child can draw using less pressure and see immediate results.) Finger painting and water coloring are other creative activities. You can mix food color and white dishwasher soap to make "paint." Mixing the different colors together teaches them how colors are formed. Gluing pieces of colored paper or small items together, and pouring rice in and out of a dump truck enthralls young children. Our sons enjoy chalking or designing with shaving cream on the sidewalks—the Garcia-Prats sidewalks are spectacularly decorated year round. Keeping these times unstructured lets the creative juices flow. We encourage and praise their works of art, even if we have no idea what "it" is.

We also take advantage of the learning opportunities readily provided outdoors. We observe ants crawling along the sidewalk, collect (and count) acorns, watch the airplanes flying overhead, pull up weeds to see the roots, and talk about the different colored leaves. The boys ride little tyke bikes, play ball, swing, and slide. We're playing and stimulating their innate curiosity all in one.

Learning By Doing

Children learn by doing—moving from the concrete to the abstract. **We encourage hands-on involvement.** The boys help add and mix the cake ingredients, roll the cookie dough, stir the food coloring into the icing, and scramble the eggs. We allow them to play and experiment with water, sand, and a combination of both—mud. (Timmy has mastered mud making and decorating.) We fertilize and water plants, mulch leaves to add to the compost pile, and plant seeds. The boys make secret potions mixing dirt, leaves, and other assorted materials. They use scissors, hammers, and screwdrivers. Even as the boys get older, we use the multisensory approach to enrich their learning experiences.

Excursions to the parks, zoo, library, science and art museums, and even the grocery store provide additional enjoyable learning experiences. During one excursion to the grocery store, David, eighteen months old at the time, amazed Cathy with his ability to infer association. Cathy's mom occasionally sent the boys care packages—usually homemade cookies packaged in brightly colored coffee cans. Walking down the grocery store aisle stocked with coffee, David pointed and demanded, "Cookies, cookies!"

Each new experience increases their vocabulary, understanding, and awareness of their world. And the amount of *time* we spend with the boys during these activities is of utmost importance. No matter what they're doing, we're teaching them it's a *red* marker, a *blue* dump truck, *green* grass, or a *round* cookie. We count while climbing up and down stairs, placing silverware in the kitchen drawer, or selecting lemons at the store. **We don't formally teach our sons their colors, shapes, letters, or numbers. They learn them by hearing the words over and over again.** One amusing "color" story happened when Tony was eighteen months old; his favorite color was "orange." Joe drove an orange Volkswagen Beetle at the time. When we asked Tony what color Daddy's car was, he'd quickly respond, "orange." Everyone was so impressed. Although Tony was a precocious child, when we proceeded to ask him what color the grass or sky was, he responded with his favorite color, "orange."

Riding in the car, whether to the grocery store or across country, we utilize the time productively. (The car is in many ways Cathy's minischool on wheels.) When Tommy was in first grade, a friend nicknamed him "Flashcard Tommy"; Tommy could rattle off math facts with incredible speed and accuracy. One mom asked about the secret of Tommy's success. Cathy explained that they play mental math in the car; she proposes a math problem and the boys solve it. Cathy also keeps paper and pencils in the car so the younger boys can write numbers and letters, sound out words, or draw pictures. Cathy calls out a letter or a word while five-year-old Jamie writes the letter or the beginning or ending sounds. Gradually, Jamie writes words. Jamie thinks we're playing a game, yet, his reading and writing vocabulary continually increases. He's learning *and* having fun—without a formal lesson or a worksheet.

Discovering Ways to Make the Learning Experience Fun

Our "teaching" style is another example of the trickle-down effect working in our favor. We started playing these educational games with the older boys, not realizing at the time the long-term benefits. It was a rewarding surprise when their brothers insisted on playing the same games. We stumbled on the idea that if we make the educational process fun, our children will enjoy learning. One summer, while waiting for their next events at a swim meet, Tony and David were solving problems in a math workbook. A mother observing their efforts commented, "I can't believe you're *making* your sons work on math during the summer." Joe, glancing at the boys, responded, "Now does it look like we're forcing them to do that?" The mother agreed. Tony and David didn't consider the math drudgery; solving the problems kept them entertained during the monotonous waits between events. When Tony began swimming in United States Swimming competitions, the swim team members often whiled away the time reading wonderful books. Many of the books passed from one swimmer to the next. Parents need to examine their attitudes on reading, writing, and arithmetic. Do our attitudes imply that learning is work? **A positive attitude and example shows our children the value and satisfaction we derive from acquiring new knowledge.**

The Garcia-Prats meals are a time to nourish our bodies—and our minds. **Conversations over family meals provide excellent opportunities to discuss what's happened in our sons' day, as well as in the world.** One topic of discussion often leads to another. A discussion of a World Cup soccer game may evolve into a discussion on Brazil's or Nigeria's location on the globe. Once, a news story on the indictment of an elected official prompted a discussion on Watergate and the infamous Nixon presidency. Fascinated by this unbelievable piece of United States history, the boys later watched the movie *All the President's Men.*

The Key to Learning: Read, Read, and Read Some More!

Although we have found many ways to foster our sons' love of knowledge, we believe the most important and effective way is by **reading** to the boys. *No other activity enriches your children's love of learning more.*

Reading to our children enriches the relationship, develops listening and memory skills, increases vocabulary and language skills, and provides experiences beyond their imaginations. **We begin discovering books with the boys before they're even one year old.** We start with books that have vivid illustrations of toys, trucks, animals, and household items. We've had to buy several copies of many of Richard Scarry's books—we wear them out from constant use. Each of the boys preferred different books; Jamie loved *The Very Busy Spider*, and Timmy can't hear enough of *Brown Bear, Brown Bear*.

Reading to the boys opens up their world, teaching them about interesting people and places. They can "travel" to China in *Ping*, to Boston in *Make Way for Ducklings*, or to England in *Lassie Come-Home*. They share the emotions of friendship in *Amos and Boris* and parents' love in *Sylvester and the Magic Pebble*. They appreciate the struggles of Helen Keller, Harriet Tubman, and Lou Gehrig, and experience racial injustice in *Roll of Thunder, Hear My Cry* and courage and devotion in *Island of the Blue Dolphins*. Their imaginations soar reading *Castle in the Attic* and *The Twenty-one Balloons*. They laugh at the antics of the characters in *Wayside School Falling Down* and the poetry of Shel Silverstein and Jack Prelutsky.

When we read to the boys, the titillation found between the pages springs to life. Why would a child want to pick up a piece of paper with a bunch of letters on it, unless he'd discovered the excitement derived from those letters? Parents do their children an injustice by *not* reading to them on a regular basis, and put them at a big disadvantage when they begin formal education. **Children who have been read to are familiar with letters, words, and sentence structure, and children who haven't been read to aren't.** It takes fifteen minutes or less to read most stories to a child under five years old. **We *must* as parents make those**

fifteen minutes available to our children. At a PTO meeting, Mrs. Landram, the principal, strongly encouraged parents to find the time to read to their children every night. After the meeting, Cathy was sarcastically asked if she read to the boys every night. When Cathy responded that she did, many parents were surprised we had time with so many children and commitments. We have time because we don't allow television, the number one intruder of reading time, to dominate our lives. Instead of watching mindless sitcoms, we choose to spend the time reading to the boys. We assure you, from our years of experience, the time invested is well rewarded.

(Cathy): *Reading played a significant role in my childhood. I can't thank Mom enough for reading to me as a child and encouraging my reading as I grew older; books have enriched my life. They were my companions;* **I learned countless lessons through the experiences of my book friends.** *A few years ago, children's literature was criticized for not providing young girls with strong role models. I don't know what books the critics read, but I learned important lessons from the young heroines (and believe it or not, the heroes) in the stories I read. I was touched by the courage of Karana in* Island of the Blue Dolphins, *and the bravery of the young girls in the "I Was There" historical fiction series. Even the "Nancy Drew" mystery series, although not considered outstanding children's literature, provided a strong, courageous, well-educated heroine. I read the biographies of Helen Keller and Joan of Arc and many other saints. In my junior high years, I was motivated and inspired reading* Quo Vadis, Profiles in Courage, Uncle Tom's Cabin, The Exodus, *and* Cry, the Beloved Country. *Because of the powerful influence of my parents, teachers, and the books I read, I have always felt confident that I can do and be whatever I choose.*

We continue to read to the boys even after they have learned to read by themselves. Children understand books at a higher level than they are capable of reading on their own. **Reading to them beyond their reading level helps to open their world and to increase their vocabularies and understanding of the English language; it also provides us with special moments together.** The importance of story time was reinforced by a comment Jamie made after a close friend's sister-in-law and nephew were killed in an automobile accident. The mother left behind two other young children. Jamie, when he heard about the children, sadly said, "Oh Mommy, who will read them stories now?" We have always cherished the time we spend reading to our sons, but with Jamie's comment, the experience is valued even more. It's obvious they treasure that time as much as we do.

Our sons also treasure the books they have received over the years as gifts. They enjoy looking at the front inside cover of a book from our home library to see if there's an inscription noting whose book it is, when they received it, and from whom. **We give books to the boys and friends for birthdays, Christmas, Easter, baby gifts, other special occasions, and "just because."** When Mark was five years old, his favorite book was *The Napping House*. His preschool teacher read the story to his class, and he thoroughly enjoyed the rhythmical words and subdued illustrations. His godmother, a school librarian, unknowingly gave Mark the book for his birthday; evidently Mary Ellen, like Mark, thought it to be an exceptional story. Many of our books are treasured, not only because of the wonderful stories but also because of the thoughtful giver.

Motivating Children to Read By Providing Reading Material Geared to Their Interests

We provide various types of reading materials for the boys to read at home: magazines and newspapers, as well as books. Although we've built up an extensive home library over the years, the public library is still our primary source of reading materials. We enjoy the time spent roaming the shelves for that special book; and the younger boys are very proud of the selections they bring home. Recycling magazines and newspapers with friends increases the variety of materials available to read. The director of our neighborhood swimming pool furnishes a basket at the check-in desk to recycle used magazines. Several of the boys' teachers over the years have organized a similar program in the classroom; each child brings a book or magazine from home to share with classmates.

Parents are often at a loss at which books to choose for their children. Cathy's background in children's literature is a definite asset, but resources are available to all parents. **Children's librarians are an excellent resource when determining the level or type of book to read at a particular age.** (The Houston libraries provide lists and descriptions of books for each age and grade level.) **Ask your child's teacher to recommend books that are appropriate.** Several years ago Cathy acquired a list of recommended books from the National Endowment for the Humanities. Although the list is extensive, it covers only books published before 1960; obviously there are many wonderful children's books published since then. **Another helpful resource for us over the years has been *The Read-Aloud Handbook* by Jim Trelease.** Cathy discovered this book in the early 1980s while browsing through a bookstore. She bought it, read it, and recommends it to all parents and teachers. We've given the book to teachers, friends, family, and many new parents as a baby gift. Mr. Trelease explains why, when, and how to read to your children; he also provides an extensive list of excellent children's literature. We wholeheartedly agree with his words of advice and his choice of books.

To help us decide on reading material for our sons, we use their interests as a springboard: sports, pets, art, current events, or experiences in their lives. When Danny was in second grade, Mrs. Jackson read *Mr. Popper's Penguins* to the class. Danny's curiosity about penguins soared. We read *National Geographic* articles and probably every book in the library on penguins, including rereading *Mr. Popper's Penguins*. He drew penguins and created a family of penguins by decorating toilet tissue rolls. Next came his fascination with the sinking of the *Titanic*. We read the book *Exploring the Titanic* and watched the National Geographic video on the efforts to locate the sunken ship and its treasures. And, as if on cue, the Houston IMAX featured *Titanica*, the 3-D film on the exploration of the *Titanic*, further enriching Danny's knowledge on the subject. He even asked for a model of the *Titanic* for Christmas. Our support of Danny's interest in the penguins and the *Titanic* encouraged him to absorb all he could about both subjects. It's amazing how much we learned in the process, too.

(Cathy): **When I taught first grade, I took advantage of my students' interests and strengths to motivate them in the classroom.** *One boy in the class had the reading readiness skills but wasn't particularly interested in reading. I noted that he loved bugs; every day at recess he found a new critter to show "lucky" me. I wondered if insects could be the key to unlocking the door to his reading. Although I could not find an insect book, I found a story at his reading level about a cat and a bug. "The cat ran after the bug," read Tommy, sounding out each word slowly and phonetically. Then he read the same sentence over quickly and excitedly. "The bug ran fast," he continued. Tommy read and reread that one little book and then moved on to books on insects. Bugs were the motivating force that triggered his interest in reading.*

When I volunteered in the school library, a fourth-grade boy asked me for help in selecting a book. He didn't enjoy reading, but he had to do a book report on a biography. I knew he was a talented young athlete so I recommended a biography on Knute Rockne from "The Childhood of Famous Americans Series." When he returned to the library the following week, he immediately found me. "Mrs. Garcia-Prats, are there any more books like the one you gave me last week?" he excitedly asked. "It was great." He went on to read the biographies of Babe Ruth, Jim Thorpe, and Lou Gehrig, other books in the series.

As parents and teachers, we're often too concerned with what we think children should read, instead of letting them read what they want. I remember a teacher I had who wouldn't let the girls in class even bring a "Nancy Drew" book to school. That's a mistake. Although we want to channel our children's reading in a challenging direction, we discourage them from reading if we don't allow them to focus on their interests. When they discover a topic of interest, like Danny with penguins and the Titanic, *they are more likely to want to read about the subject. Determining the appropriate reading level is also important. If the book is too difficult, a child will get discouraged and lose interest. On the other hand, if the book is too easy, the child isn't challenged and may get bored.* **The right combination of interest and ability level motivates children to read.**

Children of all levels of intelligence usually excel in one particular subject. **Build confidence and self-esteem using the child's strengths.** *One of my students struggled with reading, but was a master of math facts. Praising his math skills while minimizing his reading weaknesses allowed him to maintain a strong self-image.*

Our attitude, as parents and teachers, affects whether children view themselves as failures or successes. We must keep our expectations of our children realistic or they become discouraged and uninterested in learning. Some first-grade parents were frustrated by their children's inability to read at the level they thought was appropriate. I would remind them that some children walk at nine months and others at fourteen months; some children talk at a year and others a year and a half.

Children learn to read at different ages, ranging from three to eight years old. *One summer I tutored a young boy in reading. In a few short weeks, he was reading without having to stop and sound out each word. The parents gave me credit for his tremendous strides. Although I strengthened his phonetical skills, I was convinced his reading clock had clicked on, and according to his parents, it hasn't stopped ticking.*

As the boys grow older, we continue to find ways to foster their reading outside of school. **Whenever a movie based on a book is released, we have the boys read the book prior to seeing the movie.** When David was in seventh grade, the movie *The Hunt for Red October* came out. We told David he could see the movie once he had read the book. Motivation kicked in and David engrossed himself in the novel. He couldn't put the book down, and before we knew it, most of his friends were borrowing it on David's recommendation. When *The Indian in the Cupboard* was released, Mark and Tommy eagerly read the book. The boys agree that the book is almost always better than the movie. We also believe that the boys will lose interest in reading the book after seeing the movie; the experience in reverse is never the same.

Parental Involvement and School Success

Once the boys begin their formal education, our support, involvement, and encouragement is crucial to their educational development. We must demonstrate our commitment to their education for it to be meaningful. **Our children know we care when we take time to ask about their day, review their schoolwork, assist with their studies, read with them, help them stay organized, and participate in school activities.** Responsible parents accept that role in order to provide the best educational experience possible for their children. If parents expect the school to shoulder the entire responsibility, their children will pay the price. We hear too many parents complain and insist that homework is unnecessary and inappropriate—schoolwork should be done at school. Yet, study after study of successful schools and students reflect the benefit of homework and outside learning activities. **Education is a discipline, and it takes discipline to attain success.**

(Cathy): *As a teacher, I experienced firsthand the importance of parental involvement. When I asked parents to review math facts with their child for five minutes every day, I could tell which students practiced by their level and speed of advancement. When parents reviewed the spelling words over the course of the week, the student met with success. Reading improved more rapidly when the child read orally with someone on a regular basis. Children want to succeed. A child is just as unhappy with a low grade as is the parent. One father told me that he had to wing it on his own as a kid, and he expected his kids to do the same. Yet, this same father was disappointed when his child wasn't at the top of the class. Formal education takes thirteen long years. We choose to provide our sons with the tools they need to enjoy and succeed in school—we don't leave them to fend for themselves.*

Our assistance at home and our positive attitude toward school and homework inspire the academic achievement of our sons. We fully understand the time commitment reviewing schoolwork entails. We usually finish working with all the boys around 9:30 every evening. **We consider the time we spend reviewing science or math as** *quality* **time with our sons, not as a burden or obstacle to our watching television.** We know working with our sons is a better investment of our time. People discuss the use of discretionary income; maybe we need to talk about our use of "discretionary time." **We take advantage of homework as an opportunity to spend one-on-one time with the boys.** Danny reads his home reader to Cathy while Joe reviews science with Tommy. By middle school, the boys are self-sufficient regarding schoolwork. They organize their materials, take responsibility for completing assignments, and read and review for quizzes and tests. We continue to closely monitor their work to ensure they understand and retain new information. But if they need assistance, they know we're available. When Matthew needs help with an algebra problem, Cathy steps in. If Chris is confused about a chemistry concept, Joe reviews the material with him. At the high school open house, Father Leininger, a math teacher, emphasized to parents the importance of nightly review of information learned during the day. He told parents that if not reviewed in three days, 65 percent of the information is forgotten.

We attend teacher conferences to find out how our sons are achieving in school academically, physically, and socially, and how we can better assist them at home. We're amazed at parents who don't feel teacher conferences are important to attend after their child leaves grade school. We meet with teachers from preschool through high school regardless of whether the course grade is an A or a C. Our children are aware of the value we place on their education by our continuous concern and involvement. **Are too many parents, by their lack of involvement, sending the message to their children that education is a hassle and unimportant?**

The boys understand our commitment to their education not only by our direct involvement with their studies but also by our direct participation in their schools. We volunteer depending on our schedules, interests, and talents. We all can't volunteer during the day in the library, office, or cafeteria, but each of us can actively participate in the school, whether it's a one-time commitment for a special event or an ongoing commitment as a room mother or club representative. We are impressed with the long-term commitment of one Denver, Colorado, father, Fred Long; he has been reading to his son's classes since the child was in kindergarten. His son and his classmates, now entering high school, realize Mr. Long enjoys being a part of their lives. **Parental participation translates into successful schools and successful students.**

Seeking Additional Help When Needed

When we determine one of the boys needs extra help, we aren't embarrassed to seek it. Assimilating and retaining information comes easier for some of the boys than it does for others. Instead of having one of our sons struggle and feel incompetent, we make sure he receives the appropriate help. Self-confidence and self-esteem play a major role in educational success. When a child continually performs poorly or below the standards he sets, self-esteem and self-confidence plummet. Just as positiveness begets positiveness, the opposite also holds true. **When one of the boys struggles academically, we determine what it'll take to break the cycle and get him back on track.** Recognizing that we learn in different ways encourages us to present information from different perspectives, using different teaching techniques. All our sons want to do well, so we provide the necessary tools to help them achieve their goals. **If it means finding an additional program or tutor to fill in the missing gaps and rebuild self-confidence, then that's what we do.** Our additional commitment of time and money sends a clear message that we care and want the best for them.

Fostering a Positive Home/School Partnership

Teachers play a dynamic role in determining a positive outcome of the educational process. We can all think back to our own experiences to understand the impact teachers had on our level of achievement—for better or for worse. Although we support the school and teachers, we also believe we must be our sons' strongest advocates. **When we are concerned about one of the boys, whether for academic or nonacademic reasons, we meet with the teacher or appropriate person to discuss our concerns.** We are amazed at how many parents, due to fear of retaliation, feelings of intimidation, or the inconvenience, won't address a child's problem at the school. If we want change to occur, we must act.

We establish a positive relationship with the school and faculty, reinforcing our belief that the educational process is a partnership between the school and parents. **Teachers and parents must exhibit mutual respect and mutual cooperation in their efforts to educate our children.** (Parents should not criticize teachers in front of their children—negative comments affect the student's attitude toward the teacher and his or her authority.) A clear understanding of expectations improves the relationship between students, parents, and the school. At our sons' high school, expectations are spelled out "loud and clear." When a student wants to enroll in an advanced course, for example, he signs a contract with the teacher accepting the responsibilities outlined for the course. Parents and students acknowledge and adopt the school's discipline code upon acceptance into the school. The discipline and academic standards and consequences for noncompliance are well defined.

Children Will Rise to Our Level of Expectation

(Cathy): *I am very opinionated when it comes to education. My years of teaching have provided insight into the time-consuming, emotionally and physically demanding job of an educator—even in the best of schools. Were my years as a teacher rewarding? Yes, but they were challenging and demanding, too. Now as a parent, I want the best education possible for our sons. Because I've stood on both sides of the classroom door, I feel my expectations are realistic. Both Joe and I want our sons in an educational environment that respects their individuality and encourages them to reach their full potential. We want a school that fosters a love of learning by providing a challenging and stimulating curriculum. We want our sons in a school where respect for oneself and others is integrated into the daily experience. And we want our sons to grow in their love and appreciation of God. We don't think that's too much to ask of every school in our country—whether in the most affluent or the poorest section of town. I believe schools and parents have set educational standards and expectations too low, and our children are paying the price. The "can't do it" attitude dominates society's thinking—and we wonder why our children are not achieving.*

We rewatched the movie *Stand and Deliver* to confirm a belief championed by Jaime Escalante, the teacher in the movie: "Our students will rise to the level of expectations in your *molino* (mill)." The movie is based on the true story of teacher Jaime Escalante and the success of his math students in a predominately Hispanic high school in Los Angeles. In record numbers, his advanced calculus students passed the rigorous Advanced Placement Calculus exam. Mr. Escalante, in spite of the negative attitudes of the system, instilled *ganas*—desire—in his students. He told them they already had two strikes against them: People assumed they knew less because of their names and because of their complexions. He proved to the students that people were wrong. With hard work and perseverance, they too could succeed in society. But Mr. Escalante taught his students more than the rigors of advanced calculus. **His students learned self-respect and self-discipline—tools necessary for success.** Other educators at the school blamed lack of resources and the economic backgrounds of the students for the inability to effect change. Mr. Escalante raised his level of expectations and then assiduously worked with his students to help them attain their goals.

Mr. Escalante is not alone in his accomplishments. A similar story of success happened in Houston. Principal Thaddeus Lott would not accept the premise that his students at Wesley Elementary could not achieve at the same level as those students in the more affluent areas of Houston. When his students' standardized tests returned with exceptionally high scores, Mr. Lott and his teachers were accused of cheating. Even the school district's administrators found it hard to believe students from this economic and cultural background could score in the 90th percentile. **Yet because of Mr. Lott's vision, strong leadership, and high level of expectations, and the perseverance of the teachers and parents, the students excelled.**

Another school success story ran in the May 12, 1996, edition of the *Houston Chronicle*. **Principal Velda Correa of Weslaco, Texas, said she determined what the families of the school needed and how to address those needs:** "We have to get past what other people see as barriers and develop these children as whole people." The school children were described as being from "the most disadvantaged families in one of the poorest school districts in the state." However, in spite of dysfunctional families, language differences, and low economic status, two-thirds of the students passed the Texas Assessment of Academic Skills; and the school won an award for 97 percent attendance.

The Teachers' Responsibility to Be Role Models

What impresses us most about these success stories is that each involves one person's determination to overcome the barriers hindering the students' achievement level. Someone who *believed* in young people gave them the opportunity to reach their goals. Our own experiences reinforce the importance of the school and home working together—sharing in the commitment to excellence in education. **Our positive attitude and high expectations coupled with similar tenets by our sons' teachers has produced gratifying results.** We appreciate Coach Banas's confidence in and words of encouragement to Joe Pat, Ms. Stanford's understanding of Tommy's apprehension of new experiences, and Mrs. Gomez's gentle words of praise and love to Jamie, encouraging his participation in class. We're delighted that Tony was challenged and inspired by Coach LaRochelle; that David was stretched to successfully lead the Freshman Retreat by Mr. Roman, Fr. Dooley, and Ms. Riojas; and that Chris was motivated to excellence by Mrs. Jamerlan and Fr. Leininger. We thank Ms. Hutchinson for motivating Mark, the entire St. Francis de Sales middle school staff for their confidence in and affirmation of Matthew's goals,

Mrs. "Golden" Holden for enriching Danny's preschool days, and for the smiles and cuddles offered Timmy by Mrs. Burks. We appreciate the efforts of the boys' teachers (and all those not mentioned by name) to reinforce the values we've established at home while treating them as individuals and stretching them to *think* and *mature.*

A teacher's positive or negative attitude and realistic or unrealistic expectations influence children's perceptions of their ability to achieve. Joe Pat returned home his first day of first grade devastated by his inability to write his name using a new handwriting technique introduced into the curriculum. "I can't do anything right in first grade. I can't even write my name," he said tearfully. Joe Pat had been writing his name since preschool, but when he couldn't satisfactorily write the new squiggly letters, he felt like a failure. In our opinion, the new handwriting method should have been introduced in a more positive manner. **When a teacher's techniques have a negative impact on our children, we determine how we can counter the effects.** We may meet with the teacher to share our feelings, or work with our son to help him cope with the situation. Our main objective is always to help our sons achieve to their fullest potential.

When one of the boys doesn't complete an assignment or study adequately for a test, he faces the consequences—we don't blame the teacher for our son's poor performance. It's very important to distinguish between your child not fulfilling his or her responsibilities and the teacher "picking on" the child. We are supportive of the teachers' efforts; and the teachers *know* if they have a concern they can call us. A teacher fights an uphill battle when a child knows his parents will defend inappropriate behavior and inadequate schoolwork. Lack of respect in the classroom for teachers and fellow classmates disrupts the learning process for everyone.

Our biggest educational concern (gripe!) is with teachers who lack a love of learning and don't inspire, motivate, and challenge our kids. Leo Buscaglia in his book *Living, Loving and Learning* addresses teachers, "If you don't get excited every morning about getting into that room with all those little kids with their bright eyes waiting for you to help them to get to that table, then *get the hell out of education!"* Ditto, ditto, ditto! We can't understand why ineffective, uncaring teachers are allowed to remain in the classroom or why they'd want to stay when they're obviously bored. The school's primary responsibility is to the children and their total development—not to protect or maintain the status quo.

A poem from the book *The Power of Positive Students* by Dr. William Mitchell with Dr. Charles Paul Conn exemplifies the importance of the home/school relationship:

I dreamed I stood in a studio
And watched two sculptors there.
The clay they used was a young child's mind
And they fashioned it with care.

One was a teacher—the tools she used
Were book, music, and art.
The other, a parent, worked with a guiding hand
And a gentle, loving heart.

Day after day, the teacher toiled with touch
That was careful, deft, and sure.
While the parent labored by his side
And polished and smoothed it o'er.

And when at last their work was done
They were proud of what they had wrought.
For the things they had molded into the child
Could neither be sold nor bought.

And each agreed they would have failed
If each had worked alone.
For behind the parent stood the school
And behind the teacher, the home.

—*Author unknown*

Providing Supplemental Programs to Enrich Children's Education

In addition to providing our sons with a strong formal education, we supplement their schooling with enrichment opportunities. We look for programs that will enrich and enhance their natural abilities and talents. We are very fortunate in the Houston area to have available many educational programs for children at the art, science, and children's museums, in addition to our city's recreational programs. One summer Joe Pat and Matthew participated in a Space Camp, taking advantage of our proximity to NASA. Mark, Tommy, and Danny took art classes another summer. The boys enroll in sports-related camps to develop their athletic abilities. When they complete sixth grade, all our sons attend the Rice University Summer School for Middle and High School Students, where for six weeks during the summer, they enroll in three enrichment courses of their choice. They can choose from a hundred classes (on both traditional and offbeat topics), many not available in a regular school curriculum. The topics include Science—Having Fun with Chemistry; Social Studies—Too Hot to Handle: Controversial Foreign Policy Issues since 1945; Math—Geometry: The Great Shape Shake-up; and English—Crime and Punishment: Defining Justice Through Literature. Often the social studies courses correspond to a historical anniversary: Kennedy's assassination, the Vietnam War and life in the '60s, or the Holocaust. There are no grades or credit for the courses; teachers provide a narrative evaluation of the student's progress. The boys have found the experience extremely rewarding, especially when they can utilize and apply the information they've learned. The summer prior to the October 1989 San Francisco earthquake, Tony and David took a geology course. The anniversary year of Martin Luther King's death Chris, Joe Pat, and Matthew participated in a civil rights class. As parents we are excited about the program because the boys enjoy their courses and teachers—reinforcing our belief that learning is fun.

Learning from Our Mistakes

Children, like adults, learn from their mistakes. If we expect perfection from our children, they will fear failing. We want our sons to understand that making mistakes can be a positive experience. When Danny takes a practice spelling test at home and misses a word, he rewrites the word three times. He rarely misses the same word on the test at school. If Mark misses a question on a science quiz, he'll usually answer it correctly on the test. Trial and error techniques solve many problems, whether it's schoolwork, working on the computer, or repairing a car. Our children benefit from falling down and figuring out ways to pick themselves back up. We can't always be there to solve their problems, so it's important to learn "survival" techniques.

Learning: A Lifelong Process

We have encouraged all our sons to continue their education after high school. We tell them that if they work hard, doors will open for them. Both Tony and David were rewarded for their efforts by receiving partial scholarships to Saint Louis University and Creighton University, respectively. With Tony and David in college, we can look back and feel confident that we provided the boys with the best education possible, both at home and school. We invested many, many hours in their education—an investment that has earned tremendous returns. Is it worth the time? Of course it is; and we enjoyed being involved in the process.

By our example we continue to show the boys that learning is an ongoing, rewarding process. They observe us reading newspapers, magazines, and books. Joe enrolls in medical continuing education courses and reads medical journals to keep abreast of new information. Although Cathy doesn't presently teach, she continues to read educational journals and maintains membership in Kappa Delta Pi, an International Honor Society in Education. We take advantage of local seminars and classes; Cathy studied Spanish (noncredit courses) at the community college. We undertake new challenges (for example, writing this book) and continue to develop our interests and talents.

We read an interesting article, *Your Child's Brain*, in the February 19, 1996, issue of *Newsweek*. **The article confirmed our belief and experience that early learning is crucial in physical, intellectual, and emotional development.** In fact, the article offers such valuable information on the importance of childhood stimulation, we wish it were required reading for all new parents. The author, Sharon Begley, explains that "when a baby comes into the world her brain is a jumble of neurons, all waiting to be woven into the intricate tapestry of the mind." "It is the experiences of childhood, determining which neurons are used, that wire the circuits of the brain"—for math and music, language, and emotion. If the neurons in the brain aren't used by a particular age, they die. We must provide our children stimulation during these "windows of opportunity." For the "logical" brain, the window of opportunity is from birth to four years. The "language" brain has a window of opportunity from birth to ten years, and the "musical" brain has a window from three to ten years. Studies show listening to music actually strengthens the circuits used for math and logic. Isn't it amazing that all the music Cathy plays during the day improves the mathematical, logical, and musical abilities of the boys.

At the beginning of the chapter, we said instilling the love of learning is one of the most enjoyable aspects of parenting. For two decades we've had fun playing and interacting with our sons. All the stimulation has reaped countless benefits. Our sons have developed their individual talents and interests while gaining an appreciation and respect for the gift of knowledge. Our simple piece of advice—talk, laugh, sing, hug, play, and read with your children. Your children will learn—and they will love it!

Chapter 8

Faith and Family

Y ou have been told, O man, what is good, and what the
Lord requires of you: only to do right and to love goodness, and to walk humbly with your God.
                                                        –Micah 6:8

Spirituality imparts different meanings to different people. Every religion has its unique beliefs and practices. We accept and respect the fact
that our beliefs, our religious practices, and the value we place on spirituality may differ from that of other families. Whatever the tenets of your
faith, we encourage you to embrace and practice them so your children
will understand their importance. We find that our faith is an invaluable
source of strength, inspiration, and guidance in our parenting effort.

The Influence of God in Our Lives

Chapter 9 in this book is titled "Getting By with a Lot of Help from Our
Friends." And we sincerely do get by with a lot of help from our friends,
but we mostly get by with a lot of help from our God. Of all the gifts our

parents shared with us, the greatest and most valuable was their faith. Their belief in God and trust in His divine wisdom and love provided us with the foundation of our own lives. We make no bones about the influence of God the Father, God the Son, and God the Holy Spirit in our lives today—as individuals, as a married couple, and as a family. Our dependence on God and our religion is a liberating element in our lives, not the binding, restrictive experience often portrayed in our society today.

We find that happiness is a result of our faith and religious practices. And we do believe God wants us to be happy in *this* world as well as in the next. If we believe God is a God of love, then it follows that He intends us to be happy. As parents we love our sons *and* we want them to be happy. That doesn't mean we let them have or do anything they desire, but we do work hard to provide them with everything they need. We believe God, our Father, is no different. He provides guidelines for us to follow that strengthen us in our daily efforts and prepare us for life everlasting. He bestows on us our unique talents, and then we're responsible for using them to love and serve Him. He gives us a free will to choose whether to accept or reject His teachings.

People waste a lot of energy chasing the wrong dreams—power, money, fame—in the pursuit of happiness. But happiness is not attained through material possessions—that's become obvious in our world, where materialism dominates our lives and still unhappiness abounds. **Our happiness is realized when we love and feel at peace with ourselves and with God, our family, and our friends.**

John Powell, S.J., in *Happiness Is an Inside Job,* tells us it's God's will for us to be happy and enjoy life, but the responsibility for achieving that happiness falls on us as individuals. In his book, Father Powell shares a sign he posts on his mirror: "You are looking at the face of the person who is responsible for your happiness." He explains that happiness is "a by-product to loving." Basically, the more love we give and receive, the happier we are. **Thus the lesson to be learned is that to be happy you must love!**

Spending Time Developing a Relationship with God

Our relationship with God, like the other relationships in our lives, demands time and attention to develop and flourish. Our understanding of God and the role He plays in our lives evolves, grows, and matures over the years, from the time we're small children throughout our adult lives—*if* we foster the relationship and choose to follow His teachings. **Just as a marriage relationship grows stagnant with lack of time, love, and attention, our relationship with God won't strengthen and grow if we don't choose to take advantage of opportunities to develop our faith.**

(Cathy): *As a young child, my first image of God was from the Bible stories I heard from both the Old and New Testaments. I believed God was loving and just because my Dad and Mom were loving and just. (Our first impressions of God usually stem from our experiences with our own parents.) I associated their love with God's love. My parents' love and trust in God, exemplified by how they lived their lives and treated my sisters and me, influenced my spiritual development.*

*When I began formal religious education, my understanding of God and the Catholic faith that my parents practiced took on a more personal, deeper meaning. Jesus became an important part of my day. I was taught that Jesus was my friend and there to help me if I asked. Prayer was the vehicle for communicating with Him. But my prayers were formal, rote prayers, not true conversations with a friend. During my teenage years, my sister Linda gave me a book for my birthday—*Prayers *by Michel Quoist. The prayers in the book are based on everyday subjects, milestones, and experiences—friends, young love, death, loneliness, sin, fear, use of time, and so forth. The prayers are conversations with God that use simple expressions and everyday words. Guided by the prayers in the book, I began to pray in a whole new fashion. I felt like I was talking to a friend instead of a faraway entity that was indirectly involved in my life.*

One prayer in the book that helped me during a difficult time was "Lord, Why Did You Ask Me To Love?" For two years during college, I was a resident assistant for forty girls in the dorm. They came to me for advice, support, encouragement, and, many times, out of the simple need for a friend. The demands and sometimes the needs of these girls for my time, love, and attention were frightening, and, to use Abbe Quoist's words, "consuming me." I felt like "I didn't belong to myself anymore." The prayer, "Lord, Why Did You Ask Me to Love?" ends with the reassuring words, "Don't worry, God says, you have gained all, while men came in to you, I, your Father, I, your God, slipped in among them." I understood that the giving of myself to others was a giving of myself to God. **Sharing my fears, joys, hopes, and worries during my conversations with God brought a sense of peace to my days.** My sister's inscription at the front of the book reads, "Cathy, chats with God are so peaceful and fulfilling." So, so true!

Once I learned to converse with God as if He were sitting next to me holding my hands, my prayer life blossomed. Prayer was no longer relegated to a specific time of day; prayer was incorporated into my daily activities. I still set aside quiet time to pray, but the problem of "time" to pray was no longer a limiting factor or an excuse not to pray. I pray washing the clothes, making beds, cleaning the bathrooms, and driving the car pool. **Although I continue to say my favorite traditional prayers, most of my prayers during the day aren't fancy or formal, but simple words of praise, thanks, or appeal.** I praise God for the beauty of the sea and the wonders of His power while walking along the beach in Galveston. I think of Joe or the boys and thank God for the gift of them in my life and the happiness they provide. I ask God to help me be strong when the hassles of the day seem overwhelming or to protect the boys when they're out driving. In some ways, my thoughts become my prayers; I think of someone or something and say a prayer.

Being Inspired by the Example of Others

(Cathy): As a child, I loved to hear the stories about the saints. They seemed so lucky to be holy and gifted by God. Yet, over the years, I grew to understand that they were real people with real problems and imperfections just like me. What made them stand out was their extraordinary love of God exemplified through their daily attitude, approach, choices, and love of others. They didn't necessarily do one specific thing that made them *a saint;* **it was their way of life that distinguished them.** *When I read the lives of the saints, I realize how diverse they are; no two share the same talents or personalities. In* 365 Saints: Your Daily Guide to the Wisdom and Wonder of Their Lives, *Woodeene Koenig-Bricker provides a daily insight into the life of a saint and how* **we can strengthen our own lives by their example.** *I enjoy reading the simple one-page stories and find her words of wisdom inspiring and uplifting. On St. William of Eskilsoe's feast day, for example, she says, "Mornings provide us with a clean slate. No matter what we did—or didn't do—the day before, the sunrise marks a new beginning. Each one of us gets to start life anew every morning."*

Anne Gordon's A Book of Saints *serves as a reminder that the saints share with me many of the same concerns and imperfections.* **They weren't exempt from pain and suffering; they accepted their tribulations and asked how they could use the experiences to strengthen their faith.** *Instead of feeling helpless or hopeless, I feel encouraged and motivated to emulate their lives, even though many of them lived centuries ago. I empathize, for example, with the sufferings of Saint Elizabeth Seton. Her husband died of tuberculosis at a young age, leaving her with five young children. A few years later, two of her daughters died of the same disease. Gordon tells us that Saint Elizabeth "saw no sense in asking, 'Why, God?' only in asking 'How can I grow from this?'" How wonderful to have that much faith and the courage to carry on!*

Reading the lives of the saints makes me aware of how much the saints were influenced by other saints that came before them, and how our living saints of today, Mother Teresa and Pope John Paul II, are inspiring the saints of tomorrow. At St. Francis de Sales School, Mrs. Wooten, the eighth-grade religion teacher, attempted to convey the same message as Koenig-Bricker and Gordon: The saints were ordinary people living exceptional and loving lives. She asked her students to think about people in the world today who were living saints—individuals living lives of love. Mother Teresa was mentioned, as were many other religious and public figures. Then one student blurted out the name of a classmate she felt exemplified the characteristics of a saint. When Mrs. Wooten asked why she had chosen this particular student, she answered, "My friend is gentle, kind, and patient with everyone." Her classmates agreed. They also started naming people closer to home who live their faith. Mrs. Wooten was pleased with her students' understanding **that being a saint doesn't take an extraordinary act—it simply takes living a life of love.** We each have the potential to achieve that status. Our life story may not be told in a book about saints, but we'll be on God's list of saints. And isn't that, after all, where it counts?

My perfect example of a saint living a life of love is Mary, the Mother of God. She plays an integral role in my life today because, as a mother, I know she understands my concerns and listens to my heartfelt requests for guidance and encouragement. I admire her acceptance of God's will and her devotion to her son, Jesus. **And I strive to emulate her maternal example of love, faith, and devotion.** Mary became a source of inner strength when I matured in my understanding that she was my mother, too—a gift to me from Jesus, her son, on the day he died. Jesus entrusted Mary to us and us to her—mother to child and child to mother. The Rosary I had recited since I was a child was no longer simply a repetition of prayers; it had become a meaningful meditation on the mysteries of my faith.

Growing in Spirituality

(Cathy): *My understanding of my faith, whether through prayer, Mary, or the saints, would never have developed and matured if I had curtailed my religious education at the elementary school level.* **Only by taking advantage of opportunities placed before me has my faith strengthened.**

My Dad was in the Navy, so we moved every couple of years. I attended both public and Catholic schools, depending on which was available. I began high school at Bishop Kenny High School in Jacksonville, Florida, and finished my last three years at W. T. Woodson High School in Fairfax, Virginia. The education I received at Woodson High School was excellent, but I missed the active integration of religion into my day. When the time came to choose a college, I knew I wanted to attend a Catholic university. My decision to attend Loyola University was one of the best decisions I've made—outside of marrying Joe and having the boys.

At Loyola University, I was required to take four courses each of philosophy and theology. Twenty-four credit hours seemed excessive at the time, but of all the courses I took in college, the theology and philosophy courses offered me more personal long-term benefits than all my other courses combined. **I developed my conscience and learned to think for myself—really think—about my purpose in life, religious beliefs, teachings, and practices (many that I had just accepted from my parents and teachers), and about the integration of God in my life.** Courses like "Man's Search for Meaning," "Death and Dying," "The Humanity and Divinity of Christ," and "Medical Ethics" provided a new insight into myself and my faith.

I appreciated the availability of priests, professors, and friends (both inside and outside of class) to share ideas and ask questions. My friend Debbie and I spent countless hours discussing and sharing our ideas and feelings on philosophical and theological topics. Sometimes these topics related to a specific course, but more often they concerned our own personal experiences. I learned a lot about myself and conceptualized many of my beliefs from these discussions. Although we live in different cities today, I relish the times Debbie and I get together and share our deeper thoughts, feelings, and daily challenges.

My spiritual growth spurted during my college years. Every decision and choice I made was preceded by prayer—including my decision of where I would student teach and my decision to marry Joe. **Prayer still remains at the forefront of my decisions and choices.**

Making Decisions Based on Conscience

(Cathy): *Praying and listening to my conscience enables me to feel at peace with my choices. St. Augustine tells us to* **"return to your conscience, question it . . ."** *My theological and philosophical background, as limited as it is, enables me to return to my conscience when I have a decision to make.*

As Joe and I prepared for our wedding, the issue of birth control confronted us. Socially accepted practices were not accepted by our religion.

(The Catholic Church teaches that it is morally unacceptable to use artificial contraceptives for birth control.) Father Kenneth Buddendorf, S.J., the priest who married us, recommended we read the encyclical letter of Pope Paul VI, Humanae Vitae (Of Human Life), *before we made our decision. Only in reading and understanding the church's teaching could we make a responsible, conscientious decision. "Listen to your conscience, and follow it," he told us. We read it, discussed it, and made a decision that was morally right for us.*

We make the same recommendation to the engaged couples we meet with during the marriage preparation program. We don't tell them what to do, but instead recommend they listen to their conscience and follow it.

Many people today accept whatever society deems appropriate without taking time to consider the moral and ethical repercussions of their decisions. **We teach our sons that just because everyone's doing something doesn't make it right.** Their primary concern should be whether the action is pleasing or displeasing to God. Life is a series of choices—right and wrong, good and bad. **We advise them to pray and "return to your conscience" before making a decision.**

Our relationship with God helps us focus on what we believe *He* wants us to do with our lives. We pray for His guidance when making decisions, whether for ourselves or regarding our sons. One evening at dinner, our friend Father Thomas Donovan jokingly said to us, "Do you know how to make God laugh? Tell Him *your* plans for the future!" We probably all wish God would write down exactly what He wants each of us to do so we could just do it—**but God's way entails an active participation on our part through prayer and acts of love to seek His will.**

When people criticize us for having more than the two or three socially accepted number of children or believe our children are the results of ineffective natural family planning, the comments don't bother us. We know in our hearts our children are not "mistakes" but rather gifts produced by our love and the fulfillment of God's plan for us. How do we know that? We prayed and were at peace with the answer to our prayers. We learned over the years, too, that just because we thought it was time for another child didn't mean God was ready for us to have one.

(Cathy): *When Matthew, our fifth child, was fifteen months old, we decided to have another child. After trying for a year, though, I still wasn't pregnant. Yet, I truly believed God wanted another child in our lives. When I sat in the perpetual adoration chapel my one hour a week, my prayers wandered to thoughts of another child. At first, I dismissed the thoughts, "I already have five children. Why would I have more?" But the thoughts kept returning. (I imagine the experience is similar to that of a man or woman who is called to enter the priesthood or religious life.) I came to realize, after much prayer, that Joe and I would be irresponsible to not have more children. If we truly understood the definition of a responsible parent, then our not having children was for selfish reasons, rather than because we couldn't handle them physically, emotionally, and financially.*

Finally, I worked up the courage to tell Joe about my experience and to ask him if we could have another child. After a couple of weeks and a second request, Joe answered me by saying, "Cathy, you've never asked me for anything. If you feel we should have another child, of course, it's okay."

It wasn't that simple, though. Month after month, I still wasn't pregnant. I was confused and wondered if I had misunderstood what I thought God was telling me. (Only two other people knew we were trying to conceive: my obstetrician and Mary, a friend who taught natural family planning. Most people thought we were crazy to have five children. And we didn't want to deal with their comments at this point.) My disappointment each month was mixed with feelings of guilt; I knew many childless couples who were trying to conceive. Here I was with five wonderful children. Was I being selfish?

After a year, I was pregnant with Mark. The entire experience taught me many things. First, I was reminded God works according to His plans, not ours. During the eighteen months before Mark was born, Joe and I opened our home to foster children. God had set this priority for us at the time. Second, I no longer took my fertility for granted, but for the first time truly believed it was a gift from God. Third, I was able to empathize with women who have infertility problems in a way I never could before. Every time I hear of someone experiencing difficulty trying to conceive, the feelings of disappointment, sadness, and guilt return. My heart goes out to them! The experience also taught me to accept the joys and sorrows introduced into my life and to appreciate even more the importance of love, support, and encouragement from friends.

Seeing God in the Faces of Others

(Joe): *I grew up in an Hispanic, Catholic home where my parents gave God a central place in the life of our family. Likewise, my parents sacrificed to send my brother, sister, and me to Catholic elementary school and high school in El Paso. They believed the quality of education was high, but, more important, that we would be in an environment that supported our religious beliefs. I'm convinced my Jesuit education in high school and college were pivotal in the formation of my concept of God and how I should embrace Him in my life. My experiences brought me to the conclusion and the strong conviction that God was not solely a Sunday/church god.* **The Creator who made this universe is in all individuals. So I see Him and deal with Him in the people at work, the people at the store or repair shop, and in the members of my family.**

I realized the importance of the Ten Commandments and the teachings of the church, which I learned from the "Baltimore Catechism." However, from my theology teachers in high school and college, I learned that we see God in all *that He created, especially our fellow men and women. The teachers themselves lived what they taught us by the kindness and respect they showed to their students and others.*

In medical school, I decided how to approach my life with God. I acknowledged that God was in each patient, in their loved ones, and in the nurses and physicians I worked with, and that I should treat them with respect and kindness. Although I assented to this integration of God into what I did each day, it was only a very small step in the development of understanding what His love means to me. My marriage to Cathy and my love for her furthered the depth of this understanding. *God compares His love for us with the love of a husband for his wife; my love for Cathy brings this example to an intelligible level. As Cathy and I became parents, God's love, sacrifice, and protection took on a deeper meaning because of our love for the boys.*

God is in each of us, and it is this admission that makes our respect and love of each other a living example of what He would do if He were here on earth. *Our family should reflect this understanding as well. This means that all of the boys treat each other with the respect and love that they receive from their father and mother and from their God. This is how they will know that God is a "practical" God and that He lives in each of them and their brothers, as well as in all the people they encounter.* **It's scary and humbling to think that the knowledge and love of God that our children embrace begins with the love and respect we demonstrate to our spouses and those around us.**

Integrating Faith into Daily Life

How we live and love is the best example to our children and others of the importance we place on God's love in our lives. We don't think you can separate who you are and what you do from your religious beliefs and practices. **For religion and spirituality to have meaning, they must be integrated into our thoughts, words, and actions.** "What good is it to profess faith without practicing it?" (James 1:14).

How can we say we love God and then turn around and treat our spouses with disrespect? How can we teach our children that God is a God of love and then not find time to spend with our children to show we care about them? How do we teach that God is forgiving of our sins if we hold a grudge or won't forgive a wrongdoing? How do we show our children that God is first in our life if we're primarily focused on materialism? Do we attend church services once a week where we publicly praise God and then leave Him behind at the church door the rest of the week? Do we attend religious services at all? Do we take time out of the day to pray as a family?

We make God an integral part of our home. Crucifixes and religious statues are exhibited around the house. But the statues and crucifixes mean nothing if they don't remind us of God's love and our responsibility to be good people and live by God's commandments.

We grew up hearing, "The family that prays together stays together." **We don't underestimate the power of praying together as a family.** Our meals begin with a prayer of thanksgiving for the blessings on our table and in our lives. We then add individual prayer requests that vary from day to day: We pray for Tony and David away at college, for a family member or friend who has died or is recovering from an illness, for safe soccer games, for guidance on this book, for the homeless or hungry people in our community, for vocations, and for peace in our home and world.

Every evening before the younger boys go to bed, we gather as a family and pray. The boys take time out from whatever they're doing—studying, reading, or talking on the phone—so we can pray as a family. We started evening prayers when Tony and David were little; we continue to find that saying prayers together unifies and strengthens us as a family. If we or the boys have friends visiting, they are invited to share this special time with us. We took the value of family prayer time for granted until friends shared with us the impact the gathering of our family to pray had on their children. One mother told us our family prayer time had renewed her eighteen-year-old daughter's enthusiasm for her own faith, deepening her understanding of the importance and value of family prayer. Gathering to say prayers as a family consumes about fifteen minutes of our evening—worthwhile time reserved for God in the course of our family's day.

Praying is done everywhere, not just in the confines of our home or church. When we travel in the car, especially for a long trip, we ask God for a safe and enjoyable trip to our destination; and we thank Him when we arrive. If we witness an accident or hear an ambulance, we pray that the individuals involved will be okay. Even when we eat out, we say a prayer of thanksgiving. One night in between soccer games, we stopped at a fast-food restaurant for a quick meal. Even before we had our food, Timmy vehemently insisted we say prayers.

The younger boys learn the traditional prayers of our Catholic faith by saying the prayers every day. When Cathy taught preschool religious education, she asked parents to begin teaching their children certain prayers by reciting them daily—children learn through repetition. One parent questioned the need to learn the prayers at that age, saying the words of the prayers mean nothing to little kids. Cathy used the analogy of learning the alphabet to explain her reasoning behind reciting prayers with young children. Learning the ABC's is important for reading readiness; we can't read if we don't know the alphabet. Most parents teach their children to sing the alphabet song long before they learn to read. Similarly, if children know the words to the "Our Father," they will gradually understand their meaning. At home, we incorporate formal prayers with informal prayers, so the boys understand there are different ways of talking to God. **Whether they say traditional prayers or prayers from their hearts, it is essential that parents take time to demonstrate to their children the importance of prayer—talking to God.**

The Value of Church Involvement

Another expression of our love of God is attendance at weekly church services. Although God's third commandment is "Remember to make holy the Lord's day," we attend Mass on Sunday because the experience enriches our lives as individuals and as a family. Rising early on a Sunday morning and getting dressed and to church on time concretely demonstrates to our children the priority of God in our life. We'd like a morning to sleep in, too, or catch up on much needed housework or paperwork; but if we feel God is important in our lives, we must set the example and go to church. **We teach our sons that we take time out of the week to thank God for His many blessings and to ask for His guidance in the week ahead.** Although people argue they can pray outside of a church, in our faith, Catholicism, we can't experience the unique gift of the Body and Blood of Christ except through the Sacrifice of the Mass.

At a First Communion preparation class, Pat Kerwin, the presenter, asked the parents to raise their hands if they attended church every week. Less than one third of the parents raised their hands. Mrs. Kerwin addressed the parents who didn't regularly attend Mass: "Why then do you want your children to receive the sacrament of the Holy Eucharist?" She explained that it was hypocritical to have their children receive the sacrament of the Holy Eucharist and then not provide them with the opportunity to receive the Body and Blood of Christ on a regular basis. "The Eucharist," she said, "is our complete act of faith. It impels us to go out and love just as Jesus has loved us. The Eucharist nourishes and strengthens us and gives us everything we need to be the presence of God in the world." **Children grow confused by the mixed messages:** If the Eucharist is a source of strength, and frequent reception of the Body and Blood of Christ will help me be a better person, why don't my parents take me to church every Sunday? **It is through embracing and actively practicing the tenets of your faith that their importance will be understood by your children.**

Encouraging Our Sons to Share Their Time, Talents, and Treasures

Prayer and attendance at church aren't sufficient examples for children to learn the importance of God in their lives. Love and service to others, at home and in the community, exemplifies the teachings professed by our religion. We encourage the boys to use their God-given talents to help others, to make a positive difference in other people's lives. The boys' schools provide opportunities for them to share their time, treasures, and talents. **We remind the boys that God expects those who have been given much to return much, whether it be their time, talents, or treasures.** We also remind them that God prefers a happy giver. We want our sons to give from their hearts, not because it looks good.

Our sons may serve at Mass on Sundays or at weddings or funerals, assist in the church soup kitchen prior to Holy Thursday services, attend a retreat, or clean up after the bazaar. The older boys reach out through community projects, helping those less fortunate.

We show our sons little ways to make a big difference: a bouquet of flowers for a sick neighbor, a card to show you're thinking of someone, a kind word to someone who's hurting, including a person in an activity so they won't feel left out. The simple acts of kindness show God we love others and remind us of Jesus's words, "I assure you, as often as you did it for one of my least brothers, you did it for me" (Matthew 25:40).

All our sons participate in the high school Freshman Retreat program. The retreat experience impacts their lives as freshmen and again as they accept leadership roles in later years. All mottoes or themes for the retreats emphasize the fulfillment of God's command to "Love one another as I have loved you": Seize the day, live God's way; Look out to see within; To be friends is to see God in brothers. Be simple men, be men for others. Our sons' continued involvement in the retreats strengthens and enriches the spiritual dimension of their lives, reinforcing that spirituality is their first priority.

Through active involvement in our parish church and the community, we reap many blessings: We learn more about our faith, we strengthen our beliefs, and we're involved with people who share similar values and goals. There are many ministries and volunteer positions available to utilize different talents. **We are responsible for finding our niche and using our talents for the benefit of others.**

We also enjoy the social side of parish involvement, whether it be an education program, a country western dance, serving soft drinks at the annual bazaar, or painting the parish school. We value the opportunity to witness a diverse group of people sharing their talents for a common goal.

Different ministries fit into our lives at different stages and to different degrees. When the older boys were in preschool, Cathy taught and coordinated the preschool religious education program. For seven years she was actively involved in The Woman's Hospital Foundation. Joe continues his eight-year involvement with the Houston Chapter of the March of Dimes. We've worked with our diocesan marriage preparation program for fourteen years. In the first ten years, we met with four to five couples a year, but as our family commitments became more time consuming and demanding, we reduced our commitment to one couple during the summer. We anticipate increasing the number of couples again when time permits.

While our involvement benefits others, the rewards flow both ways. The marriage preparation ministry, for example, is extremely rewarding: We enjoy the time shared with couples as they begin their journey together, and we enrich and strengthen our marriage as we move from one of life's stages to the next. Also, it's satisfying to know that those March of Dimes programs that are designed to increase the number of healthy babies by providing pregnant women with prenatal care and education to prevent birth defects are actually succeeding.

Discovering Ways to Strengthen Your Spirituality

Most careers and areas of specialization require continuing education to strengthen and update skills. In today's fast-paced world of technology, we quickly fall behind if we don't take time to learn new skills or improve our understanding of new research findings and technology. Computers are an excellent example of the importance of learning to use new technology—almost every job requires some understanding of computers. **Our spirituality needs this same type of reinforcement through prayer, religious education programs, retreats, and spiritual reading.** Spiritual exercise, like physical exercise, invigorates the mind, body, and soul. We can't imagine facing the challenges of parenting or life itself without God's grace and love. Times can be hard with His help—and hopeless without. The time spent enriching our spiritual life is time well invested.

We established spirituality as a top priority in our lives, as individuals, as a couple, and as a family. **Because it's a priority, we find ways to strengthen our faith.** We can't always attend the adult education classes offered in our diocese, but we do find time to read the Bible and religious books, newspapers, and magazines in order to learn new concepts, reinforce our beliefs, and find encouragement in our daily lives. Reading a page from Woodeene Koenig-Bricker's *365 Saints* or a daily meditation from Pope John Paul's *Lift Up Your Hearts* takes a few minutes, yet motivates our minds and hearts. If what we're reading is inspiring, it creates a positive effect on our lives.

We visit the perpetual adoration chapel of a nearby parish as often as possible. When the boys were younger, we went on separate evenings. Now we're pleased to be able to go together as a couple. The one hour spent in quiet prayer or spiritual reading provides a sense of peace—a special intimacy with our Lord.

Educating our children in our faith provides additional opportunities to expand our understanding of its teachings and reinforce our beliefs. As parents we're responsible for the spiritual development of our children. We are the *first* educators of our children, and as in most other areas of their lives, they learn from our example. **If we don't practice our faith or understand our faith, how can we pass it on to our children?** We must fill in the gaps in the areas that are hazy and in the areas we don't understand or maybe never learned about. When we were in school, Bible study was not a priority; it is today. Our sons' biblical background is strong. Studying and reviewing with the boys strengthens our biblical knowledge. We work in cooperation with the religion teachers to prepare our sons for different faith developments and the reception of the sacraments. We read and utilize the information provided by the teacher as well as material we may find on our own to enhance our knowledge of the particular subject.

(Cathy): *I expanded and strengthened my understanding of the role of the Holy Spirit in my life while preparing Christopher, Joe Pat, and Matthew for the sacrament of Confirmation. My increased understanding of the Holy Spirit's influence allowed me to prepare them for Confirmation better than I had prepared Tony and David.*

At the time the boys were beginning their formal studies for Confirmation, I received the Winter 1995-96 edition of Windows, *a magazine published by Creighton University. (Our son David attends Creighton University.) I read an article titled "Finding God in Daily Life" by Professor of Theology, Richard J. Hauser, S.J. The article, and later his books* In the Spirit *and* Moving in the Spirit *pulled together in a concrete fashion my religious beliefs and their effect on my attitude and approach to life, especially regarding the influence of the Holy Spirit.*

Father Hauser encourages us to find God in daily life by "recognizing and responding to the movements of the Holy Spirit." We must learn to recognize the temptations for evil and the opportunities for good that confront us every day. God gives man a free will to choose between right and wrong. He doesn't force us to do good—the choice is ours. It's not only choosing to do good, though, that matters. Our "quality of heart" and our "desire to love" are essential. Our good deeds mean nothing to God unless they're performed with love. "If I give everything I have to feed the poor and hand over my body to be burned, but have not love, I gain nothing" (1 Corinthians 13:2-3).

*God expects us to live lives of love by putting our faith into action on a daily basis with everyone we encounter and in every experience. He didn't leave us to our own resources to accomplish that goal. We are sustained by the gifts of the Holy Spirit—wisdom, understanding, counsel, fortitude, knowledge, piety, and fear of the Lord. And the more we live in the Spirit, the more we experience the fruits of the Spirit: charity, joy, peace, patience, kindness, goodness, generosity, gentleness, faithfulness, modesty, self-control, and chastity. The "perfect" person lives a life encompassing all these fruits. **Our goal then is to strive to attain "perfection" by living a life of love.***

Basing Our Philosophy on Our Faith

Our religious beliefs and faith *are* our family philosophy. One is indistinguishable from the other. God's influence, His grace, permeates all aspects of our family—our marriage, our individual lives, and our role as parents. **God is the purpose for what we do and how we live.**

Our discipline is of God—we teach our sons that God gives us a free will to choose right from wrong. He is a merciful but just God. He holds us accountable for our choices—for what we do and for what we don't do.

The education of our sons is of God—we provide our sons opportunities to learn, develop, and use their God-given talents to love and serve Him.

Respect is of God—we teach our sons that God created everyone; therefore *all* people deserve to be treated with dignity as children of God. Respect begins at home. We must respect ourselves by fulfilling our physical, emotional, intellectual, and spiritual needs. Eating, drinking, and exercising appropriately and adequately, and not abusing food, alcohol, drugs, and sex, demonstrate respect for ourselves.

Our values are of God—we teach our sons to establish priorities with God being the number one priority. And we remind them that all things are possible with Him at our side.

Love is of God—we teach our sons to love God with their whole hearts, souls, and minds, and to follow His commandment to love ourselves and others.

Our home is filled with love and happiness because God is an integral part of the equation. We strive to stay focused on what we feel God wants us to do, individually and as a family. We don't have a magic formula; we live by Jesus's example. He taught us that He is the way, the truth, and the life. **It's up to us as parents to show the way, the truth, and the life to our children.** Our love, commitment, and respect for one another teaches our sons, more than anything else, of the love of God and the joys available to those who love Him.

Developing Support Systems: Getting By with a Lot of Help from Our Friends

A *faithful friend is beyond price; no sum can balance his worth.*

–Sirach 6:15

Lord, make me an instrument of your peace; where there is hatred, let me sow love; where there is injury, pardon; where there is doubt, faith; where there is despair, hope; where there is darkness, light; and where there is sadness, joy. O Divine Master, grant that I may not so much seek to be consoled, as to console; to be understood, as to understand; to be loved, as to love; for it is in giving that we receive; it is in pardoning that we are pardoned and it is in dying, that we are born to eternal life.

–St. Francis of Assisi

"No man is an island," wrote John Donne, and nowhere is that more true than in a family. We need each other to reach our potential as individuals and as a family. With each other's love and support, we attain our dreams and true happiness. Our extended families, and our circle of friends and acquaintances, enrich our lives even more. The welcome mat outside our back door reads, "Blessings come in many ways, but the nicest come as friends"—and family, of course!

We often read about the importance of developing support systems to provide emotional and physical help during difficult times. We've learned that support systems are important *all* the time—in good times and in bad. We all need support sometime in our lives. We're not ashamed to admit we can't do it alone; and we don't feel guilty about "imposing" on someone else. **When we need help, we ask for it; and when someone needs help, we provide it.** Asking for help isn't a sign of weakness; it's a belief that we're all in this world together and that if we help each other the struggles and stresses will be minimized and the joy increased. The saying "Friends double our joy and divide our grief" exemplifies our feelings for our friends and family. It's wonderful having family and friends who you know love and support you, as you do them.

Our Primary Support System: Each Other as a Couple

Throughout this book, we've expressed the important role our relationship plays in the success of our family—and our happiness. **We lift each other up when we're down, we empathize with each other's difficulties, we share in the responsibilities of our home and children, and we encourage each other in our endeavors.** There's no greater sense of security than knowing—deep-down knowing—your spouse is there for you in good times as well as bad, for richer or for poorer, in sickness and in health. After all, isn't that the essence of commitment?

(Cathy): *Joe's support of my role at home makes my parenting experience so much more rewarding. He understands and doesn't criticize me on days that don't go according to plan (and we have our share). He listens to my frustrations—the inability to generate change in one of the boys' schools—and my jubilations—my pride and excitement at Fr. Brian's invitation to be the first woman to speak at Strake Jesuit's annual fund drive dinner. Instead of complaining when dinner is late, he pitches in by making the salad or playing with the boys so I can finish cooking. It seems so simple, yet his actions tell me he appreciates what I do for him and the boys.*

Joe recognizes my need to be involved in activities outside the home. His support and encouragement of my time at the boys' schools and in the community allows me to enjoy the experiences. He accepts the extra responsibilities my involvement entails; he doesn't make me feel guilty or selfish.

Joe's also supportive of my feelings. Early in our relationship, he was baffled by my emotions and tears. He now asks, "Are they happy tears or sad tears?" He determines why I'm upset and angry, and doesn't assume he did something wrong. His thoughtful hugs tell me that he's there for me and that he cares. Actually, Joe's emotional support strengthens me more than all the physical help he provides.

Experiencing firsthand the value of Joe's support of my needs encourages me to be equally supportive of his needs. **Take the time to think of ways to be supportive of your spouse on a daily basis.** *Your support is another sign of your love.*

(Joe): *I cannot imagine taking on each new day without knowing and understanding that Catherine is there for me. During the rough years of my training, her support strengthened me. During a demanding Labor Day weekend soccer tournament (with five of the boys' teams competing), her support of my efforts to keep things organized and in perspective eased my mind. And, I guess, it's her unselfish support that makes things possible.* **That support and love provides the serenity that keeps me moving in the right direction during hectic times.**

A Circular Flow of Support Within Our Family

Support within our family flows from parents to children, from children to parents, and between siblings. Our parents taught us the importance of being there for family. The world is tough enough without going it alone. **We encourage and teach the boys to support each other as we do them, and in the process they've learned to be sensitive to our needs, too.**

Cathy appreciates the three o'clock phone call from one of the high school sons: "Mom, we don't have practice today. We'll pick up our brothers at St. Francis de Sales." They know it means Mom won't have to wake up one of their younger brothers from his nap. Or they walk in the door after school and can sense it's been a marathon day; they gather their little brothers together and go upstairs or outside to play. They even suggest Cathy take a break, go for a walk, or read for a few minutes while they watch their brothers. Cathy remembers the afternoon Chris came home to find her sitting in the overstuffed chair with his three youngest brothers wrapped around her—running fevers and miserable. "Mom, this is pitiful," he said leaning down for a kiss. Chris knew his brothers wouldn't leave their mom, but he took the initiative to help his other brothers get an after-school snack and start on their homework.

A couple of weeks after Jamie was born, parent-teacher conferences were scheduled at the boys' high school. We both wanted to attend the first conference; we like knowing who our sons are with during the day and their teachers' expectations. We worried, though, that the responsibility at home would be too much for Tony and David: getting their younger brothers to bed, taking care of three-week-old Jamie, and studying. When we suggested a baby-sitter, they told us they could handle the evening and not to worry. We attended the conferences and returned home to find a calm, serene house. Tony was propped up on the sofa reading while Jamie slept across his legs; David was upstairs studying; and everyone else was asleep. We were impressed—and touched.

Joe Pat put his culinary skills to work one evening when Cathy was tied up with two back-to-back soccer practices at fields thirty minutes away; Joe was on-call at the hospital. Joe Pat realized dinner would be very late if he waited for Mom to get home from the practices. He offered to prepare dinner. Cathy explained how to cook the chicken, and Joe Pat took over. Cathy returned home to a much appreciated, delicious meal.

Our family runs the soft drink booth during the two days of our parish bazaar. With a little one around most years, we need the help of the boys to make it a successful and enjoyable experience. The older boys take turns watching the younger brothers. At one bazaar, Tommy, eight years old, offered to walk Timmy, eighteen months old, around the grounds in the stroller. When he checked in with us an hour later, we expressed amazement that Timmy had been cooperative for that long. Tommy proudly explained his ingenious method, "I give Timmy one Tootsie Pop—only twenty-five cents. It lasts twenty minutes. Three pops—one hour!" We were impressed with his creative scheme.

Children can learn and appreciate the value of supporting each other, as long as their parents demonstrate their appreciation of this mutual support. (Children don't want to be taken for granted any more than we do as adults.)

The Boys' Love and Support of Each Other

The boys' support goes a long way toward making our family experience a joy—from their supportive actions toward us to their love and support of each other. We share *their* excitement over each new pregnancy and the thrill upon the birth of their brothers. They take pride in each other's accomplishments, whether major—Matthew's Principal's Award—or minor—Danny's two soccer goals in one game. They feel blessed to have each other.

Tommy's first-grade class was asked to draw a picture of their families. Mrs. Kearns, the art teacher, observed Tommy sitting pensively, not yet drawing. Thinking he was overwhelmed by the task of drawing twelve people, Mrs. Kearns suggested he just draw some of the family. A little later Mrs. Kearns noticed Tommy still wasn't drawing. "Tommy, are you okay?" she asked. Tommy sadly looked up at her and asked, "Mrs.

Kearns, *who* don't I draw?" She encouraged him to draw everyone and arranged for him to have extra time to complete a now treasured, framed drawing of the GP twelve. Chris, in third grade, caused quite a stir with one of his drawings. Mrs. Rapp's reading class was reading stories about wishes. She asked each student to illustrate one wish for a "wish book." Chris drew our family with an additional baby flying in the air—his wish was for another brother. The phone rang off the hook for several days with friends asking if we were expecting again. Cathy was confused until one parent told her about Chris's picture.

As our sons leave home to attend college, family emotional support is extremely important. Cards, letters, care packages, and the magic of e-mail bring everyone a little closer. There are times when Tony or David call and we sense they're down or lonely. It's rewarding when, after talking with them for just a few minutes, you feel their spirits lift. When they call, they want to talk to as many brothers as possible. Timmy's conversations are hysterical—he can't help but raise your spirits. We are pleased that Tony and David, in spite of their hectic schedules, keep in touch with each other and their other brothers over the course of the semester. The younger boys draw pictures or write letters to them, and in appreciation, Tony and David jot a quick note in return. Danny beamed when Tony wrote that he'd hung Danny's drawing on his bulletin board. Simple gestures of love and support.

The Support of Our Extended Families

Our extended families provide a tremendous source of support. Neither family lives in town, so our connections are primarily long distance. We enjoy calling and sharing our experiences with our parents, sisters, and brother, and relish the times we get together. Cathy's mom visits most often, since she flies in from Virginia every time Cathy delivers one of the boys. Her dad teases us, "You don't have to keep having babies for Mom to visit. She can visit any time." **With all the commitments and stresses in all of our lives, it's important to remain connected to families, whether they live in town or far away.**

(Cathy): *Besides the emotional support we receive from our families, we appreciate the times they lend a helping hand. My sister Paula lived in Houston during my pregnancy with Joe Pat. She was like a second mom to our sons. How they loved Aunt Paula! Paula was a nurse at the Texas Medical Center and often stopped by on her way home from work to give me a few minutes of rest or to help me prepare dinner, knowing how hard it was for me to look at food during my early months of pregnancy. Her sensitivity to my needs, emotionally and physically, was greatly appreciated.*

When I needed urgent eye surgery to repair a detached retina, I didn't hesitate to call my parents in Virginia to ask for help, even though I knew the inconvenience my mom being away would cause for my dad and sister. My mom was on a plane early the next morning to take care of Tony and David during the two weeks I stayed in the hospital. (Friends, especially Libby and Karen, provided additional help by watching the boys so my mom could spend time with me in the hospital.) Following surgery, the doctor advised me not to bend or lift for three months. Tony was fifteen months old and David three months old at the time of the surgery. There was no way I could care for them without bending or lifting. I flew with the boys to Virginia where my entire family pitched in during a very difficult time. My sisters even rotated their vacations to look after me, Tony, and David. Never was family more treasured!

Cathy's parents willingly take care of the boys so we can attend one of Joe's out-of-town medical meetings or just catch some R and R. We think they prefer to visit when we're away; they don't have us regulating the amount of "grandparent spoiling" being dispensed. From the beginning of our marriage, Cathy's parents encouraged us to have special time as a couple. We appreciated the "gift" of a dinner, especially after we had children, sent with the thoughtful note "Enjoy dinner on us. Wish we could be together." **It's the simple, nonmonetary gifts—their concern, encouragement, and kindnesses—that we treasure.** Most important, we value their undying love for our sons—who of course, unlike us, can do no wrong.

(Cathy): *My sisters, Linda, Patrice, Paula, and Michele, have always been my best friends. We may live a thousand miles apart, but we're near in heart and soul. I thank God for the creative talent of Alexander Bell that enables me to hear their voices and share the continuing chapters in our lives. Together we laugh and cry, and listen and encourage each other. Above all, we know that whenever the other needs us, we're always there—emotionally if not physically. Knowing how much I treasure my sisters, I'm thankful the boys have each other.*

Family members, especially parents, should distinguish between support and interference. We never cease our role as parents, but there comes a time when "parenting"—making our grown children's decisions, telling them what to do or expecting them to mirror our lives—is no longer appropriate.

The Treasure of Grandparents

As our family grew, it logistically became easier for the grandparents to visit Houston. **We encourage these visits and love to see their relationships with our sons flourish.** Papa Musco's trips to Shipley's Donuts are a welcomed treat. Grandma Musco's suitcase full of goodies make it Christmas whenever she comes. Grandma Garcia always brings a new game or two to enliven an already lively house. And Grandpa Garcia thoroughly enjoys talking with the boys about their latest adventures. The boys are blessed with special grandparent memories. Grandparents enrich children's lives and the unique grandparent-grandchild relationship helps young people appreciate the elderly, whether in their own families or in society.

David wrote an essay on grandparents in a seventh-grade creative writing class. He wrote: "When grandparents are near, there always seems to be excitement and joy. They are there when I need them. When my grandparents come to town, it's like rags to riches at our house. They spoil us, but I don't mind. My family seems closer together. They are the missing piece that makes our family one."

The Need for Friends

Our circle of friends is ever widening—a perk of having ten actively involved children. In our early years of marriage, our friendships revolved around people at work. When we began our family, our circle of friends expanded *and* changed. Before children we could make spontaneous plans; now we had to arrange for a baby-sitter. Our needs and focus differed from those of our friends with no children. We began organizing activities with families in similar circumstances, families who understood and shared our parenting experiences. There's so much you can learn from other people, and it's reassuring to know you're not the only one going through a particular stage—whether with a newborn, toddler, or a teenager.

(Cathy): *When Tony was born, most of my friends were the teachers I had worked with; they were still working and not available during the day. Our neighbors were mostly retired couples, so I often felt isolated. Gradually, I met other mothers who were also home with their children. I was grateful for the friendships of Libby and Carol; I had someone to ask all those "silly" parenting questions to. We arranged activities together during the days and helped each other out when one had a doctor's appointment or other commitment. In that first parenting year, their friendship and support kept me going. And, most important, **I learned to reach out for support and, at the same time, to be available to others when needed.***

*When we moved into our present neighborhood (we've lived here almost twenty years), there were other young families to interact with on a regular basis. Having other mothers to talk to and share my days with was a blessing—and my support system. Since my sisters and parents lived far away, I needed to develop a support system—friends—close to home. **I can't stress enough the importance of sharing your time and feelings with other parents.***

I made wonderful friends when the boys attended a neighborhood mothers-day-out program. I met moms through church activities, and *during the summer at our neighborhood pool. **I found activities for the** **boys in which other young children, and their moms, were involved.** One of my dearest friendships began on a rainy February morning at the Meyer Branch Library. Tony, three years old, David, two years old, and I went for story hour. After the story and art activity, we hopped into the car, but the engine wouldn't start. We rushed back into the library through the pouring rain to call Joe for advice. A mom approached, noticed I was flustered, and asked if she could help. I explained the problem, and she offered to take us home. She was actually glad my car had died; she wanted to meet this lady who had two sons her child's age. She had just moved into the neighborhood and hadn't met any children for her son to play with. Tony, David, and Ryan became a threesome. They played together for hours on end. My friendship with Alethea blossomed from that day on. The day she and her family moved to Fort Worth was a sad day for the Garcia-Prats.*

*More recently, a wonderful friendship developed thanks to a phone call. A mom, referred by another friend, called for advice regarding a school decision. She wasn't sure which kindergarten program was in her son's best interest. We talked about what she and her husband were looking for in a school and then I shared my experiences with the different programs. She stopped by a few weeks later to tell me her final decision and to thank me for listening. She also offered to drive Chris to his summer job (which was near her home) after dropping her son at a summer play group. Monica's friendship is unique and special—widening my circle of friends. I've especially appreciated her support and encouragement during the time I've been writing this book. She'll even pick up Jamie and Timmy to play with her children so I can have a few extra child-free hours to write. **I'm thankful Monica didn't hesitate to make that simple phone call seeking support and advice.** We've both been rewarded many times over with mutual caring and support.*

Countless Ways for Friends to Help Each Other

Our friends' support over the years manifested in many ways. After Matthew, our fifth son, was born, friends organized to provide meals for our family for three weeks. One friend gave us a gift certificate to a neighborhood restaurant so we could have a few minutes to ourselves—the first in weeks—while she prepared dinner for the boys. Friends continue to support us during the pregnancies and after the boys' births. Another friend, Susan, remembering her own nausea during pregnancy, brought dinner for us in the early months when Cathy has trouble with nausea. During the last weeks of Cathy's pregnancy with Tommy, another friend, Afife, stopped by to lend a helping hand. She threw clothes in the wash and mopped floors, certainly going beyond the call of friendship. We knew we probably would never have the opportunity to reciprocate many of these acts of kindness. **We promised ourselves that whenever we knew someone who needed help, we'd take advantage of the opportunity to prepare a meal, run an errand, or take care of a child, in return for the kindnesses bestowed on us.**

(Joe): *I'll always remember our friend George at soccer games. Our sons played on the same team, so we spent many Saturday mornings watching their games. Tommy, about a year and a half, would come to the game with his brothers. One Saturday I wanted to shoot a video of the game, but Tommy wanted me to hold him. George, sitting on the sidelines in his chair, offered to hold Tommy. Tommy was reticent to sit with George until George brought out a bag of grapes. Tommy loved the grapes and proceeded to eat all of them. George wryly asked me if I fed my children on a regular basis. This was the first of many Saturdays that Tommy sat with George at the soccer games and enjoyed whatever snack George brought along. Needless to say, Tommy and George became special friends. To this day George's favorite question of us is, "Don't you feed those kids?"*

The people I work with are supportive as well. Eunice, my secretary, makes sure I receive the important phone calls from Cathy, especially when she's pregnant, or messages from the boys' schools. Lalo, a longtime friend and colleague, thoughtfully brings soccer photos for the boys from magazines he finds while traveling to medical meetings outside the country. Ginny, a physician assistant, and Tim, a neonatologist, both close friends and colleagues, share stories about their kids, and support the notion that our children are a priority.

Our friends lend a hand in countless ways. One afternoon, our neighbor Carol stopped by for a visit only to find Cathy in the midst of getting five children ready to head to the pediatrician to check Joe Pat's infected ears. She immediately offered to baby-sit the four healthy boys so Cathy could take an obviously uncomfortable Joe Pat to the doctor without the others in tow.

Although we've mastered the art of "divide and conquer," we haven't figured out how to be in two places at once. (Cathy's working on it!) When we have four soccer games at ten o'clock at four different soccer complexes, we need help. Our friends' willingness to provide a ride and supervision for one of the boys is greatly appreciated. The boys are grateful, too, because they know it would be impossible to do what we do without our friends' assistance. **We remind them that when they get the opportunity to help others, they should volunteer immediately.** And there are times when we do provide a ride, or have a friend spend the night—**whenever we can help, we help.**

Our friends and families set an excellent example for our sons on both the value of true friends and the importance of supporting others. Jody and Jack gave Chris a gift certificate to the restaurant where he made reservations for homecoming night to thank him for driving their son to school. My sister Michele and her husband, Steve, organized a Christmas skating party for their children, Dan and Erica, and their friends. They rented the skating rink and invited the children for a free afternoon of skating. The guests were asked to bring a gift to share with the less fortunate children in their community. The children enjoyed the afternoon while helping others—a beautiful example of the Christmas spirit.

Our sons will always remember the year Misty and George invited our family, quite a commitment, for Thanksgiving dinner. Halfway through dessert, a couple of the boys started vomiting profusely—*not* due to the food, we might add. A few months later, they summoned the courage to invite us again, but with a little forethought. As the boys entered the house, a grinning George handed each one a little brown bag—just in case.

Your Pediatrician: A Great Source of Support

(Joe): *Parenting concerns change as our children move from the toddler years through the difficult middle school years to the teenage years. We continue to develop support systems to reflect those changes. Our pediatricians have been a tremendous source of support, medically and non-medically, at all stages of our children's development. (Over the twenty-one years we've needed a pediatrician, we've sadly seen two retire—we're on our third.)* **Their advice and support encourages us in our parenting efforts.** *People assume that because I have a pediatric background we don't need a pediatrician; I remind them I'm the boys' father, not their doctor. Although I do check the boys' ears and throats, their pediatrician assumes the primary responsibility of our sons' medical care. Over the years, their wisdom and support on major and minor issues has strengthened us as parents. We are ever grateful for Dr. Plessala's advice and support when Cathy decided to breast-feed Tony. Tony was a voracious eater, causing Cathy's nipples to crack and bleed. Without his advice and support, she may not have continued to breast-feed Tony. And nursing all the boys evolved into one of Cathy's most rewarding experiences as a mother.*

We remember Dr. Curtis's thought-provoking talk to the boys, at a routine physical exam when they were sixteen years old, on the responsibilities associated with driving a car. He reminded us that no question was ridiculous if we as parents were concerned. **Don't be embarrassed or unwilling to admit you need help.** *When Mark broke out in an unusual rash one Halloween night, I didn't hesitate to take him across the street to another pediatrician in the group, Bob Boyd, who diagnosed shingles. Another evening I rushed Timmy over to have Bob look at his fingertip, which he had injured in the chain of the exercise bike. Even after ten children, we called Dr. Kate Campbell, our present pediatrician, when we needed advice on determining whether one of the boys had a nervous stomach or a stomach virus.*

Depending on Teachers For Educational Advice and Support

When the boys start school, we depend on the teachers for advice and support. They are with our children seven to eight hours a day. Teachers observe how our children perform academically, socially, physically, and emotionally in the school environment—if they can't tell you how your children are doing in all four areas, you need to know why. **We have developed strong parent-teacher relationships because we depend on each other to make the educational process function successfully for our sons.** The teachers know we care about our sons and we *know* they care. Mrs. Cassidy, a third-grade teacher, taught four of the boys. We knew the boys were in an academically stimulating environment (Mrs. Cassidy had parents enthralled during open house sessions), but even more important, we knew she would develop the whole child. She had a unique ability to motivate her students, to foster their individual strengths. She listened to our concerns about each son, not comparing them but recognizing their differences, especially regarding learning styles. She suggested viable ways to help our sons at home and, most important, she was honest, caring, and straightforward in her approach—not only with the parents but also with the children. We've been blessed with exceptional teachers for our sons, too many to name individually. They know who they are because they haven't been just teachers; they are also our friends.

Getting to Know the Families of Your Children's Friends

Another important support system involves the families of our sons' friends. We make the effort to meet the boys' friends and their parents. **We want to know who our sons are with and feel comfortable that they share similar values. Having fellow parents know our feelings on different activities proves beneficial.** Joe Pat and a friend decided they wanted to attend a dance that we had already vetoed. The boys were determined to go; they figured if Joe Pat spent the night with his friend, not mentioning to us they intended to go to the dance, we wouldn't know. His friend's mom was aware of our attitude on attending dances in sixth grade, so was surprised by the boys' plan. Confused, she called us. Needless to say, Joe Pat didn't attend the dance, and he didn't spend the night. Instead, his weekend was filled with "hard labor"—cleaning gutters, working in the yard—to remind him of the importance of trust and honesty.

We're pleased to see the boys developing their own support systems with friends and teachers. They value their friendships, too. Tony and David's best friend, Robby—often referred to as our eleventh son—is a special gift to our entire family, with his bright smile and jovial manner. Our college-aged sons enjoy returning to the high school to visit teachers, teachers who are now friends.

Teaching Our Sons to Be There for Others

We teach the boys that it's often the little actions, the gentle word or the warm smile, that brighten the day for someone else. Just as we appreciate kind words and gestures, so do others. If everyone would live by the golden rule, "Do unto others, as you would have others do unto you," what an incredible world we'd have. The golden rule is more often associated with preventing negative behavior, but we give it a positive slant: **Do good deeds for others as we appreciate the good deeds showered on us.**

We want the boys to experience the joy of giving as well as the joy of receiving. When you bring joy to another, the experience returns joy to you. One evening, after a spring soccer game, Cathy and Mark saw a young mother struggling to carry an infant and lawn chairs to the soccer field. Mark ran over and offered to help the mother, who gratefully accepted and appreciated his assistance. When he ran back to the car, his face beamed with the rewarding feelings his deed had brought. Cathy told him that he had done a thoughtful thing and that she would have appreciated someone's help in a similar situation. When Danny was in second grade, he was asked to lead a kindergartner to the front car pool area. Danny was proud and excited because Mrs. Kehoe, whom he loves, had asked *him* to help her student.

Empathizing and **listening** to another's concerns are also important ways to express support of a friend. Cathy's mom, not one to talk up a storm or seek attention, has mastered the art of listening. As a good listener, she empathizes and listens with her heart, yet also deciphers the meaning behind the words. Friends and family know Mom will share her gift of listening with anyone who needs her.

Supporting each other is imperative in today's world, where we hear about injustices and violence daily. **Instead of making each other's lives miserable, we must try to make each other's lives happy and fulfilling—starting with our families.** There are so many ways to provide a helping hand to someone you know, or don't know, to ease a burden or show you care: Share responsibilities in the home, watch a friend's child so she can go to the doctor or her child's school program, pick up groceries or medicine for an ill friend, bake cookies for a thoughtful teacher, collect mail for an out-of-town neighbor, share an inspiring book with a colleague, or *listen* when someone needs an ear.

Leigh, a good friend, told us how Tony had eased her worries about having "back-to-back" children with one simple sentence: "David and I are less than a year apart and we're best friends,"—as are her daughters today. Mrs. Jamerlan, Chris's biology teacher, was touched when Chris offered words of concern on a day she felt sick. **We need to learn to be sensitive to others' feelings and concerns.**

(Cathy): *A friend told me of two inspiring books,* Random Acts of Kindness *and* More Random Acts of Kindness *by the editors of Conari Press. The acts of kindness shared in the books lift your spirits and inspire you to do something, anything, for someone else. Interspersed through* Random Acts of Kindness *are suggestions on ways to practice kindness, in case you're short of ideas.*

When I think of specific acts of support and kindness that have left a lasting mark on me, two experiences stand out. When Tony and David first started grade school, I wanted to participate as much as a mom could with younger kids still at home. Parent involvement at the school, though, was limited at the time. From my own teaching experience, I knew the impor-

tance and value of parent participation. When a new principal was hired at the school, I broached the subject of a parent volunteer program with her. She was eager and willing to give it a try. To participate during school hours, I needed someone to watch Joe Pat and Matthew. Our neighbor, Mrs. Cruz, offered to help. She had always been actively involved in her own four children's schools and understood the importance of volunteering. Every week for a couple of hours, Mrs. Cruz shared her time and love with my sons while providing me the opportunity to help the second-grade reading class. Her kindness benefited many: I had a chance to share my teaching skills again and develop a long-lasting friendship with Ms. Renken, the teacher; Joe Pat and Matthew grew to love their special time with Mrs. Cruz—another "grandmother" in their lives; and the students in the reading class blossomed with the extra attention.

My other experience came during my student teaching in New Orleans under Margie Herberger. Margie had a unique way of making her students and friends feel special and loved: Margie shared "a happy"—usually a small gift or note given for no specific reason. She would say with a smile as she presented her "happy"—"Just because." She would bake a batch of cookies for the children to share or pick up paperback books for the students to keep for their own. For some children, Margie's gift was their first personally owned book—the sparkle in their eyes was reward enough. I treasure the "happy"—a set of silver demitasse spoons—Margie excitedly gave me shortly after my engagement to Joe. Margie died a few years ago from breast cancer. I know, though, that Margie lives on through the "happys" her friends and former students now share with others.

Producing Positive Results Through Simple Kindnesses

Words of encouragement, praise, and support need to be regular expressions used in our families, with our friends, and with people we meet. Reassure the new parents that they're doing a good job with their baby (don't offer unsolicited advice) or share words of encouragement with the mother pregnant with her fourth child. Write a note of thanks to the teacher who prepares an exciting lesson or enhances a learning experience for your child. We remember the simple kindness shown Chris by Mrs. Kubik, his third-grade teacher, on the first day in his new school. He was nervous about making new friends and adjusting to a new routine. Mrs. Kubik assured us she would assign a special partner to help him through the transition. Chris came home from school excited about his new friend, Shane. She couldn't have made a nicer choice.

We hear many parents complain about teachers not being positive and supportive with the students, yet how many parents make the effort to be positive and supportive with the teachers? Kindness works both ways. If all we ever hear are negative comments, we begin to feel as though we can't do anything right. **We know from our own experiences how motivating a compliment or thoughtful praise can be— especially regarding parenting.**

After an article on our family ran in the December 1996 issue of the *Ladies' Home Journal,* we received thoughtful cards, calls, and letters expressing appreciation for sharing our story with others. The Great American Puzzle Factory sent puzzles and games to fulfill Tommy's Christmas wish for a 1000-piece puzzle. David received cherished Rockets tickets. We also enjoyed hearing from other large families who share similar values and experiences. One family from Brewster, Nebraska, who have ten children, thanked us for "showing what real love, commitment, and priorities are all about." Another family from Kutztown, Pennsylvania, who have eight sons, jokingly thanked us for supporting their business—they live on a dairy farm. Although we've never met these families or the individuals responsible for the gifts, we feel a kinship with them. Their words and acts of kindness touch our hearts and inspire us in our parenting efforts. We are grateful for the support—we all need it.

The controversy over women working outside the home versus staying home to raise children is a divisive issue in our society. **Parents, especially women, need to support each other in their roles and not criticize and judge individual choices.** Many women have a true choice in whether they work outside the home; others do not have a choice—the need to work is dictated by economic circumstances.

Rather than "which is better," the issue should be about how we as individual parents accept our role and provide for the emotional, physical, and spiritual well being of our children. **Support of each other is what we need to grow and improve as parents.**

Each one of us can change someone else's day with a kind word or gesture. **We don't need to spend a lot of time, money, or energy for the kindness to be of value.** Never underestimate the power of a smile. The simple smile brightens almost anyone's day. People enjoy being around people who exhibit a zest for life.

We continually learn new, simple acts of kindness from our friends and families: Papa's and Grandma's thoughtful care packages to Tony and David in college; Afife's quick, thoughtful phone calls to wish us Merry Christmas, Happy Mother's Day, or just to say, "I'm thinking of you"; Mary's freshly baked breads gobbled up by the boys in minutes; Dawn's delicious shrimp jambalaya to thank Joe for his continued support; and the little notes of thanks or praise that we receive. **We *can* make our world a better place for our children to live in, one kindness at a time—and we need to start in our homes with our spouses and children.**

We could survive having ten sons without family and friends, but our days would be harder, longer, more stressful, and less enjoyable—for us and for the boys. We assure you it's worth the time and effort to develop support systems. We treasure our family and friends and appreciate the many blessings they bestow on us with their love and friendships. **After all, supporting each other, especially within the family, is an expression of love.** "Lord, make me an instrument of your peace," prayed St. Francis of Assisi. If each of us strives to become an instrument of His peace, the lives of our families, friends, and communities can't help but be filled with love and joy.

Chapter 10

Coping with Time, Fatigue, and Life's Stresses

I *am not asking you tonight, Lord, for time to do this and then that, But your grace to do conscientiously, in the time that you give me, what you want me to do.*
                                        –Michel Quoist

The way in which a man accepts his fate . . . gives him ample opportunity–even under the most difficult circumstances–to add a deeper meaning to his life.
                                        –Viktor E. Frankl

Striving For Parental/Family Sanity in Today's World

"How do you keep up with ten sons *and* stay sane?" We must get asked that question or one similar five times a week. Even we're amazed some weeks that we've accomplished everything we have—and that we and the boys are still intact. Stress, to some degree, has probably always been a part of family life. In today's society, though, stress seems to overwhelm too many families. Families are frazzled about household chores, finances, careers, and children.

We have our share of stress, but we've learned to handle and reduce it in constructive, positive ways: We organize and prioritize; maintain *realistic* expectations of our time, energy, finances, and abilities; establish goals for the day, week, and year; and trust in God. Our children are our first priority, and so we dedicate the majority of our time, energy, and money to their development.

Maintaining Balance Through Time Management

We can't emphasize enough the importance of spending time with your children. There's a quote by Daphne Rose Kingma in *More Random Acts of Kindness* that deserves sharing: "Time is the one commodity above all that is our true possession. . . . Time's most important quality is that it passes, that we have only a finite amount. Therefore, be aware of its value and know that when you give your time, you're giving of your life."

We usually hear, though, that there's not enough time to do everything. We agree—that's why we prioritize and organize. Every family has basic needs and responsibilities to fulfill: eating, sleeping, taking care of our children, working, buying groceries, preparing meals, washing clothes, cleaning house, and paying bills and taxes. We can't dodge these responsibilities, so we accept that they need to be done. We also want time to relax and enjoy each other. **Our goal then is to prioritize and organize the "have to's" in a manner that enables us to have time for "fun-too." Perfection is not one of our goals.** Our house is not as clean today as it was twenty years ago, but our children's needs are met—and we're happy.

Since no two days are exactly alike in the Garcia-Prats household, we must stay on top of the various schedules and commitments. The large calendar over the desk in the kitchen indicates the obligations for each day. Whenever a new activity is scheduled—a doctor or dentist appointment, a meeting, a practice, cookies to be baked, parent-teacher meetings, soccer games—we write it on the calendar. At the end of each day, we check the calendar to plan the next day's schedule. Cathy lists the activities for the day, along with phone calls to be made, letters to be written, or any out-of-the-ordinary commitment. People complain they don't even have time to make a list, but the time we save by being organized is much more than the ten minutes needed to compile the list. **Once we know what needs to be done, we decide who does what, when, and how.** This is when the "divide and conquer" technique, in context with *respect* for each family member, pays huge dividends. There's no way Cathy can be expected to manage the entire home routine on her own—the physical demands would overwhelm her, not to mention the emotional pressures. **It's imperative that all members of a family share in the responsibilities, whether both parents work or one stays home.**

In the mornings, the boys wake up, clean their rooms, eat breakfast, gather their school paraphernalia, and complete their individual chores. While Cathy or Joe prepares breakfast, the other fixes the lunches or separates the wash. (The boys make their own lunches and wash their own clothes once they begin middle school.) By seven-thirty in the morning, the beds are made, the bedrooms and bathrooms are straightened up, and the kitchen is cleaned. We've established certain days for certain chores: Mondays and Fridays are the **big** wash days; bed linens are changed on a rotating schedule; Cathy cleans different areas of the house each day; ironing is done during the evening news. **Flexibility is woven into the routine.** If there's a school program on Monday morning, the wash is done at another time; if one of the boys is sick, everything's placed on hold; if it's a beautiful day for playing at the park, the bathrooms can wait. **The children's needs and activities take priority over a clean house.** The house doesn't stay clean for long anyway, and a family's wash is never really caught up—is it?

(Cathy): *When I was in high school, I developed a friendship with Mr. Buskirk, the assistant principal at W. T. Woodson High School in Fairfax, Virginia. He often told me, "Cathy, **organization is the key to success.**" As*

I became more and more involved in extracurricular activities, I learned the value of his advice. The organizational skills I developed helped me in high school and college, and they continue to help me as a parent. **I prioritize and organize what I need to do.** *Laundry is started first thing in the morning. By starting the wash early, I can fold the clothes on and off during the day, while I'm placing phone calls or watching the boys. (Many days Joe and I fold clothes late at night, because other activities take precedence.) Because folding or ironing clothes doesn't tax my brain, I do it while watching the news, chatting with family or friends on the phone, or listening to music. I consider the portable phone one of the greatest conveniences of our time. I can make calls while washing dishes, folding towels, or peeling carrots, especially when I'm put on hold.*

I've learned which chores to do with the boys around and which ones are better suited for "mom alone"—*for example, washing the kitchen floor. I wait until the boys rest to make business-type phone calls so I can concentrate. I only get frazzled with the boys if I need it quiet and they aren't. When I open the mail, I have a pen in hand to write due dates on bills, the word file, or special instructions. If we don't need the information, I toss it immediately so we won't have to deal with the paper again. Many of our techniques derive from effective business practice. We eliminate having to do something twice whenever possible. When the boys bring home permission slips or forms, we sign them and hand them back to the boys immediately. It's too easy to lose track of the papers if we don't. School newsletters and information are filed in the appropriate school folder. At the beginning of each school year, I organize a folder for each of the schools our sons attend. I don't throw away the notes from school until the end of the semester or year, depending on the information—the note you tossed in the garbage is always the one with the information you need down the road. Although the first few weeks of school are hectic and time is at a premium, we save time and hassles in the long term by preparing the school folders right at the start. We also create folders for the boys' extracurricular activities. When we need a schedule or phone number, we know where to look without spending a lot of time searching for the information. I keep scissors, tape, pencils, and paper on the desk in the kitchen and in my room, enabling me to easily jot down information from a phone call or* *add an activity to the calendar. School calendars and schedules are posted on the bulletin board or doors. (We're gradually running out of room to post all the schedules!) We find that many hours a week are lost to families due to the lack of simple organizational skills. Joe and I prefer to have that time for ourselves and our sons.*

After Tony was born, I made the tough adjustment of learning what was reasonable to accomplish with a little one around. **I learned to keep my expectations simple and to focus on caring for the boys and meeting their needs.** *What benefit is a spotless house if your children are falling apart? Although I had my list, I learned that the chance of completing everything was remote. I set my expectations high, but I didn't berate myself when all the tasks weren't completed. I still maintain that philosophy. Unlike the business world, where experts recommend tackling the more difficult or the least pleasant tasks first, I usually tackle some of the easier chores first because this provides me a sense of accomplishment. If I'm unable to do anything else the rest of the day, at least I've accomplished something.*

My organizational skills help me accomplish a lot in a small amount of time. Since I don't like a messy house, I concentrate on those areas that make the most difference with the least amount of time expended: making the beds, wiping down the bathrooms, vacuuming, dusting, and basic straightening up. I keep the sink full of sudsy water to facilitate cleaning dishes throughout the day. **There are only so many hours in the day, so I decide which tasks are more important and do the best I can.**

Adapting and Being Flexible as Family Routines Change

We rethink and adapt our routine as our life changes. Time commitments and physical and emotional demands with a newborn or toddler (or both as is usually our experience) differ from those during the elementary school years and the high school years. When you're chasing a two-year-old day after day, you can't imagine ever having a relaxing moment again. The physical demands of parenting a newborn or toddler—waking up during the night and providing constant supervision—lessen as the children grow, but other parenting demands and concerns—school, extracurricular activities, friends—replace them.

As the boys grow older, they pitch in by making their beds and helping in the kitchen at night. So although we have more children to take care of, we also have more hands sharing the responsibilities. In the afternoons when the boys return from school, they play with their younger brothers, allowing Cathy to pay bills, make phone calls, or prepare dinner. With the older boys' support, many aspects of our daily routine have become easier. We gain an extra forty minutes in the mornings and some afternoons when the older boys drive their younger brothers to and from school. We appreciate the extra time and put the minutes to good use. We're relieved to now have a "built-in" car pool, but it took us sixteen years to get to this point. Cathy remembers all too well how hard it was before Tony could drive, getting all the boys up and out in the morning, even those not yet in school (especially when Joe was on-call and not home in the morning to help).

On the flip side of the coin, the boys' participation in outside activities increases the amount of time we spend away from home. **With the additional commitments, we reorganize the routine to maintain a sense of balance.** We review the entire week's schedule on Sunday so we are prepared to meet our commitments. We know if Joe's on-call one night, Cathy may need help getting the boys to practice or a game. Cathy plans meals around the week's different functions. If the boys have a soccer game after school, she prepares a meal that will be ready when they walk in the door, otherwise the entire evening gets thrown out of sync. During school soccer season, we eat a lot of soups and chili; Cathy fixes the soup early in the morning and lets it simmer until dinner time. When Cathy prepares spaghetti sauce, she doubles the recipe and freezes a portion for a hectic night; when barbecuing, Joe smokes extra chickens for the same purpose.

Avoiding and Eliminating the Stress Potholes

Although we reduce our stress level by staying organized and planning ahead, we also lower our stress thermometer by *avoiding* situations that create tensions and frustrations. And when we do feel stressed, we sit back and determine why or what is causing the stress. **Once we identify a situation as a source of stress, we determine how to relieve the pressure.** If the stress is caused by a nonessential activity, we re-evaluate whether it's in our or our sons' best interest to continue—if not, we eliminate the activity. If the activity is essential, then we determine what adjustments need to be made to ease the burden. Although change doesn't always come easy, our experiences prove it's worth the reduced stress.

The initial school the older five boys attended created a tremendous amount of stress in our lives. The academic program was challenging but stressful because of the educational techniques, approach, and environment. Tony's first year of school was a disaster. We had a gifted, sensitive, well-disciplined child who dreaded the thought of school each day. Tony enjoyed his preschool experience, so we knew his feelings weren't related to separation. We thought seriously about changing schools at the time, but we were very active in the parish and wanted to continue our involvement. Plus, we thought we could be advocates for change. After five more stressful years and four more sons, we realized it was in our best interest, especially that of our sons, to find another educational program. We *knew* schools could be academically strong, yet loving and nurturing at the same time. After visiting several schools and meeting with the principals, we chose the elementary school our sons still attend. We were amazed at the different attitude the boys developed about their school experience. Tony and David had three times the homework but never complained about the increased work load; their motivation for learning returned. The experience was refreshing for us, too. We dropped off the boys each morning confident that they were in an environment that nurtured the values we wanted to instill. We also felt like we could work *with* the school instead of fighting the system. Although we now had to drive the boys to school each day versus them walking, the reduced stress in all our lives was worth the extra energy and time. The school experience should be positive and enjoyable—that doesn't mean easy—for your children and you. If we have one regret as parents over the years, it's that we waited so long to change schools.

We learned a lot from that experience. **We're not afraid to make a change if we find ourselves in a stressful situation.** When Tony and David needed orthodontic work, we chose a highly recommended orthodontist. We soon discovered, though, that his office was inefficiently managed. We'd wait an hour or more for the boys to be called for treatment. We had eight sons at the time. To sit in a waiting room for a long period of time with young kids, one an infant, was unreasonable. Cathy discussed the problem with the orthodontist several times, but nothing changed. She dreaded taking the boys in for their appointments and left angry after every visit. When our dentist recommended Chris be evaluated for orthodontic work, we asked for new referrals. Along with finding a new orthodontist for Chris, we intended to switch orthodontists for Tony and David, right in the middle of treatment. Cathy chose Dr. Donald Morgan, an extremely competent, "patient friendly" orthodontist: His personnel are pleasant and the office runs efficiently with a waiting time of fifteen minutes or less. An added benefit was Dr. Morgan's personal interest in the boys—beyond their teeth. The experience was a thousand times more positive than Tony and David's initial ordeal. Cathy and the boys no longer dreaded orthodontic appointments: She could realistically estimate the time commitment and felt confident the boys were in exceptional hands.

Cathy has dropped out of school car pools because they created stress instead of making her life easier. One mother couldn't manage to pick up the boys on time, so they were continually late the first couple of weeks of school on her driving days. One morning, she totally forgot to pick up the boys. When she called to assure Cathy it wouldn't happen again, Cathy *assured* her, "No, it won't happen again. I'm no longer carpooling with you." Although driving every morning was difficult, Cathy preferred driving the boys herself so they would arrive on time. When children are late for school, they feel stressed, just as adults are when they're late for work or an appointment. Another parent insisted on smoking in the car during the ten minutes it took to drive to school, knowing it bothered the children. The twenty minutes Cathy saved a day weren't worth subjecting the boys to the irritating smoke.

We also avoid everyday situations that inevitably create stress. Cathy avoids the grocery store if the boys are cranky or tired; she knows it makes the excursion difficult. When the boys have doctor appointments, she brings her "bag of tricks" along to entertain them: crayons, pencils, paper, small cars, a favorite story. Children get restless and bored with nothing to do, so we keep them busy. Cathy witnesses frustrated parents with children in tow wherever she goes. The parents are frustrated because their children are restless and getting into mischief or picking at each other. Almost every incident could be avoided by providing the children with something simple to do. **To ask children to sit and do nothing is unreasonable, unrealistic, and a definite stress builder for the parent.**

One morning Cathy took the Suburban for an oil change. Sitting in the waiting room was a mother with a three-year-old son and an eleven-month-old baby. The mother wouldn't let the three-year-old budge from his chair or free the strapped-in eleven-month-old from his stroller. The twenty minutes it took to change the oil was a marathon for that mom (and for the rest of us sitting in the waiting room). If she had brought some toy cars for the boys to play with or crayons to draw with or had at least taken the baby out of the stroller so he could move around, she would've avoided the constant screaming and whining by the children and ultimately herself. The Boy Scout's motto, **"Be prepared,"** is one motto parents need to adopt and integrate into their parenting skills.

When difficulties arise or the days are out of sync, we address the problem quickly so it won't continue to drain our energy. As mentioned previously, the boys arguing about where to sit in the Suburban caused every trip to start off with a hassle. By assigning seats, we eliminated one frustration from our day (probably more than that, since some days we live in the car). When the original kitchen clean-up routine wasn't working due to changes in soccer practices, we sat the boys down to rework the schedule. We didn't care who cleaned which night or week, we just wanted it done timely and correctly. The boys understood and rectified the situation. They didn't want to return home after practice and face a dirty kitchen in addition to a couple of hours of homework, so an adjustment in the schedule was appreciated, eliminating a frustration for all of us.

The Need for Routines and Responsibilities

We follow routines, allowing room for flexibility. **Children function better when organization is a part of their life.** The boys know our routine and what their responsibilities are in the mornings, after school, and in the evenings. By all of us fulfilling our responsibilities in the evenings, for example, we eliminate stress and chaos in the mornings. **We avoid a tremendous amount of stress by establishing bedtimes and ensuring our sons receive adequate sleep.** When the boys are tired, they are cranky, whiny, and more difficult to deal with—whether twenty-one years old or a toddler. A good night's sleep is a *must* for children. By maintaining a calm daily routine, we help our sons maintain reasonably unflustered days.

(Cathy): *A national magazine ran a profile of a working mother who was so overwhelmed she didn't have time to enjoy her days. I empathized with her; I also thought about how I would approach her day differently.*

There are aspects of my day I can't change, but I can alter my approach and attitude. Joe and I want our days to be joyful, so with heartfelt determination we decide how to accomplish that goal. In our chapter on positive parenting, I mention how, through prayer and positive thinking, I focus on creating a positive day for myself and my family. The mother in the magazine story wakes up dreading the day, her tensions building as she showers and anticipates the frustrations ahead. She and the father of her son argue each morning about who will take the baby to daycare, automatically starting the day off with tension. Joe and I would work out a compromising solution to the problem, reducing the morning stress. Just as our sons organize a schedule to clean the kitchen after dinner, this couple could establish a rotating schedule for who's driving the baby to daycare. None of our sons enjoy washing dishes, but they need to be washed. The baby in the story needs to be driven to daycare. Determining ahead of time who's responsible for that day or week would eliminate the arguing every morning and reduce the morning stress for the couple and the baby. Children sense our tensions, and their moods often reflect ours. Deciding who takes the baby to daycare won't deliver instant happiness to this couple, but it will remove one area of stress from their day.

After reading the article, we understand even more the important role prioritizing and organizing plays in minimizing stress in the Garcia-Prats household. **We whittle away the stresses that inevitably creep into our days or we make the best of difficult situations.** The summer of '95 was our "summer from hell." The schedule for the first six weeks of the summer was incredibly hectic: Matthew attended Rice University's summer enrichment program, Joe Pat took enrichment courses, Chris held a job across town, David lifeguarded, and Tony worked at a Baylor College of Medicine laboratory. The drop-off and pick-up schedule was constant throughout the day, especially the morning. Tony and Matthew rode city buses, but Chris and Joe Pat needed to be driven to their activities. Without the older boys at home to baby-sit, the five younger boys spent most of the morning in the car. We were determined, though, to make the best of a crummy schedule. The boys played games in the car, worked on art projects, or read books for the library's summer reading club. In the afternoons, when we had a baby-sitter, we took "field trips": the art, science, and children's museums, IMAX, Space Center Houston, and a tour of the tunnel system under downtown Houston. The summer wasn't ideal, but we stayed focused, survived, *and* enjoyed being together.

The Ultimate Finance Lesson: Prioritizing Your Goals and Living Within Your Means

One of the most common stressors for families revolves around finances. Raising children is expensive. We laugh, though, when we read estimates of the total cost of raising a child from infancy through college. The numbers are mind boggling, and by our estimation and experience, inflated. Our numbers are based on the financial choices we make and the lifestyle we choose to live. Many people assume because Joe's a physician, we live on easy street, buy what we like, and have no financial worries—even with ten children. Although Joe's salary is above the norm, **we've made significant financial and nonfinancial choices that allow us to raise ten well-adjusted sons**. Joe's decision to practice medicine in a medical school setting versus a more lucrative private practice meant considerably less income; but, of more value, the choice provided treasured time for Joe to spend with the family.

Early in our marriage and as we started our family, we established financial goals so Joe could continue to practice academic medicine. We chose to live a more modest lifestyle in order to reach our goals; we wanted more children, not more "things." We learned to save for big ticket items and not accrue debt. **Our home wasn't furnished instantly via MasterCard; we bought what we needed over many years.** Our home mortgage and car loans are the only items we pay over time. The cars we drive are practical, not filled with fancy paraphernalia or luxury models; we drive them until they are no longer safe or, as was the case years ago, we need more seats. We despise car payments, so we avoid them as long as we can. We have lived in the same house for twenty years, instead of "buying up," although we added two bedrooms and a bath to accommodate our growing family. The clothes we buy are practical, in style, and well made, but not necessarily brand-name or trendy. We hand down clothes from one son to another whenever possible.

Groceries, especially sale items, are bought in bulk to save money. Family vacations consist of simple trips to nearby Galveston Island or excursions to the older boys' out-of-town soccer tournaments. A trip to Northern Virginia to attend Cathy's parents' 50th anniversary celebration was planned well ahead of time. We deal with unexpected financial demands, too: the hot water heater that had to be replaced a few weeks before Christmas, car repairs, Chris's soccer shoes splitting apart right before a big tournament—all with tuition bills due. When unexpected expenses stare us in the face, we sit back and figure out how to redistribute the limited dollars. **Coping with family finances is difficult and stressful, but when we remain focused on the essentials, and choose to live within our means, we manage to make ends meet and ease the worries.**

Our parents taught us by their example how to live within our means. They established goals for their families, and, in order to make them a reality, they made tough financial choices, too. Education was a primary goal and expense for our parents. They went without extras for many years in order to provide us with the best education. We know if we had not planned ahead financially for the stage we're now in—two sons in college, three at the Jesuit high school, three at our parish school, and two in preschool—we could not afford to send our sons to the schools of our choice or provide the extracurricular activities. The decision early in our marriage to prioritize our financial obligations and live a modest lifestyle makes this feasible.

We're bombarded in today's society by the media and advertisement industry telling us what we "need" to make our lives more enjoyable, more fulfilling, and more worthwhile. **Our society confuses needs with wants.** Two or three television sets with cable, the latest stereo system, a luxury car, or a more elaborate home won't determine whether our children grow up compassionate, well educated, responsible, and respectful. **Money, and the things money buys, do not make or break the good parent. Good families—good parents—can be found across all economic strata, just as dysfunctional families span the entire income range.**

We don't want to sound like we're minimizing the stress caused by finances, but as with all aspects of parenting, we must put finances in perspective to provide our children with a happy, loving home. **Hearing parents argue about money is a difficult experience for children,**

especially if they are made to feel responsible for the hardships incurred by the family: doctor bills, medicines, clothes, shoes, school supplies. If parents continually complain they deserve "the better things in life," children grow up confused about what qualities define a good person.

Do we wish our government would provide some financial relief for families? We do, and we know it's in their power to do so—if our government would only prioritize our country's needs versus fulfilling wants. As families most of us have to postpone buying what we don't have the money to buy; our government should do the same. We've wanted a nice dining room table since we moved into our home, but other expenses continue to take precedence over the table. We need new flooring throughout the downstairs, but our priority for now is paying the boys' tuition. We could charge the table or take out a loan for the flooring, but then we'd be stressed every month paying the bills. We'd rather wait on the table and floors than create unnecessary stress.

Minimizing Personal Stresses by Organizing and Prioritizing

(Joe): *My sources of stress are the demands at work and at home and the need to integrate both. My work stresses are related to my administrative duties and deadlines and the needs of the intensive care staff. In addition, I am responsible for the care of critically ill newborn infants and the concerns of their worried parents. I prioritize and organize in order to handle and reduce the stresses at work. I cope with the emotional stress (the death of a newborn whose life I've worked so hard to save) by establishing a support system with my colleagues. Sharing my feelings lightens this heavy burden and allows me to continue to effectively handle the rigorous duties in the intensive care unit.*

*The stresses at home are related to fulfilling the needs of the family within the time constraints that we have. **The stresses are lessened by several factors: the ability to prioritize and organize (sounds like a*** *broken record); my closeness to Cathy; and our ability to work together and enjoy doing so.* When Cathy and I aren't communicating well or have conflicts within our relationship, the stress level increases dramatically. I feel the stress and I'm convinced the boys do as well. Resolving our differences and strengthening our relationship reduces the stress in our family and increases the enjoyment that Cathy and I have of the time we share together and with our sons.

(Cathy): *My personal stresses result from fatigue, excessive demands and responsibilities, lack of control in a situation, or just being in a crummy mood. Since I want to minimize stress for myself and family, I work hard to reduce and eliminate its causes. When I'm overwhelmed by too many responsibilities at one time, I sit down and prioritize. While trying to complete this book and meet a December deadline, I also needed to prepare for Christmas, write and mail Christmas cards and packages, and get ready for out-of-town company. I decided to complete the chapter I was working on and then spend the week before Christmas preparing for the holidays. Once I made that decision, I felt a load lift off my shoulders.* **We like to think we can do it all, but we can't.** *I had to rein in my expectations so Christmas would be enjoyable for the family.*

The holidays are a perfect example of a stressful period of time, often generated by our own actions and decisions. Father Michael Berlowski, our parish priest, gave a homily a couple of weeks before Christmas on how "consumerism has consumed Christmas." People have lost focus on what Christmas is all about—the gift of the Christ Child. Father Mike told us that when we allow the secular focus of Christmas to dominate the religious dimension, we demonstrate our lack of appreciation for God's greatest gift—we throw His gift away as if the birth of His son wasn't adequate or what we truly wanted.

Over the years, we've learned to focus on what's truly important during the Christmas season and eliminate the excess baggage. Before any holiday decorations are brought out, we place the Advent wreath (a wreath with four candles symbolizing the long wait for the Messiah and the hope He would bring) on our kitchen table and an Advent mural on the kitchen wall. Our evening prayers and a reading from the Old Testament are recited around the wreath. Then the younger boys place a missing piece on the Advent mural each evening until Baby Jesus is placed in the manger on Christmas morning. The lighted candles during meals and the prayers in the evenings remind us every day during December of the true meaning of Christmas.

We celebrate the joy and fun of Santa, too, but we keep it in perspective. The boys' Christmas lists are modest: puzzles, books, posters, CD's, soccer paraphernalia, and clothes. Our Christmas shopping is done in one day. Joe takes a day off during December and with the ten boys' lists in hand we have a ball. One woman stopped Cathy in the toy store as she was flipping through the boys' lists and asked, "Are you Santa?" When Cathy looked perplexed, she smiled and said, "That's quite a list you have."

Cathy's "Stress Reduction 101" Course

(Cathy): **When I focus on what's important for myself and my family, I automatically reduce my stress and enjoy my days.** *Something as simple as leaving five to ten minutes early to pick up the boys from school or for a doctor's appointment, instead of at the last minute, relieves the anxiety of arriving late.*

Since fatigue is one of my worst enemies, I make the effort to get adequate sleep. When the boys are little, getting a full night's sleep is difficult, so I make *myself go to bed earlier. When the boys are infants or I'm pregnant, I rest when they have their afternoon quiet time or when the older boys arrive home from school and can help with their brothers. Resting may mean I don't finish all the day's projects, but the price the entire family pays when I'm exhausted isn't worth having my day's list completed.*

Joe and I are both exhausted after our nonstop days. When we finally sit down to watch the ten o'clock news or read, whatever energy we have left drains right out of our bodies. Most nights we don't stay awake through the entire broadcast; the older boys wake us up and send us to bed. During the summer Olympics, Joe and I sat down to watch the news, quickly nodding off, only to distantly hear Matthew tell Joe Pat a few minutes later, "Look, Joe Pat, synchronized sleeping."

Since time is a precious commodity and I enjoy time for my interests and commitments, **I've found ways to fulfill one responsibility while involved in another.** *Because I spend hours in the car taking and picking up the boys from school or sports practices, I carry a tote bag in the car filled with reading material, stationery, notecards, and pen and pencil to take advantage of the five-minute wait that turns into twenty. (If the younger boys are with me, they have their special bags, too.) Our Christmas cards, for example, are written while waiting for the boys to finish soccer practices—a few cards here and a few cards there. When Tony was swimming, I took the Christmas cards to swim meets and wrote them during the long intervals between his events. The boys help me by placing the stamps and return labels on the envelopes.*

I take advantage of any opportunity to exercise. *Walking and other sources of exercise are not only physically beneficial, they relax me and give me time to think and pray. When I exercise, I have more energy, less fatigue, and a better attitude. Joe and the boys appreciate my need to exercise and are rewarded with a happier wife and mother.*

The boys are required to arrive for a soccer game forty-five minutes before game-time. If weather permits, I spend the time walking. If I don't walk, I read. When Timmy or one of the other boys is with me, I put Timmy in the stroller for the walk or play with the boys while we wait for the game to start. The same holds true for soccer practices. Because several of the boys practice a half hour or more from home, Joe or I may wait in the vicinity of the practice fields for them to finish. I use that time to walk, read, or run quick errands. The system works for me, providing those extra few minutes of time to meet my needs and reduce any stress.

When I feel down in the dumps, angry, or moody, I determine what's causing my mood and then work to change it. *I start with a prayer asking for guidance and help to refocus on what's important and necessary. "Jesus help me," "Jesus strengthen me," "Jesus guide me," are* simple, but effective prayers. What a wonderful feeling knowing He's there to help me!

Often changing what I'm doing improves my mood. I may go outside and work in the yard, play a game with the kids, call a friend, bake cookies—anything to change the mood.

Music also helps alter my mood, relaxing and uplifting me. I listen to music most of my day, whether at home or in the car; music eases the drudgery of routine household chores. Someday I hope to learn to play the piano as a way to express my feelings and moods. I remember my sister Michele expressing her emotions through the piano—you could tell her mood by how and what she played.

Sometimes these moods are caused by frustrations out of my control. The phone calls I make to straighten out someone else's mistakes are annoying because they take away from my precious time to do what I want. I work hard to control my annoyance because like all stress, it just saps your energy. **I've learned to speak up when a problem needs addressing. I also present a possible solution to the problem, rather than just complain.** Our neighborhood grocery store never seemed to have enough checkers or baggers. A quick run to the store for five gallons of milk took twenty minutes because of the inefficient system. I wrote the management and asked them to consider providing more checkers and baggers during peak hours. The management responded to my request by increasing the personnel all day and thanking me for my interest. The few minutes it took to write the letter have been returned a hundred times over. I've learned that often businesses or schools are unaware that a procedure is inefficient or inconvenient. Bringing the problem to the right person's attention can produce positive results, eliminating the frustration or inconvenience in the process.

Teaching Our Sons How to Cope with Their Stresses

The same techniques we use to change our moods or reduce our stress, we employ with the boys. If the boys are in "rare" form, we determine why, and then how to get them back on course. **A distraction or a change in activity often makes a dramatic difference.** On a restless afternoon, Cathy may give the younger boys an early bath. Playing in the tub is fun and always seems to calm them down. An afternoon excursion to the neighborhood park releases some of the excess energy accumulated over the course of the day. **We strongly believe, as parents, pediatrician, and educator, in the importance of** *physical activity* **for children.** Just as exercise benefits our physical and mental well being, exercise produces healthy results in our children. We noticed when Tony was on a break from swimming, he was more restless and fidgety. The swimming provided the physical outlet and stimulation he needed.

Children are under incredible, yet often unnecessary, stress in today's society, especially as they advance to the middle school and high school years. **As parents we need to eliminate the stress in our own lives so that we will reduce the stress in our children's lives.** If we wake up in the morning and the day begins in chaos because of our disorganization and poor planning, our children start their day on a stressful note. As parents we have control over the day-to-day operations in our homes and the decision to provide a secure, loving environment for our children. We need to ask ourselves several questions. Are we providing a loving, secure environment for our children? Are we placing too much pressure on our children to succeed, academically, artistically, or athletically? Are the expectations and the responsibilities we urge our children to fulfill realistic and age-appropriate? Are our children involved in too many extracurricular activities? Are we providing our children with time to be children or are we structuring every minute of their day? Depending on our answers to the above questions, we may be increasing our children's stress instead of relieving it.

(Joe): *Parents add to their children's stress by the expectations they have of them. The boys have been blessed by their athleticism and their enjoyment of competition. I specifically stress "the enjoyment" of competition because as parents we can sour this enjoyment very quickly. Participation and competition in sports is a very positive experience for girls and boys. They learn to work with teammates to achieve a common* *goal. They develop self-discipline. They learn to diminish individual needs for the greater good of the team. And there is the social benefit of playing with friends. Parents forget this very quickly when winning is the primary emphasis. When a young athlete is berated by his parents after a less than stellar performance or a team's loss, the look on the child's face says it all. The child who faces constant parental criticism won't enjoy competing for very long. Children should enjoy a sport (or any activity), knowing that their parents will be supportive (even if they are just sitting on the bench) and accepting of their best effort. **Respect your child's efforts and let the sport or activity be a source of enjoyment and learning, not a source of stress.***

It's our responsibility as parents to help our sons deal with the stresses in their lives. **We provide a loving, secure environment, eliminating a major cause of stress for children.** If yelling, screaming, fighting, and disrespect are an everyday occurrence in your home, your children pay the price. We keep our expectations and their responsibilities age-appropriate and realistic. Our sons know they are loved for who they are and not for what they accomplish. We're amazed at how many parents expect a child to make straight A's or be the perfect trumpet player or basketball player. When we were in school, only a few of our classmates earned straight A's, were exceptional musicians, or were gifted athletes. Where did all these perfect students, athletes, and musicians—now parents—come from that they expect perfection from their children? Are our children requesting all the extra activities or are parents overextending their children to fulfill their desire to create the perfect child?

When Tony and David were in their early school years, they took piano lessons and were engaged in a sport, which varied depending on the season. After a year of running from one activity to the next, Tony and David asked to drop the piano lessons. "We never have time after school to just play," they said. We finished out the lessons and learned to keep the days simple for our sons. Today the younger boys choose one activity at a time; the older boys determine their degree of involvement within reason. The boys prefer to have time for themselves and to play with their brothers; it also reduces our running around. If each of the boys were involved in two or three activities at the same time, we'd find it difficult to handle the commitments. Talk about stress! **Parents, by encouraging their children to do it all, create undue stress for their children, and ultimately themselves. Pick and choose, we advise.** We constantly remind ourselves and the boys that we can't do it all. Better that our children grow up relaxed and secure than overwhelmed by the demands placed on them, especially if we expect them to be the best at whatever activity they're involved with.

Discussing Societal and Peer Pressures with Your Children

We talk to the boys about societal and peer pressures and influences. When Cathy was a resident assistant in the college dorm, she was amazed at how many of the girls didn't know how they felt about drugs, sex, smoking, or drinking. A young person may not be prepared to handle the pressures of sex, drugs, or alcohol if they've never taken the time to think about what they'd do in a particular situation. **Take advantage of the opportunities provided through the media to convey your feelings about controversial issues facing your children.** Discuss how to handle awkward situations, reminding them you're available to help as needed. We stand our ground when it comes to our values and beliefs and teach our sons through our example that the right choices will increase their enjoyment of life, not reduce it.

Trusting in God

We also teach the boys not to get upset or worried about the little things in life. We place a tremendous amount of trust in God, and we share these feelings with our sons. We know God doesn't ask us to do more than He knows we can handle, even though some days we feel stretched to the limits. With that faith, we use the twenty-four hours He shares with us to complete what He wants us to do in the best way we can. We keep focused on our marriage relationship, our children as individuals, and our family as a whole. Everything else revolves around these three priorities. God tells us to hand over our burdens to Him, so we do. We are confident, for example, that if He wants us to educate our sons in Catholic schools, He will help us accomplish our goal, as long as we stay focused on what's right in His eyes. We believe that "God helps those who help themselves."

Our organizational and prioritizing skills and our responsible choices, along with our faith and trust in God, eliminate most of the anxieties that could overwhelm us. We take to heart the words of St. Francis de Sales: "Do not fear what may happen tomorrow. The same loving Father who cares for you today, will care for you tomorrow and every day. Either He will shield you from suffering or He will give you unfailing strength to bear it. Be at peace, then, and put aside all anxious thoughts and imaginings." If we abide by the concepts in this prayer and teach our children to do the same, we can live joyful, less stressful lives.

Chapter 11

Traditions, Memories, and "Fun"-damentals

T*here is an appointed time for everything . . . a time to laugh.*

—Ecclesiastes 3:1,4

". . . ritual and symbol are as necessary to human beings as air and water. They mark us as human, and give us identity."

—Kathleen Norris, The Cloister Walk

(Joe): Arugas *is a Spanish word for wrinkles, as on a bed sheet or piece of clothing. One simple word, yet how I laugh and think of my brother, Vic, every time I hear* arugas. *Vic and I shared a bedroom (we shared a double bed as well) growing up. I still chuckle remembering how my brother insisted on our sheets being wrinkle free when my parents put us to bed; the wrinkles didn't bother me. Ten to twenty minutes after lights were out,*

Vic would jump out of bed, and make me get up as well, to straighten out the sheets to get rid of the arugas. *After the sheets were straightened to his satisfaction, he would jump back in bed and go to sleep. Boy, if you wanted to make him mad, just jump on the bed before going to sleep and produce a bunch of* arugas. *Even today, my parents, Vic, my sister, Christine, and I laugh about it when we get together. Vic is still very particular about all that he does and, as an emergency room physician, this trait serves his patients well.*

Memories and traditions are the unwritten history of a family. Each family shares unique memories and traditions created from their culture, religion, race, family makeup, and the special and ordinary events that encompass their lives. The memories we conjure up of our past experiences may trigger joyful as well as sorrowful emotions.

Since the routines of family life and the traditions we embrace play a strong role in whether we hold loving memories of childhood, we strive to create traditions and experiences that will foster happy memories for our children. We make our daily routine and events enjoyable so our children will fondly remember the days they had with us, their brothers, and their grandparents. Our fondest family memories are the fun times we share with our sons, parents, siblings and friends. We associate "fun"—there's really no better word to express it—with the everyday routines and responsibilities of family life. We enjoy being together—not only on special occasions but each and every day.

(Joe): *Cathy is a frequent instigator of a bit of friendly razzing or witty joking with the boys. She never lets any of us get too serious about the responsibilities or the hectic pace. She keeps the atmosphere around our home light and enjoyable.*

Creating Memories from the Moments We Spend Together

It's our daily interactions that create the joy in our home. We will always remember the special birthday parties, Christmas celebrations, and graduations, but it's the *everyday laughter* that sparks the overall sense of happiness when we think of our family. The tumbling and wrestling on the floor, the healthy teasing, the lively dinner conversations, sharing tales of our daily experiences, the three-, four-, or five-way hugs, the home movies or videos, the family photos, and the singing and dancing lighten our spirits and bring joy to our hearts. We face enough stress and frustrations out in the world; **we want our home to be a haven where we can relax and enjoy each other.**

Experiencing happiness and building memories is difficult when family members rarely interact. **Parents and children can't get to know and *enjoy* each other if they never do anything together.** Interaction must be a daily occurrence. We bake cakes and cookies, make play dough, play board games (Scrabble, Sequence, Candy Land, Sorry), make puzzles, ride bikes, swim at the neighborhood pool, play soccer, and go on picnics. All these activities allow us to relate as individuals, while having fun. **This interaction creates a closeness that is measured by the comfort each of us feels being around the others.**

That's one reason we're concerned when we hear people tell us they bought a TV and VCR for their child's bedroom. It seems that in more and more families, each member lives in his own little world, doing his own thing. Children and parents aren't spending time together but retreating to their individual rooms. We all need "space," but enough is enough.

The first time we took David to Creighton University in Omaha, Nebraska, we had the opportunity to meet his former high school biology teacher, John James, and John's parents. John is the youngest of ten children, so we struck a natural affinity from the beginning. While visiting his parents, we talked about family and "space." Mrs. James pointed out that they had one living area, one television, and two bathrooms, which were shared by everyone. They were "forced" to interact to some degree, but in a healthy manner. We agree. We have one television in our home for all of us to share. The boys must agree on what to watch (if they argue about it, the television is shut off), and whatever program they're watching must be appropriate for whoever's up at the time. (This system is somewhat limiting and means that usually the television isn't on.) With the television off, though, we find opportunities to interact with each other. After school, the boys play a pick-up soccer game or street hockey. The younger boys ride bikes or make up a game. In the evenings, we read aloud. We have wonderful memories in our family of time spent reading *The Very Busy Spider* by Eric Carle and *The Little Mouse, The Red Ripe Strawberry, and the Big Hungry Bear* by Don and Audrey Wood. We don't have many memories related to watching television.

Memories flow from the times spent together. Happy memories are little harbors of laughter and tranquility in our daily maelstrom of bustling and stressful days. And like the memory of Vic and the *arugas,* we have special memories and funny stories unique to our family.

One morning we couldn't find Christopher. His bed was empty and he was nowhere to be found. What an eerie and scary feeling. After scouring the house for twenty minutes, we found him—asleep under his bed. Chris had a habit of falling out of bed and not waking up. This particular morning he had fallen out of bed and rolled under it. His brothers tease him about being a "serious and focused" sleeper.

Matthew's still trying to convince his brothers he was attacked by a lizard in his bed when he was five years old. He insists he felt something on his leg, looked, and saw a lizard. Jumping out of bed, he ran to his older brothers for help. When his brothers investigated, they found no lizard in his bed or in the room. The "attack lizard" story lives on.

David, too, still tries to convince everyone he was "pushed" into the pond at the zoo when he was seven years old. He has a hard time convincing anyone because he was standing alone at the time. The picnic lunch had to be postponed because of a soggy David.

Decorating the Christmas tree every year revives the story of "Tony and the Falling Tree," captured on video for posterity. Tony, as the oldest, was asked to place the star on the top of the tree. Although we encouraged him to stand on a stool, he felt he didn't need one. As Tony leaned and reached over to position the star, the tree and Tony toppled. Happily, both were saved by his brothers—as is the memory today.

Thus, when the "dubious" honor to place the star on the tree was bestowed on David, he wisely chose to use a chair to reach the top. David, though, wanted to be sure the star didn't fall off the tree, so he gave it an extra push. Crack went the star! Placing the star on our tree became hazardous to the star, tree, and the oldest at home. So now we top the tree with a wooden angel that was made by Jamie in preschool.

We laugh now, too, about the Easter Eve that we were "invaded" by a cat. Our home was being remodeled at the time, and a black canvas was all that covered one opening for an outside wall. While we were dyeing Easter eggs, the cat snuck under the canvas to his and our surprise. The boys screamed, the cat went wild, and a chase ensued.

Another evening, we were sitting in the den sharing stories. Danny, four years old, couldn't get a word in edgewise. Determined to arouse our attention, he loudly piped up with "When I was a dog!" Not only did he get our attention, we laughed for hours.

Making Children Feel Special by Observing Traditions

Part of raising our children and the enjoyment of family life includes observing traditional holidays and the holy days of our Catholic religion. We also recognize meaningful events in the course of the year that have special significance for the family or for one of us in particular: First Communions, graduations, spring breaks, family trips. Remembering these times elicits memories of the fun and the emotion associated with the event.

We'll always remember Chris's ninth birthday celebration. Cathy's Uncle Sab, her dad's twin brother, was in town. He offered to take us to dinner to celebrate the occasion. Our trip to Carrabba's, a Houston Italian restaurant, could've been just another birthday dinner. But Uncle Sab added a touch of frivolity by continually thanking Chris for being so thoughtful and generous to take us all out for his birthday. Chris's eyes would double in size each time Uncle Sab complimented him. The waiters played along the entire evening, even handing a surprised Chris the tab at the end of the dinner. Chris's face went from "Oh, no" to "Oh, yes" as Uncle Sab, with a big smile on his face, handed him a wad of bills under the table.

The Fourth of July is filled with new traditions for our family. When Tony was five years old and David was four, Cathy spontaneously made a sheet cake decorated as an American flag. Since then, the boys expect and look forward to a flag cake every Fourth of July. Decorating the cake and licking the bowls with the many colors of icing is fun, as well as an opportunity to reinforce for the younger boys the colors and shapes of the flag. The brightly decorated cake arouses interest in the many reasons we celebrate the Fourth of July: acknowledging our personal and religious freedom, commemorating those who have fought for our country, remembering those individuals who are members of our government, and reflecting on the privilege of voting. As the boys grow older, the cake and the memories associated with it prompt discussions of what this privilege of freedom demands of us and what people experience who live in countries where individual freedoms aren't allowed.

Traditions can be simple: Friday night videos at home with popcorn; puzzles on a rainy day; weekend barbecues or picnics; planting flowers in the fall and spring; carving the Halloween pumpkin; decorating Easter eggs. **The shared experiences impart lasting values and memories.**

Establishing Your Own Traditions

We didn't intentionally "establish traditions" or even give it serious thought until a telephone conversation with Cathy's father. We had just told him we wouldn't be able to spend Christmas in Virginia nor would we be traveling to El Paso (Joe's parents' home) to spend the holidays. (Traveling during the holidays to either of our parents' homes became logistically challenging as the family grew, not to mention expensive. Plus, hauling the boys' Christmas presents to Virginia or El Paso and then home again after Christmas, along with the gifts received from relatives, was difficult.) Cathy's dad said he understood firsthand the difficulties of traveling with a "large family" but, more important, he said it was time we established our own family traditions.

(Joe): *In retrospect, I found that advice to be very important and insightful. It made me remember the traditions I experienced growing up and also consider the importance of establishing traditions for our own family.*

I enjoy recalling the many happy memories I have of my own family. The ones that stand out are usually those of our family traditions. My mother's family organized an annual Fourth of July picnic at a local park. There were always large tubs full of ice, soft drinks, and watermelons. My mother comes from a family of nine brothers and sisters, so there were many cousins, aunts, and uncles to spend the time with. The park had a steep grassy hill that we climbed and rolled down over and over again. We usually ended up dirty and itchy from the grass and nauseated from tumbling so many times, but we thoroughly loved the whole event.

I also have fond memories of the dinners we enjoyed celebrating graduations or other very special events. (We didn't go out to eat as a family very often because it was expensive, so these dinners were very special.) We dressed up, and my parents took us to their favorite restaurant, usually on a Sunday. As my brother, sister, and I got older, my father would offer the one being honored the chair to his right.

I also remember quite vividly that my father and mother would stop at our parish church on the way to my aunt and uncle's New Year's Eve party to say a prayer of thanksgiving for the year that was ending and a hopeful prayer for the year to come. My brother, sister, and I didn't necessarily want to stop at the church; we considered it a little "hokey." My parents, though, didn't give us a choice. My father would remind us that we were very fortunate to have the many gifts God had given us over the past year and that we should pray and thank God for the blessings in the year to come. So, although we were "forced" to participate in this thanksgiving, I cherish the memory today.

I also remember a tradition that was passed down from my father's parents. Each night before we went to bed, my brother, sister, and I would come to say good night to my father. We kissed him and then he blessed us by making a small cross over our foreheads. This was his way of showing his love for us and expressing his wishes for God's care for us as we slept. When he visits our home, he continues the tradition, blessing our sons when they come to say good night.

Teaching Values and Culture Through Traditions

Today as adults, we hold very special the many "traditions" that our families established while we were growing up. **Our parents emphasized those values that were especially important—family, education, and the acknowledgement of our dependence on God—and we follow suit with our sons.**

Evening prayers are recited as a family before the younger children go to bed. The boys learn their prayers in this manner, and we hope the message resounds loudly to each of them of the importance of recognizing the Good Lord's hand in our day. We hope remembering the centrality of God and his blessings on each day is a tradition that the boys will continue with their own families.

The Christmas season in our household is a very festive time. But the preparation for Christmas begins four weeks before Christmas Day, with the beginning of the Advent season. This month-long period in the Catholic liturgy focuses on our spiritual preparation for the birth of the Christ Child. With all the commercial influences of the Christmas season, we use this focus to remind the boys of the real reason for our happiness during the Christmas celebration. As previously mentioned, we place an Advent wreath on our dinner table as a centerpiece. Each night a candle is lit during dinner with each week increasing the number of candles lit until all four candles are aflame the week before Christmas. Our evening prayers include a Scripture reading associated with each day of Advent.

Another special tradition for our family is our Advent "mural." The mural—a self-decorated painting of the Nativity scene—hangs on the wall in the kitchen. Each evening following the Scripture reading, one of the boys pastes a piece of the Nativity scene onto the mural. The boys color the background scenery of the mural as well as the many figures that compose the Nativity scene (shepherds, animals in the stable, angels, sheep). The younger boys love coloring the mural and taking turns pasting the components of the scene. Since even the youngest participate in the coloring project, we end up with some interesting figures—an orange sheep, a purple shepherd, a green donkey. But each of the boys is proud of his creative contribution to the mural. The Advent mural is as much a part of the Christmas season as the tree, decorations, and Christmas wreaths. What began as a simple, one-time project, evolved into one of our most treasured traditions.

Another Christmas highlight for our family is cutting down our own Christmas tree. The Houston area has several Christmas tree farms. We choose a Saturday or Sunday before Christmas (finding a day free of soccer or school activities can be a real challenge), pack a picnic lunch, several soccer balls, and a football, and off we go. We ride a tractor to the field with a measuring stick and tree saw in hand. Then the fun begins—getting twelve opinionated people to decide on the "perfect" tree—a true lesson in consensus building. Once the tree is placed in the car, we eat lunch and play soccer and football. Although we sometimes have to cajole the older boys into going, once we're there any misgivings they might have had quickly fade. We *all* have a great time.

People: What Memories Are All About

Thanksgiving has become one of our family's fondest holidays. With Tony and David home from college and friends and family sharing our table, we are reminded of God's blessings and abundance. We don't remember the menu from year to year, but we do remember the people who touched our lives. **And it is people who make the memories special,** from the simple associations—Papa and Shipley Do-nuts, Grandma and ice cream cones after school at Baskin-Robbins, or Uncle Vic and the Mardi Gras King Cake he sends from New Orleans—to the visits by the boys to Grandma and Papa's house in Virginia during the summer or our spring breaks spent on Galveston Island.

(Cathy): *My parents' 50th anniversary was a celebration of family and love. Aunts, uncles, cousins, and friends from both sides of the family—the Muscos and the Johnsons—gathered as one. We laughed, danced, reminisced, and remembered those no longer with us. The celebration reinforced the value of family and the ties that bind us, in spite of the distance that separates us. It was so rewarding watching our sons enjoy themselves with the children of my cousins—dancing, talking, laughing, and playing soccer. It brought to mind my memorable summer visits to Niantic, Providence, and Windsor Locks. Love was everywhere—and you felt it!—then and now! There's no greater feeling than to be surrounded by that much love.*

Cathy's father's advice to begin *our* traditions reflected his understanding of the value of memories and traditions to the family. Families without traditions or happy memories may survive in this hectic world, but they'll lack the ties that connect their family's past and their present experiences. **Traditions and memories, even when initiated for the first time, connect us with our past.** The connection may be with a person such as a parent, brother, sister, aunt, or uncle, or it may be with the deeply rooted values and tenets that our family entrusted to us in their own special way. Traditions endear us to these special people and, more important, to the special values that they instilled.

A family without traditions is a family without history and without living examples of the values they espouse or any introspection of those values. And a family life without laughter is a life filled with the rigor of rules and responsibilities without the enjoyment of what those rules and responsibilities can bring. Rules and responsibilities balance freedoms and privileges, enabling us to enjoy each other. Love without laughter soon becomes drudgery.

Treasure the time you spend with each other. Create and foster traditions and memories that build your family's identity and bind you together through seasons and generations. And, of course, celebrate laughter every day of every year.

Chapter 12

The Boys Talk—
"Our Two Cents"
By Tony and David Garcia-Prats

O*ne person can make a difference; together in Christ we can make a change.*
—Strake Jesuit Freshman Retreat theme '94

And now here is my secret, a very simple secret: It is only with the heart that one can see rightly; what is essential is invisible to the eye.
—Antoine de Saint-Exupéry

Appreciating Our Family

After being at college and away from home for a couple of years, we've had a chance to reflect on our family, and how and why it works. Living so closely with other students in the dorms, we share many experiences with them. Often talk drifts away from topics like sports and music and turns to more personal experiences like hard times, relationships, and families. Through these discussions, we have gained a greater appreciation for the loving family we enjoy at home. Many of our friends talk about not wanting to go home on breaks because they dread seeing their nagging parents or bothersome siblings. We, on the other hand, can't wait to return home to spend time with our parents or play soccer with our younger brothers. It's at these times **we realize how much our family means to us and how truly blessed we are to have a family that loves, cares for, and respects one another.**

Working Together to Fulfill Our Responsibilities

As the two oldest of ten, we are aware that it takes a concerted effort by all twelve members of the family to make our home the loving place it's grown to be. **By following the daily example of our parents, we've learned how important it is for each of us to do our part to keep the family running smoothly and successfully.** Without this team effort, it would be impossible for us, or any family, to succeed.

We each have chores and responsibilities around the house. They are assigned according to ages and schedules, and there is always something each of us can do to help out. These chores, we've learned, are done best when done willingly and with a smile. Our Mom has reminded us countless times that "Jesus loves a happy giver." **Whether it's an "assigned" chore or something extra we're able to do to help out, the willingness and smile go a long way toward making the family run smoothly.** Recently, Joe Pat noticed that the grass in the front yard was dying due to its excessive use as a soccer field—and a baseball field and a football field. He took the initiative to resod and regularly water the grass to make our yard look as if there weren't ten boys constantly playing on it. No one asked him to do this; he just went out of his way to get something done that needed to be done.

Most family chores are assigned according to age. Those of us who drive take the younger brothers to and from school and practices and run errands for our parents; Mark, Tommy, Danny, and Jamie set and clear the table, or feed and walk Princess, our golden retriever. Everyone willingly helps out so the family will benefit. Even Timmy, the youngest, tries his best to pitch in, whether it's carrying in a loaf of bread when Mom or Dad return with the groceries, dumping food into Princess's dish, or turning on the water hose for any reason.

The youngest five aren't expected to do their own laundry, but they are expected to make their beds in the morning, keep their rooms clean, and put the clean, folded clothes in their drawers. The oldest five share the responsibility of mowing the yard, with Matthew currently doing most of the mowing. We've each seen the day when we graduate from merely raking leaves to mowing the lawn. The younger ones still have this to look forward to. We've realized, too, over the years, that we're lucky to have so many brothers to divide the work load; if there were just two or three of us, we'd have to mow the yard or wash the dishes more often or do the whole job ourselves. Although there's more to do with ten of us, dividing and conquering lessens the time involved—plus it's more "fun" having someone to do the chores with.

Another way to help out at home is to accept the responsibility of taking care of ourselves. Our parents started teaching us how to take care of ourselves at an early age. They taught us the little things we can do for ourselves. We learned the basics of hygiene—brushing our teeth, good grooming, tying our own shoes, preparing our clothes—and then moved on to bigger things like making our own school lunches or doing our laundry. Because we keep up with these personal responsibilities, our parents don't have to worry about them.

In addition to taking care of ourselves around the house with chores and hygiene, we also assume responsibility for our schoolwork, sports practices, and other school and church activities. Just as we know that our beds should be made every morning, we realize that getting our homework done is our responsibility, too. It's up to each of us to bring home the right materials from school, so that we get the work done well and on time. We're also responsible for knowing when and where sports practices and games are, and if for some reason our parents can't drive us to a practice or game, we find a ride. That's not to say our parents won't do everything they can to assist us, but the main responsibility falls on us. If our parents had to find rides for all of us, it would take them forever, and they'd end up feeling stressed trying to accomplish everything. **So by taking care of ourselves, we help the entire family.**

Learning to take care of these basic needs turned out to be an advantage for us now that we're in college. Our parents aren't physically there urging us to keep up with our studies, meet deadlines, or make sure our clothes or rooms are clean. But because we learned the importance of school at an early age, as well as self-discipline and responsibility, we make sure we keep up with all our assignments. And though our parents call to see how we're doing, they aren't there looking over our shoulders making sure papers and projects are completed. We see to it on our own that what needs to be done is done. (Our dorm rooms? Now, that's a different story!)

Learning the Difference Between Rights and Privileges

Many kids don't understand that with responsibilities comes freedom. They may gripe about cleaning their rooms, mowing the yard, or having to pick up their brother or sister at school, but they don't realize that by doing these little things they gain trust and privileges. **There is a difference between rights and privileges.** We don't have to play sports or drive the car on the weekend or have our laundry done for us. These things are privileges, not rights. But many times these privileges are taken for granted. When we were younger, our mom did all the laundry for us. It seemed like she never stopped doing laundry. Washing, drying, and folding—only to have us pick up the neatly folded clothes and throw them on our beds to be put away later. Pretty soon those neatly folded clothes were no longer neat or folded. We were repeatedly warned about this trend, until one day Mom shifted the responsibility of laundry to us. We were in shock! Us? Do laundry? We didn't even know where to start. Out of necessity, the older five quickly learned, and now we're experts, which proved to be a blessing for us in college.

As we've grown older, our financial responsibilities have grown with us. We've never been overwhelmed by these responsibilities, though, because our parents' expectations are reasonable. If we want to drive, we are required to pay part of the car insurance. In high school, we paid the additional fees outside of school tuition and were responsible for our own entertainment expenses. In college, we're responsible for paying part of our tuition and buying our books. Money for entertainment is solely our responsibility. We work during the summers to earn the money we need to meet our expenses. We also hold part-time jobs on campus during the school year now that we're in college. (Our parents didn't allow us to work while in high school, except during the summer.) Learning to save, budget, and sacrifice is not always easy or fun, but being able to responsibly handle our money has proven beneficial to us now.

We all enjoy athletic activities and being involved at school and church. If we want to play sports, we have to do well in school. "No pass, no play" was a rule enforced in our home long before the Texas Legislature got involved. Actually, the rule in our house is more like "Do your best, or no play." Sports and extracurricular activities come second to school. So doing well in school means being able to play sports. We've also learned that developing the habits of discipline and responsibility in our schoolwork carries over into sports and vice versa.

Our willingness to drive our younger brothers to and from school and soccer practices earns us the privilege of using the car on weekends or when needed. Driving the car and playing sports aren't necessarily rewards gained, but they are a result of trust gained. If our parents can depend on us to get our homework done or pick up our younger brothers, they can trust we'll be responsible when we go out with our friends, respect curfews, or be prepared for school the next day, even though there's a big game or practice.

Respect: A Two-Way Street

Respect in the family, as in any relationship, is vital. We are respectful to our parents and each other, and our parents return that respect. We demonstrate our respect by obeying them and their rules while we are "under their roof." They reciprocate that respect by providing us our privacy and allowing us to grow up and make our own responsible decisions. **We obey the rules and guidelines that they establish because we understand they don't make rules or set guidelines to control us; they make them because they love us and want the best for us and the family.** And many times, Dad and Mom *do* know best.

But just because we respect our parents doesn't mean we always like or agree with their rules. Just like other teenagers, we've lobbied for longer curfews and our own style of music and clothing. **We don't always get what we want, but our parents never blow us off. They do listen to our reasoning.** They've been in our shoes before—as hard as that is to imagine—but we've never been in theirs. Sometimes one of us will walk into our bedroom after talking with our parents about a controversial issue, such as curfew, and be displeased with their decision. Hoping for the other brother's support, we'll rant and rave about how unfair they're being. (In addition to our home being a secure and great place to vent our frustrations, we always have our brothers to talk to about what happened.) Sometimes we both agree that our parents are being unreasonable, but other times one of us doesn't think they're being unfair. We may sit the other brother down and say, "Hold on. Have you looked at it from their point of view?" The answer is almost always no. Seeing it from the parental point of view helps us understand where they're coming from, even if we still don't totally agree. **We've learned, too, that our parents have to look at situations in the context of the family as a whole.**

Being Role Models for Each Other

Being the older two of the bunch, we realize that we are being looked up to on a daily basis. Like it or not, we are role models for our younger brothers. Everything we do, whether at home, school, or on the soccer field, is watched and frequently imitated by them. When our brothers see us studying hard for a test, they realize that it's okay to study, and they can do the same. Likewise, if they see us disobeying our parents, they think that it's okay. We can't remember how many times our parents have reprimanded us for something our little brothers have done because they saw us do it first. One afternoon, one of our younger brothers told our parents that he was "going to take a piss." Mom and Dad sat our brother down to explain that what he said was inappropriate; they also sat us down to remind us that our brother didn't learn the language from them and that we needed to clean up our act.

There are other aspects of being a good role model besides having good study habits, and appropriate language and behavior. Our brothers observe how we treat each other and our parents. **If they see us show respect to the family, our friends, and others around us, they begin to develop that same sense of respect.**

We also try to pass down our sense of good sportsmanship to our younger brothers. We're all extremely competitive. But there is more to sports and life than just winning. When we were younger, two-on-two basketball games became so competitive that they usually ended up with one player not talking to the other, because of a bad call or a hard foul. As we've grown older, we've learned that when playing sports, especially with our brothers, our goal isn't winning or losing, but having a good time. Now in our friendly soccer games at the neighborhood field, we have an unwritten rule: We never keep score. The games are still competitive, but they always remain fun, because it doesn't matter whether or not the last goal counts or who wins or loses.

Since we're all close in age, sometimes our younger brothers have to compete against each other in soccer or race each other in a swim meet. After the meet or game, they always congratulate each other, no matter who won. They are genuinely happy for the other.

We learn a thing or two from our younger brothers, too. Last summer, ten-year-old Tommy won a Ping-Pong championship at a neighborhood Fourth of July party. He was excited, as were the rest of us. We watched as he graciously accepted his first-place prize—two gift certificates for ice cream—and joked about who he was going to take with him to the ice cream parlor. Then Tommy walked over to the runner-up, congratulated him, and handed him one of the gift certificates. It was one of the kindest gestures we've ever seen, and a moment we'll never forget.

We've also noticed times when Danny, our eight-year-old budding artist, will be drawing with one of his younger brothers and they will show him some indecipherable scribbles and ask, "Danny, how do you like my dinosaur?" Without hesitating for a second, he always compliments the work. The younger one proudly returns to his art with a smile on his face. **It's amazing to see the results that can be produced by a positive compliment from a sibling.**

We are supportive of each other and free from sibling rivalry because of the way our parents treat us. It's almost impossible to feel genuinely happy for someone when you feel that your skills and abilities are inadequate. **Our parents never compare us with each other, rather they celebrate our differences.** They've never announced someone's straight-A report card or ridiculed another son's less stellar grades. We each excel at different things, and we know we're loved because of who we are and not because of what we accomplish. Our parents accept us as individuals and encourage us to develop our own talents. They help us to build self-esteem and confidence in our abilities. As older brothers, we try to imitate our parents in how we treat our younger siblings. **It's easy to be supportive of each other when we are secure with ourselves.** We're sad to see other people be jealous of their siblings' accomplishments. We feel sad because we know that the person has little confidence in himself or herself, but also because often our proudest moments have not been about our own accomplishments, but about our brothers' successes.

Stepping into Our Parents' Shoes

Last summer we gained a unique perspective into how much our parents do for the family. They took a well-deserved vacation to Italy for almost two weeks. (Our dad had received the Golden Teaching Award from Baylor College of Medicine's Pediatric Department. Part of the award was an expense-paid trip to any medical meeting in the world. Dad chose a meeting in San Remo, Italy. The trip out of the country was a first for our parents.) The oldest five volunteered to run the show while they were away. Four of us had jobs and one of us attended a summer enrichment program, so it took a lot of organization and teamwork. When we weren't at our jobs, we were home making lunch and putting the little guys down for naps. After a long day we would drive everyone to their soccer practices, fix dinner, and put everyone to bed. After about a week we remembered that we were supposed to be bathing everyone, too. With a lot of help from friends and more than a couple of meals cooked for us, we all survived.

We learned a lot from the experience and gained a true respect for what our parents accomplish on a daily basis. **First of all, we learned how physically taxing being a parent is.** Somewhat to our surprise, we were exhausted every night, and there were five of us dividing the workload. We still can't figure out how our parents accomplish what they do. **Second, we learned how important it is for each individual to cooperate in order for the group to function as a whole.** Even if just one of our little brothers acted up, it made for an especially long day. On the other hand, when everyone helped, the day ran smoothly. **One person acting selfishly creates a negative effect on the whole, just as someone's compassion, generosity, or self-sacrifice has a positive effect.** This is a lesson our parents have tried to explain to us, but it took firsthand experience to truly understand the concept. Third, we learned that being a parent is very stressful. Usually when we baby-sit, we are responsible for everyone, but we know that as soon as Mom and Dad return we can hand that responsibility back to them. However, being responsible for our little brothers, knowing that Mom and Dad weren't coming home for a while, was overwhelming at first. We found that kind of twenty-four hour responsibility to be very stressful. **Finally, we learned that being a parent is very rewarding.** Yes, it was exhausting and stressful driving across town to an all-day soccer tournament, with the rain pouring down, unclear directions, and five rowdy brothers in the backseat. Our parents must have experienced similar situations many times over many years. But we also realize what gets them through the stress. Once we arrived at the game, watching our brothers play was so enjoyable, and we were so proud of them, that the hassles involved in getting to the game faded from our memory. The warm, satisfying feelings make everything worth the work.

Choosing Family and Spirituality as Top Priorities

To do things well, and to get things done, we've learned to establish priorities. Following our parents' example, we make spirituality, family, and education our top priorities.

Our parents' emphasis on each of us to develop our spirituality has been a great gift. During high school, we were both involved in the Freshman Retreat. (A group of upperclassmen organize and run a three-day retreat for the entire freshman class.) The retreat focuses on building the freshman class into a community and stresses the importance of God's influence in our lives. The retreat leaders bring the class together and work to develop their spiritual growth, emphasizing that each individual can make a difference with the help of God. The Freshman Retreat was something we felt strongly about because our involvement was a way to put our faith into action.

When we were younger, our parents took us to Sunday Mass every weekend, but now we attend Mass every weekend—not because our parents want us to, but because *we* truly want to go. In college and especially during finals, many students are tempted to blow off church, but we've found that going to Mass is one of the most rewarding things we do. That one hour gives us a chance to put things into perspective. We find ourselves more relaxed and ready to go after gathering at church to worship and thank God. **The spirituality our parents gave us has gradually become our own.**

We observe the same process happening to our younger brothers. Our high school brothers are now actively involved in the Freshman Retreat. And we see signs of them maturing spiritually in the little things they do every day, whether it's contributing meaningful prayers at dinner or patiently helping their brothers or friends.

Sensational stories about dysfunctional families make the headlines and evening news, and cause lots of banter about "family values." But looking around, there are more subtle signs that many parents and children need help, that they aren't making family a priority. **Parents *must* make their family a priority.**

This summer, while at our neighborhood pool, we saw a ten-year-old girl taking care of her five-year-old sister day after day without parental supervision. As lifeguards, we couldn't let the five-year-old swim because she was without adult supervision, a pool rule. We can't imagine our parents expecting Mark or Tommy to care for a younger brother all day. We felt genuinely sorry for those girls. Other times we notice parents in the video store who let their children rent violent or explicit movies because they don't want to take the time to set boundaries. Once we noticed a young girl, around twelve years old, pleading with her father to let her rent *Schindler's List*. Her father objected saying that she couldn't handle it yet, but after some whining and arguing, the girl walked out with the movie. **It's as if parents don't want to say no to their kids or accept their parental responsibilities.**

Saying no is tough, especially with younger brothers. When we babysit, sometimes we have to tell our brothers they can't have an ice cream cone or watch a certain movie, even though we know we may have to tolerate their whining and complaining. **We understand that saying no is the right thing to do, although maybe not the easiest.**

Brothers and Best Friends

Before we left for college, we took for granted the friendships that we share with each other. Not only are we brothers, but we're truly the best of friends. We hang out and joke around just like any other group of friends. It's great, too, having built-in friends to spontaneously play a game of basketball with or go with to a movie. And if one brother's not interested, we can usually find another one who is.

When Tony left for college, the house felt empty, not just because we lost a brother, but because we lost a friend. And every time we leave for college, we miss our best friends. People are amazed and surprised at how close we all are to each other. We remember the time when we were in high school and both played in a volleyball league with our church youth group. Tony had been playing since the beginning of the league, and David joined the team a couple of weeks later. During the week after David joined the team, the youth director approached our mom to find out more about Tony's friend. He noticed that we got along well and had a great time together; he was unaware that we were brothers. When Mom told him we were brothers, he was shocked. He figured we were best friends—and, in fact, we are.

Because we are such good friends, we respect and value each others' opinions. Our high school brothers ask our opinion about teachers and courses we had in high school, knowing we will help them out as much as we can. When we see them do something we approve of, or disapprove of, we let them know. When they need our advice about a situation on the soccer field or in the classroom, or about anything else, we are always there to support each other. We know that while we are away at college, we can pick up the phone and call home and there will always be a friend to talk to, whether it's our parents or a brother. Our brothers know they can call us, too, when they need to talk.

Our Loving Family Shapes Our Life Decisions

Coming from a large and loving family has helped to shape our decisions about school, work, friendships, spirituality, and the way we live our lives. **Choosing to make our family a priority in life is the best decision we've ever made.** We also know that when we start families of our own, we'll make our children our number one priority, just as our parents have made us theirs. Sure, it takes a lot of work and some sacrifices to become a happy and loving family, but we wouldn't want it any other way.

Mission Accomplished— and the Beat Goes On

B*e the change you want to see in the world.*
— Gandhi

You give but little when you give of your possessions. It is when you give of yourself that you truly give.
— Kahlil Gibran

One chapter ends, another begins—whether we're referring to a chapter in this book or a chapter in our lives. The chapters are all interrelated— what happens in one affects what happens in another. We strive to make the early chapters build and strengthen the ones to follow.

Writing this book was a challenge—from finding the time to write to finding the appropriate words to share. (We often felt like the Apollo 13 astronauts: "Houston, we have a problem,"—time!) As the words flowed, we were reminded of the hardships and the blessings associated with parenting: the interrupted sleep, the days without rest, the worries, the decisions, the fears, and the tears coupled with the warmth of love, hugs, kisses, laughter, successes, pride, and joy!

Parenting is the greatest responsibility bestowed on anyone. How humbling to be entrusted by God to foster the physical, emotional, spiritual, and intellectual development of another individual. *Every day* we face so many decisions and choices—some easy and some difficult— that affect our children. We choose what words to speak to our children and how we treat them. Are we kind or unkind, respectful or disrespectful? We choose to love our children. Do our sons feel our love from the moment they wake up in the morning until they fall asleep at night? We determine how much time we spend with our children. Are they a priority in our lives and do they know they are? We choose to share our faith with our children. Are we examples of God's love in the world? Do they understand the importance of God in their lives and live according to His commandments?

"To love somebody is not just a strong feeling—it is a decision, it is a judgment, it is a promise," wrote Erich Fromm. If we believe that statement, then loving our children is a decision and a promise. Along the same lines, St. Thomas Aquinas tells us, "To love is to will the good of another." As parents, we must decide to make our family a priority and to make choices that enable and encourage our children to develop physically, emotionally, intellectually, and spiritually—to be the best that they can be!

Parenting isn't easy. It's demanding, challenging, and constant. We can't decide to fulfill our role one day and not the next. Our children need and depend on our *constant* love and attention—every day! We can take a week's vacation physically from our children, but we can't take a sabbatical from the emotional and spiritual vows of parenting.

We realize how quickly the years go by. We look at Tony, the oldest, and remember him as Timmy is today. The realization that the years fly by so swiftly encourages us to relish the time we spend with our sons, from oldest to youngest, because quickly they are grown and on their own. As Tony approaches the next chapter in his life, we are filled with mixed emotions. We're proud of who he is and the choices he's made, and we're excited about his future opportunities. At the same time, we close a chapter in our lives with Tony. We'll always be his parents, but we no longer need to "parent." We pray our years of love, guidance, and emphasis on God will sustain him, and all the boys eventually, as they move on with their lives.

The week we returned from taking Tony to Saint Louis University his freshman year, the mother in the comic strip *For Better or For Worse* also experienced her son's first year away at college. She wonders why a lighter load—fewer places to set at the table, fewer clothes to wash, one less bed to make, less to worry about—feels so heavy. That is exactly how we felt—less day-to-day responsibility yet a heavy heart. We experienced the same emotions when David left for school. And we continue to experience them each time the boys return to college after a break. We know they'll always be an integral part of our lives, but a change is evolving. We know—we were there at one time.

Years ago a mother of four grown children expressed her amazement that we would have five children in today's world when we could do "something" about it. When we told her we wanted our children and enjoyed them tremendously, she responded, "Yeah, you say that now while they're little. Just wait until they're older. You'll think differently." Another woman, the mother of two grown sons who was privy to the comments, leaned over and told us, "I enjoyed my sons when they were two, twelve, and now twenty. They were good boys then; they're good now. Your boys won't be any different." And, you know, she's right. We have enjoyed our sons at all ages.

We observe too frequently how parents allow the stresses of life to interfere with their enjoyment of their children. Or we observe parents setting priorities that don't include their children. Work, social functions, and the accumulation of wealth and "things" are more important than time spent with their family. With the deaths of relatives and close friends, we are reminded how precious and limited our time together is.

We want to give our children the most love we can in the time God provides. We don't want to waste our time worrying or chasing the wrong dreams. We want to enjoy the moments at hand.

As parents, we can't sit back and let someone else fulfill our parenting responsibilities, and then wonder, "What happened?" "Where did I go wrong?" Children need their parents to love and care for them all the time, not just when it's convenient. We can't make excuses for why we're not fulfilling our responsibilities. Instead, we need to decide how we're going to make our families function so that each individual can reach his or her full potential.

If changes need to be made, there's no better time than the present. Change doesn't always come easy, yet if we want our families to be positive experiences full of love and joy, we must be willing to change our attitudes and approaches. As we said in the prologue, **"Successful parents do what unsuccessful parents are unwilling to do."**

Remember, we're not alone in our parenting efforts. The God who blessed us with our children is always ready to help. We just need to ask for His help and *listen* to His response.

His help enabled us to successfully complete this book. We teased about writing the book in "our spare time" and, yet, we've been amazed at the "spare time" He provided us. The support and words of encouragement by our friends, from a simple, "How's the book coming?" to providing a child-free morning to complete a chapter, were signs of His encouragement and support.

We look back and laugh at the ironic experiences we encountered through the year as we worked on this book—a dislocated thumb, a broken finger, an appendectomy, and two fractured ankles; the five youngest boys being sick with 103-degree fevers for six days (as we were sharing our thoughts on maintaining a positive attitude, regardless of the circumstances); the ice storm in Houston, Texas, that caused a six-hour electrical outage (with the pressures of meeting a looming deadline). On one occasion, Jamie, when asked if his mommy worked, proudly told his preschool classmates, "My mommy doesn't work. *She* writes a book!" We also remember the time Cathy told Tony, as he left for school, to take good care of Kari, his girlfriend. He jokingly responded, "No, Mom, she takes care of me." Cathy teasingly reminded him, "Tony, it doesn't work that way." And he quickly answered, "I know, Mom, I know. I read your book!"

Writing about our parenting experience has helped us to better understand how and why we do what we do. We had never taken the time before to conceptualize how we created a loving, happy family. It helped us to reaffirm our values and our love and commitment to each other. Throughout, we maintained our priorities—we just added another commitment to our schedule. Everyone pitched in, even more than usual, to make the book a reality. We know the boys are proud and glad to be a part of our family. They realize they don't have as many material possessions as many of their friends, but they know that what they do have is more rewarding and longer lasting.

When David was twelve years old, he wrote an essay entitled "A Happy Family." We share the draft of his essay, with his permission. (We couldn't find the final copy.)

A happy family is but an early heaven. This means a lot to me for many reasons but the most important reason being my special family.

Heaven is a place where happiness prevails. My family stays together like a horse and carriage and that's why it is an early heaven. Why should I wait until I die to reach heaven when I can have it now? Each member of this elite group makes it possible for each other to obtain joy here on earth. In my family it is apparent that we work together to strive for an even happier household.

We care for the family and we care for others. This makes the house an easier environment to live in. Each person is like an angel helping and caring for each other. God plays an important role in our family and my parents emphasize religion. Therefore, heaven isn't just a farfetched reward somebody imagined. It's on earth right here and now.

Is your family an early heaven? If not, try and make it one. Hopefully, someday I'll be resting on clouds, but why wait for someday?

David's right! Why wait to enjoy heaven when a piece of it is right here on earth with those we love? The love we have for each other binds us together and fosters our happy home. Our greatest reward as parents is knowing the boys love each other, us, and their God.

The book comes to a close, but our parental responsibilities continue—the beat goes on. We know we'll face new challenges in the years to come because each of our sons is unique and no two days are ever the same. We're confident, though, that if we maintain our priorities and make the right choices, we'll continue to be happy.

We come full circle and end as we began: Respect, love, appreciate, and enjoy your children. Parenting is challenging and demanding, but when done well and with love, there is no greater reward for ourselves and for society.

The choice is yours!

May God bless each and every one of you and guide you in your parenting efforts.

Suggested Reading from the Garcia-Prats' Home Library

A Book of Saints, Anne Gordon

All Grown Up and No Place to Go, David Elkind

The Art of Loving, Erich Fromm

Familiaris Consortio (On the Family), Pope John Paul II

The First Twelve Months of Life, Frank Caplan

Habits of the Heart, Robert N. Bellah

Happiness Is an Inside Job, John Powell, S.J.

Hey! Listen to This, Edited by Jim Trelease

Hide or Seek, Dr. James Dobson

The Hurried Child, David Elkind

In the Spirit, Richard J. Hauser, S.J.

I've Got to Talk to Somebody, God, Marjorie Holmes

Lift Up Your Hearts, Pope John Paul II

Living, Loving and Learning, Leo Buscaglia, Ph.D

Loving Each Other, Leo Buscaglia, Ph.D.

Man's Search for Meaning, Viktor E. Frankl

Miseducation, David Elkind

The Moral Intelligence of Children, Robert Coles

More Random Acts of Kindness, Conari Press

Moving in the Spirit, Richard J. Hauser, S. J.

Poverty of Spirit, Johannes B. Metz

The Power of Positive Students, Dr. William Mitchell with Dr. Charles Paul Conn

The Power of Positive Thinking, Norman Vincent Peale

Prayers, Michel Quoist

Quiet Places with Jesus, Rev. Isaias Powers, C.P.

Random Acts of Kindness, Conari Press

Read All About It!, Edited by Jim Trelease

The Read-Aloud Handbook, Jim Trelease

Read to Me: Raising Kids Who Like to Read, Bernice E. Cullinan

The Road Less Traveled, M. Scott Peck, M.D.

365 Saints: Your Daily Guide to the Wisdom and Wonder of Their Lives, Woodeene Koenig-Bricker

Solve Your Child's Sleep Problems, Richard Ferber, M.D.

The Strong-Willed Child, Dr. James Dobson

Touching, Ashley Montagu

Unconditional Love, John Powell, S.J.

The Way of the Heart, Henri J. M. Nouwen

What to Expect When You're Expecting, Arlene Eisenberg, Heidi Eisenberg Murkoff, and Sandee Eisenberg Hathaway, R.N.

The Garcia-Prats' Play Dough Recipe

Two cups flour
One cup salt
Four teaspoons cream of tartar
Two cups of water
Two tablespoons of salad oil
Food coloring

Mix all ingredients together. Cook over medium heat until a soft ball forms. Knead until smooth.

Index

affection
    showing, 27, 50
age appropriate
    activities, 73-75
    expectations and consequences, 57
allowances, 93
arguing
    ineffectiveness of, 66

baby-sitters, 15
behavior
    adults as examples of responsible,
        108-110
    consistency in discouraging nega-
        tive, 59
    teaching acceptable and appropriate,
        57-59
    teaching that negative is ineffective,
        65
beliefs
    teaching without hesitation, 73
birth control, 151
books. See reading

career
    balancing family and, 18, 28, 182
changes
    accepting and adapting to, 8, 103
characteristics
    inheriting moral and emotional
        from parents, 98-99

childbirth, 19-21
child-proofing, 62
children
    adjusting to life with, 22-23
    celebrating uniqueness of, 34
    comparing, 107
    developing sibling love vs. rivalry,
        104-108
    developing intellectual abilities, 83-84
    developing talents, 84-85
    encouraging to make good choices, 67
    faith and, 85-86
    feeling important in parent's lives, 27
    finding the best education for, 29
    fostering confidence in, 48
    fostering self-esteem in, 35
    getting to know friend's families, 178
    importance of interaction with, 34
    learning the importance of God, 158
    moral and emotional development,
        98-99
    nurturing intellectual abilities, 83-84
    peer pressure and, 73, 205
    positive reinforcement for, 43-46
    praise and, 46
    protecting, 82-83
    providing positive environments
        and role models for, 46-49
    providing realistic responsibilities
        for, 94-95
    raising self-disciplined, 57

reading and, 83-84, 127-132
self-esteem and, 35, 94-95
self-reliance and, 94-95
setting good examples for, 108-110
sharing faith with, 85-86
sibling rivalry and, 104-108, 224
societal pressures, 73, 205
stepping into parents' shoes, 225-226
teaching how to cope with stress,
    202-205
treating with respect, 26
using positive language to encour-
    age, 49
choices
    encouraging children to make good,
        67
    making responsible parental, 86-87
    making the best of each day, 38
church
    value of involvement in, 157-160
coaches
    attitudes and approaches of, 46-49
communication
    developing effective skills, 7
    encouraging honesty and openness
        in, 70
    establishing lines of, 70
    marriage and, 2, 7
    respect and, 8
    sharing feelings, 7
    talking with children, 121-123
community service, 89
competition
    good sportsmanship and, 223-224
    healthy, 107
confidence
    fostering, 48
conflict
    dealing with, 7
consequences
    breaking rules and, 62
    enforcing, 7, 66
    implementing relevant, 63-67
creativity
    furnishing art materials to encour-
        age, 124

learning by doing, 124-126
providing a stimulating environ-
    ment for, 123-124
decisions
before starting a family, 18
    explaining reasons behind, 70
    making based on conscience, 151-154
discipline
    adapting as children grow, 62
    age appropriate, 52
    authority and, 52
    building blocks of effective, 56
    effective, 8, 68
    father's role in, 68
    following through , 52
    positive learning experiences and,
        51-53
    time-out, 52
diversity, 114-118

education
    attending teacher conferences, 134
    commitment to children's, 134
    depending on teachers for advice
        and support, 178
    finding the best, 29
    fostering a positive home/school
        partnership, 135-136
    homework and, 134
    instilling the love of learning, 119-143
    involvement in children's, 133-135
    Jesuit, 29, 40, 89
    making the learning experience fun,
        126
    participation in children's, 134
    providing supplemental programs, 141
    school success and , 133-135
    seeking additional help, 135
empathy, 72
encouragement
    children's choices and, 67
    creativity and, 124
    kindness and, 181
    trickle down effect and, 51
    using positive language , 49

environments
　　providing stimulating, 123-124
　　providing positive, 46-69
examples
　　setting good, 108-110
expectations
　　children rising to parent's level of, 136-138

faith
　　basing philosophy on, 162-163
　　happiness as a result of religious practices and, 146
　　integrating into daily life, 155
　　sharing with children, 85-86
　　strengthening, 150
family
　　adaptability and flexibility in routines, 189
　　appreciating, 217-218
　　balancing strengths and weaknesses, 13
　　choosing as top priority, 226-227
　　decisions prior to starting a, 18
　　elements that strengthen, 18
　　financial security and, 18
　　forgiveness, 13
　　grandparents, 171-172
　　meetings, 70
　　memories and traditions, 207-216
　　praying together, 156-157
　　support from extended, 170-172
　　support from within the, 168-169
fatigue
　　coping with, 185-206
　　exercising to reduce, 201
　　getting adequate sleep, 200
favoritism, 106-107
financial responsibilities
　　earning money from jobs, 93-94
　　living within your means, 196-198
　　prioritizing goals, 196-198
　　reasonable expectations and, 221
financial responsibility
　　obligations and, 93
　　teaching, 92-94

friends
　　developing a support system with, 165-183
　　need for, 173-174

games
　　educational, 126
goals
　　helping children to accomplish, 63
　　prioritizing time and needs, 30
　　materialism and societal, 86
　　tempering individual, couple, and family, 9
God
　　conversing with, 148
　　developing a relationship with, 147-148
　　influence of, 145-146
　　prayer and, 147, 156-157, 201, 214
　　seeing in the face of others, 154-155
　　trusting in, 205-206
guidelines
　　adapting with age, 63
　　setting and reinforcing, 62
　　setting limits and, 69

happiness, 112-113
　　faith and, 146
　　memories and, 207-216
　　traditions and, 207-216
health
　　taking responsibility for children's, 82-83
　　women's, 80
honesty, 102
household duties
　　sharing, 9, 23-26, 42, 59, 187-189, 218-220
humor
　　using to diffuse difficult situations, 77

inconvenience
　　accepting, 64
　　fear of imposing consequence because of, 66
　　long-term benefits of a temporary, 64

individuality
adapting to each child's, 21
respecting, 19

jealousy, 51

kindness
producing positive results through,
181
knowledge
teaching appreciation for, 119

labor and delivery, 19-21
language
reading and development of, 128
setting standards, 61
talking to children, 121-122
teaching politeness, 58, 60
using positive to encourage children,
49-50, 60
learning,
hands-on, 124-126
instilling the love of, 119-143
lifelong process of, 142-143
mistakes and, 142
process of, 120
limits
guidelines and, 62-63, 69
setting, 76
love
developing sibling, 104-108
expressing, 14, 120-121
gift of, 29
happiness and, 146
teaching respect and, 27
unconditional, 28, 35

marriage
adjusting to, 3-7
communication skills and, 2
elements that strengthen, 18
influencing components of, 11
preparation programs for, 11
primary support system in, 166-167
prioritizing the relationship, 14
memories

creating happy, 208-211
family history, 207-216
mornings
establishing a routine for, 42
motherhood
activities and schedules, 22
career vs. staying at home, 18, 182
finding time for self, 22
Mothers Day Out programs, 23
music, 122, 143

nagging, 66
nap time, 64
needs
fulfilling physical and spiritual, 10-11
fulfilling spiritual, 11
negativity, 41

parenting
developing techniques for, 55
expectations of children, 95-97
five L's of, 76
fulfilling responsibilities, 79-99
learning, 55-56
learning to be adaptable, flexible,
and prepared, 37-39
maintaining a positive attitude and
approach, 39-41
recognizing responsibilities, 79-99
shared responsibility of, 23
successful, 234
peer pressure, 73, 205
Play Dough recipe, 239
possessiveness
fostering, 43
language and, 49-50
maintaining, 39-41
mornings and, 43
parenting and, 37-53
providing role models and environments that foster, 46-49
reinforcement of, 44
trickle down effect and, 51
praise, 50
prayer, 85-86, 147, 156-157, 201, 214
pregnancy, 19-21, 87

prejudicial attitudes, 114
priorities
    differentiating between wants and
        needs, 30-33
    establishing, 30-33

quality time
    physical care-giving vs. emotional
        parenting, 33-34

reading, 83-84, 127-129
    age appropriate books, 130
    choosing books based on interests,
        130
    providing a variety of material, 129
    suggested, 237-238
recipe
    Play Dough, 239
respect
    between parents and children, 222
    communication and, 8
    discipline and, 60-62
    teaching love and, 26-28
responsibilities
    demonstrating for others, 87-88
    financial, 30, 93-94, 221
    fulfilling parental, 79-99
    fulfilling in community, 111-112
    handing down through generations,
        95-97
    learning to accept, 90
    need for routines and, 194-195
    new parents and, 22
    parental, 19
    parental choices, 86-87
    personal belongings and, 92
    positive reinforcement and, 44
    providing realistic, 94
    recognizing parental, 79-99
    rights vs. privileges, 220-221
    self-respect and, 80-81
    setting examples, 87-89
    sharing parental, 9, 23
    teaching, 66, 93
    teaching about financial, 93-94
    working together to fulfill, 218

role models
    providing positive, 46-69
    siblings as, 222-224
routines
    stabling morning, 43
    memories and traditions, 207-216
    need for responsibilities and, 194-195
rules
    establishing standards and, 69
    setting and reinforcing, 62

sanity
    striving for, 185-186
schedules
    accommodating everyone's needs, 71
    adaptability and flexibility in, 188-
        190
    central calendar and, 186
    family meetings and, 71
    time management and, 186-189
schools
    meeting the needs of children and
        family, 29
seat belts, 82-83
self-control
    maintaining, 5
self-esteem
    fostering, 35, 50
    providing realistic responsibilities to
        augment, 94-95
    security and, 224
self-love, 10, 80-81
self-reliance, 94-95
self-respect, 10, 80-81
sensitivity
    fostering, 61, 113
sex
    providing time for and attention to,
        15
    teaching children about, 113
sharing
    household duties, 24-26
    parental responsibilities, 19, 22-23
    siblings and, 106
siblings
    developing love, not rivalry, 105-108

friends as well as, 228
love and support of each other, 169-170
skills
developing children's, 84-85
societal pressures, 73, 205
socioeconomic conditions, 19
spirituality
choosing as top priority, 160, 226-227
faith and family, 145-163
growing in, 150
strengthening, 160-162
standards
establishing rules and, 69
setting fair and workable, 106
stress
avoiding, 191-194
avoiding situations that create, 193
changing the task to improve mood, 202
coping with, 185-206
eliminating, 191-194
enjoying interests and commitments simultaneously, 201
exercising to reduce, 201
holidays and, 199
making changes to eliminate or reduce, 191
minimizing by organizing and prioritizing, 198-200
presenting solutions vs. complaining, 202
teaching children how to cope with, 202-205
using music to uplift, 202
support
extended families and, 170-172
friends and, 165-183
grandparents and, 172
parents and, 166-167
pediatrician and, 177
siblings and, 169-170
within the family, 168-169

talents
developing children's, 84-85

talking
language development and, 121
tantrums
dealing with, 65
teachers
attitudes and approach of, 46-69
depending on for advice and support, 178
meeting with, 136
parental involvement and school success, 133-135
responsibilities as role model, 138-141
setting examples as, 110
techniques and impact on child, 139
teaching
values and beliefs, 73
teens, 75
television, 6, 74, 209
time
coping with not enough, 185-206
making choices, 31-33
prioritizing, 31
quality, 33-34
using productively, 125
time management
maintaining balance through, 186
organization and, 187
using a central calendar, 186-187
toys, 123-124
traditions
children and, 211-212
establishing, 212-214
family history and, 208
teaching values and culture through, 214-215
trickle down effect, 51, 61, 126
trust, 13

uniqueness
celebrating each child's, 34-36

values
communicating through conduct, 101
teaching, 73, 102-104, 214-215
traditions and, 212